BATTLE
OF THE
BISMARCK
SEA

Other books by Lex McAulay

Into the Dragon's Jaws
When the Buffalo Fight

BATTLE
OF THE
BISMARCK
SEA

LEX
McAULAY

ST. MARTIN'S PRESS   NEW YORK

This book is dedicated to all the members of the Allied Air Forces, both flight crews and ground staff, who served in the South West Pacific Area theater of operations between 1942– 45, and to the memory of the many men who have no known grave in those seas, mountains and jungles.

BATTLE OF THE BISMARCK SEA.
Copyright © 1991 by Lex McAulay. All rights reserved. Printed in the United States of America. No part of this book may be used or reproduced in any manner whatsoever without written permission except in the case of brief quotations embodied in critical articles or reviews. For information, address St. Martin's Press, 175 Fifth Avenue, New York, N.Y. 10010.

Editor: Jared Kieling
Production Editor: Eric C. Meyer
Design by Jaye Zimet

Library of Congress Cataloging-in-Publication Data

McAulay, Lex, 1940–
    Battle of the Bismarck Sea / Lex McAulay.
        p. cm.
    ISBN 0-312-05820-9
     1. Bismarck Sea, Battle of the, 1943. 2. Naval convoys—Japan—
History—20th century. 3. World War, 1939–1945—Naval operations.
4. World War, 1939–1945—Aerial operations. I. Title
D774.B59M32 1991
940.54'26—dc20   90-26943
                                          CIP

CONTENTS

**BATTLE OF THE BISMARK SEA
2-4 MARCH 1943 ·**

ADMIRALTY I.

BISMARK SEA

Wewak

NORTH EAST

NEW GUINEA

Rabaul

Sakar I.

Umboi I.

NEW BRITAIN

PAPUA

Malahang

Finschhafen
Cape Cretin

Lae
Salamaua

(4) (7)

Wau

Cape Ward Hunt

Dobodura

Trobriand I.

Goodenough I.

OWEN STANLEY RA.

PORT
MORESBY

Milne Bay

SINKING TRANSPORT

SINKING WARSHIP

100	0	100	200	300	400	500	
							km
							miles
50	0		100		200		300

THE GLADIATORS

THE AIRCRAFT, THE MEN

When General George C. Kenney took command of the U.S. air units in Australia on 4 August 1942, he had many problems confronting him, and little good news. However, if the right man for the job, at the right time, was needed, then that man almost certainly was George Kenney. Only 5 feet 6 inches in height, with short-cropped hair, Kenney was full of enthusiasm and confidence in the potential of air power in war. After growing up in Massachusetts at the turn of the century, and study at the Massachusetts Institute of Technology, he joined the U.S. Air Service in World War I, became a pilot, flew 75 missions, shot down two German aircraft and was shot down once. Captain Kenney finished that war with the Distinguished Service Cross and the Silver Star.

In the twenty years between 1919–39, he studied developments in aeronautics and the development of aerial warfare, both in practise and theory, and, most importantly, kept an open mind. To increase firepower, Kenney fitted machineguns to the wings of biplanes and 'invented' the parachute-retarded fragmentation bomb. He also demonstrated the practical uses of air-lifted troops in peacetime exercise. All of these, and more, were to be used in one way or another in his new command. Kenney was perhaps the most innovative of Allied air commanders, and the achievements of his force were limited only by the capabilities of available aircraft and equipment.

In 1940, Kenney was ordered to take over the aircraft production program. He did so, with the request that if and when the United States joined the war he be given a combat command. However, no promises had been made by air forces commander, General H.H. Arnold, and in February 1942 Brigadier Kenney was promoted to Major General and sent to San Francisco to command the 4th Air Force, a division with both a heavy training load and the responsibility for off-shore reconnaissance. On 7 July 1942, Kenney was told to report to Arnold in Washington on the 12th—Kenney found he was to command the air forces in Australia. After talks and briefings, he was aware just how big were the problems he would face on the far side of the Pacific.

When Kenney arrived in Australia to take command, he first had to gain the confidence of the Allied Supreme Commander South West Pacific Area (SWPA), General Douglas MacArthur. From the first day of the Japanese attack on the Philippines, and after the attack on Pearl Harbor, MacArthur and his staff—most particularly the abrasive Richard K. Sutherland—supposedly had been disappointed in the performance of their Air Force. Before the attack MacArthur had refused permission for his air commander, Major General Lewis Brereton, to send photo reconnaissance flights over Formosa (Taiwan). When news of the attack on Pearl Harbor reached Manila, General Brereton met Sutherland at MacArthur's headquarters and demanded that he be allowed to launch the strong force of B17s against Formosa. Brereton was told to go to his office and await orders.

Even after the first reports of Japanese attacks on the Philippines had been received, MacArthur did nothing. When the main Japanese attack force arrived, the U.S. Air Forces in the Philippines were still not dispersed or even airborne. They were destroyed on the ground, and only a small number remained flyable. Blame for the subsequent poor performance of U.S. air units faced with superior Japanese numbers was heaped on the airmen themselves.

It was not enough that the performance of MacArthur's air forces had been judged unacceptable. General MacArthur is alleged to have accused the U.S. air commander in Australia, General Brett, of disloyalty. As commander of U.S. forces in Australia Brett had been suggested as Allied Supreme Commander in the South West Pacific by the Australian government and service chiefs and was obviously seen as a threat to MacArthur's position. Brett was not one of the exclusive club of Bataan veterans who had also been evacuated from the Philippines. When MacArthur arrived in Australia, Brett was among those who met the General at the Melbourne railway station. MacArthur snubbed him and said bluntly that he did not wish Brett to accompany him to his accommodation. A week went by before MacArthur met with either Brett or the then commander of U.S. air units, General Royce. Those not members of the Bataan clique soon realised they were outsiders.

In the early part of 1942, the Australian people and government were made painfully aware that Britain would be unable to come to their aid even as the Japanese appeared to be about to invade Australia. Australians were shocked by the knowledge that Britain's Prime Minister Winston Churchill had strongly resisted repositioning Australian combat forces that had first been sent to help fight the Germans and Italians. Australian Prime Minister John Curtin realised that an American theater commander was vital if men, machines and supplies from the United States were to help stop the Japanese from pouring into the southern Pacific area. President Franklin D. Roosevelt appointed MacArthur as Supreme Commander SWPA, and directed him to leave the Philippines to take up his new post. MacArthur apparently believed that he would find in Australia a large balanced force with which to launch an immediate counter-offensive in the Philippines. Where he thought Roosevelt had conjured up this force has never been satisfactorily explained.

Never one to allow unwelcome facts to interfere with his image, MacArthur, his public relations staff, as well as others close to him, created one of the myths of his wartime achievements: the great fighting defence of the Philippines. In fact, the Japanese used only two divisions to defeat the ten available to MacArthur, and needed to do very little fighting to force the defenders back to Bataan. The heaviest action occurred when the Japanese began to attack the peninsula. There was, however, a lull for some weeks before the final offensive on 24 March, and the surrender of General King on 9 April 1942. MacArthur had arrived in Australia on 18 March. Within 24 hours, some 12,000 defenders on the supposedly impregnable island fortress of Corregidor were defeated by approximately 1,000 Japanese assault troops in 24 hours, 5–6 May 1942.

Another MacArthur myth alleged that when the General arrived in Australia, thinking was defeatist and planning was defensive, centering around the southern areas of Australia. But the fact is that while MacArthur was still in the Philippines, Australian, New Zealand and U.S. commanders, including Brett, had decided to fight as far north as possible in New Guinea. At the time of MacArthur's arrival in Australia, most Australian and U.S. formations were based in the more developed southern end of Australia. North of Brisbane, Queensland, there were no military barracks areas or modern harbors and only a single railway line. The network of airfields to come in the north was not completed. As facilities north of Brisbane developed, units began to move there and use them, staging through to New Guinea, which itself was unprepared for wartime activity.

When MacArthur arrived in Australia to take over as Supreme Commander SWPA, he quickly saw to it that General Brett and some other senior officers were removed from the Australian theater. Personal charisma and skillful command of public relations helped MacArthur to establish a good working relationship with Australian Prime Minister Curtin. The two were as different as chalk and cheese. MacArthur was a flamboyant military commander determined to fulfil his destiny; Curtin was a quiet working class man who had risen through the political ranks. Yet both men worked well together to prosecute this war against the Japanese invader. At first MacArthur was truly idolised by the Australian public, and a generally high opinion of him was maintained throughout the war years. The fact that MacArthur asked for, and was given, full powers of censorship over the radio and newspapers worked well to ensure that he was always presented in a good light. People with a more detached view of the times believe Curtin was completely fooled by MacArthur, and thus manipulated by him. Almost certainly, Curtin had never met or worked so closely with such a character.

When MacArthur arrived in March to find that his command was limited to Air Corps and service troops and no combat-ready fighting units, he immediately began agitating for enough men and units to launch a counter-offensive against the Japanese. The SWPA, however, was given low priority status—the 'Europe First' policy prevailed.

The Japanese already had occupied the strategic harbor and airfield at Rabaul, New Britain, and landed on the north coast of New Guinea, where they had captured airfield sites at Lae and Salamaua. Air raids were often made on the harbor, town and airfields of Port Moresby on the southern coast of New Guinea, and the Mitsubishi A6M Zero fighter, flown by experienced pilots in the Tainan Kokkutai at Lae, proved a difficult opponent for the RAAF and U.S. pilots defending Moresby in their P40s and P39s. The manoeuvrable, long-ranging Zero had proven itself in China, but Western Intelligence refused to believe that the Japanese could produce an airplane with such outstanding characteristics. The Curtiss P40 and Bell P39 were rugged and could absorb greater punishment than the Zero, but until the Allied pilots learned not to dog-fight with the Japanese, they were outclassed by their opponents in the air.

The naval Battle of the Coral Sea in May resulted in a tactical draw for each side but a strategic victory for the Allies, when the Japanese invasion force for Port Moresby turned back to Rabaul. In June, as air battles continued overhead, Australian militia units sent to garrison Port Moresby worked to improve defences and had little time for jungle warfare training. The high, unmapped Owen Stanley mountain ranges north of Moresby acted as a screen which blanked out the early radar installed there, and the Japanese aircraft often were not detected until only minutes before they began their bomb runs. The U.S. P39 fighter squadrons were often unable to climb fast enough to intercept, and

■ 5

could only manage to get out of the target area. The ground troops thought of a number of uncomplimentary names for the fighters as they watched them speeding away from the Japanese and out to sea.

All this was to change with the arrival of the Lockheed P38 Lightning twin-engined fighter. The P38 could climb to greater heights and with greater acceleration and more destructive fire-power grouped in the nose of the plane. Although not operational until late 1942, the P38 destroyed the myth of the invincible Japanese Zero.

On 21 July 1942, as General Kenney was en route to his new command, the Japanese landed the first elements of a major force ordered to cross New Guinea from the north coast, through the unknown mountains, to Port Moresby. From Moresby, Japanese air and naval units could dominate the southern oceans and cut off Australia from the U.S. So began the Kokoda campaign, named for the largest village and government station between Buna and Port Moresby. No roads crossed New Guinea, and only a native foot trail went through the mountains. Everything the Australian infantry ate, wore or fired had to be carried by humans up that trail, in tropical rainstorms, over unbridged mountain torrents and up mountain slopes which rose and fell as much as 2,000 feet or more. The march from the edge of the mountains to Kokoda took seven exhausting days after which the men had to engage in jungle combat.

Although the Kokoda campaign is outside the scope of this book, a brief description is necessary. The Japanese, with combat and construction engineers, 2,000 pack horses and six battalions of infantry, mountain guns and mortar and heavy machinegun support, fought their way to the northern base of the last ridgeline before the lowlands around Port Moresby. There they were finally held by Australian infantry. Supply problems limited the number of Australian battalions sent along the trail, and in the mountain battles the Japanese were always superior in number and fire-power.

Uninformed people looked at the total number of Japanese estimated to be advancing and the total number of Australian and

American troops in New Guinea, and could not understand why the larger Allied force could not stop the enemy. The reality was that most of the troops around Port Moresby were headquarters, air force, air service, construction and supply troops that performed vital duties and had no combat potential. Also, Moresby had to be garrisoned with some combat force in case another Japanese seaborne invasion force appeared. The Australians were not assisted by the opinion of MacArthur's chief of Intelligence, Willoughby, who believed that the Japanese did not want Moresby, but only airfield sites on the north coast.

As air power was of little use against the Japanese on the Kokoda Trail, but was more effective against the distant airfields and the beachhead and storage areas around Buna, Kenney placed a greater weight of attack on those targets. The Australians forced the Japanese back to Buna, on the north coast, and were then joined by U.S. units of the 32nd and 41st Divisions in the bloody fighting against formidable Japanese defences there. In January 1943, the campaign was over, with almost total annihilation of the Japanese force, but the Australian and U.S. formations were exhausted by battle casualties and sickness. There were more Japanese farther west at Salamaua, Wau, and Lae, and it was clear they would be reinforced with units from the Philippines and the major base at Rabaul. While this fighting had been raging, General George Kenney had been achieving significant gains for air power in general and for his U.S. air units in particular.

On arrival in Australia in July 1942, Kenney was well aware of the difficult situation he was about to enter and understood that first of all he had to assure MacArthur of his respect and loyalty, and that of the air units and staffs, before he could get on with the business of fighting the Japanese. Kenney soon realised that because there was little naval presence, and with the tremendous difficulties hampering land movement, air power would have to become the primary arm of attack. Kenney was intelligent, energetic and perceptive, and must have realised that in the SWPA he was being given an opportunity to demonstrate what mature co-ordinated use of air power could achieve. If he could gain MacArthur's support, great things would be possible.

Everything was in short supply, as the South West Pacific

was down low on the priority list. Materials, aircraft, parts, and personnel were greatly lacking. Kenney found a rather confused system of joint operations and administration involving Australians and Americans at all levels, including aircraft crews. He soon set about separating the systems into Australian and American, thus building a definite and separate U.S. air presence. General Brett had been happy to create a totally integrated Australian-American force, but this was just what General MacArthur did not want, and Kenney supported him.

On paper, it seemed Kenney had a considerable number of aircraft of various types, but on closer inspection, most of the planes were either obsolete or grounded by lack of parts and maintenance. 170 of the 245 fighters shown as available were actually grounded for maintenance or repairs. None of the 53 light bombers were ready to fly, only 33 of his 70 medium bombers were operational, and 19 of 62 heavy bombers were undergoing maintenance. Of the 36 transport planes, 19 different types in all, only half were flyable. Of the 51 miscellaneous small commercial and training aircraft listed, none could be used in combat.

Although the aircraft Kenney did have were not what he would have chosen for the theater, he was happy to take anything he could get. The heavy bombers which would fly the missions against the Bismarck convoy were the Boeing B17 and Consolidated B24. Originally designed for long-range reconnaissance from the coasts of the USA, they were adapted for heavy bombardment use. The B17 entered U.S. service in the mid-thirties, the B24 in 1941, both were constantly modified and improved, and they comprised the major daylight bombing force. Both bombers were at the forefront of aviation design, could take great punishment, and brought many crews safely home. The attack and medium-level aircraft in the SWPA were the Douglas A20, the North American B25, and the Martin B26, all of which were modern, fast twin-engined aircraft. However, these planes were relatively unsuccessful in the designed role of medium-level bombing. When used as low-level attack airplanes, they achieved better results in the SWPA than in other theaters. Kenney's fighters were, at first, the Curtiss P40 and Bell P39, neither of which was consistently successful against the agile Japanese fighters. But when the advantages of superior diving speed and ruggedness were exploited by the Allied pilots, respectable numbers of Japanese were destroyed. The most admired fighter in Kenney's force in 1942–43 was the Lockheed P38, briefly described earlier, which climbed to fame in the SWPA when it demonstrated its ability to master anything the Japanese could put against it.

The RAAF had 22 squadrons, but most of these were training planes. The combat element available was a mere two fighter squadrons, with about 40 Curtiss P40 Kittyhawks, and three reconnaissance squadrons with 30 Lockheed Hudsons. The RAAF, like the Australian Army and Royal Australian Navy, had been concerned with training men and units to take part in the war in Europe, the Mediterranean and North Africa. The first RAAF fighter squadron to receive P40s had done so on 4 March 1942, been declared operational fourteen days later, and then gone straight to Port Moresby. Some of the fighters were not fitted with gunnery sights. This unit, 75 Fighter Squadron, had defended the area alone for 44 days, before the U.S. Army Air Corps' 35th and 36th Fighter Squadrons arrived with their Bell P39 Airacobras.

For decades, Australia had been assured that Britain would defend her. In the late 1930s, when it became obvious that this would be impossible, the best that Britain could do was provide the plans to allow Australia to begin building obsolescent aircraft such as the Bristol Beaufort bomber. Earlier, British senior air staff and industry had been annoyed when Australia selected the North American NA33, known as the AT-6 Texan in the United States. The RAAF called it the Wirraway, an aboriginal word meaning 'challenge.' Armed with three .303-inch machineguns, the Wirraway training aircraft was classified as a fighter, and young aircrew flew it, many to their deaths, against the formidable Mitsubishi Zero. Some of the Wirraways were even modified for use as dive-bombers.

Australia, like the other Dominions and colonies, supplied raw materials to British factories, then bought back the manufactured articles. Australia had gained independence in 1901 and had its own parliament, but until the late 1930s, important foreign relations and defence matters were really decided by Britain on Australia's behalf. The Royal Australian Navy was, in fact, the Australian Squadron of the Royal Navy, with a British officer as its head. Although British officers also exerted influence in their senior ranks, much to the dismay of many Australians, the Australian Army and RAAF were more independent. By 1940, Australia began to make more of its own decisions on behalf of all branches of its military.

More relevant to the subject of this book and the wartime role of the RAAF was the way in which Britain tried to control every aspect of recruitment, training and employment of all ranks, as well as the equipment they used or flew. The RAAF was to follow RAF methods, and make use of British equipment, no matter what else was available. The Inspector-General of the RAF visited Australia in 1939 at the time the NA33 (the AT-6) was being tested. When the commander of the RAAF, Air Vice-Marshal Williams, told him to look up as the NA33 was about to be demonstrated, the RAF officer refused to do so, and demanded to be taken to see administration procedures. Soon after, by political agreement, Williams was transferred to the RAF for a two-year attachment, and a retired RAF officer, Air Chief Marshal Sir Charles Burnett, was brought out to head the RAAF. His role was clear: control the RAAF as a training organisation for the supply of manpower to RAF in overseas theaters, and delay or prevent the creation of operational squadrons and an RAAF command structure.

Australia had long been worried by the militarism of Japanese society, but Britain had repeatedly referred to Singapore as a fortress and that strong naval forces would be based there at times of need. Senior Australian officers who questioned this promise, and pointed out shortcomings, were disciplined.

A flood of catastrophes from 1940 to 1942 had washed away the facade of British military supremacy and Australia found herself in a desperate situation. All her combat-ready forces were overseas, and all that was available for the defence of the nation were training units and organisations. Despite this lack of defence, British Prime Minister Winston Churchill went so far as to redirect to Burma the Australian divisions returning from North

Africa—without informing the Australian government. Only strong action and defiance on the part of Australian Prime Minister John Curtin got the Australians turned back on course for home.

If the British were less helpful than expected, the arriving Americans soon began to demand more than some Australians thought necessary. An American theater commander was one thing, but it was another when the arriving U.S. commanders demanded total control of many matters in the host nation. As early as March 1942, when they represented little more than the remnants of a defeated force, MacArthur and Brett began to agitate against the system which had Australians commanding regions, camps, barracks, depots and airfields in their own country. No one on MacArthur's staff seems to have contemplated for a moment the reverse situation: What if, for example, Australian forces had arrived in the USA to help defend the Panama Canal Zone, the U.S. West Coast or Hawaii and they had demanded not only that things be done their way, but that they be allowed to command the field formations, airfields and installations of the host nation. At the unit and personal level, Australians and Americans almost always got along well, but at the higher levels where egos, ambitions, and careers clashed, the question of command and authority was never really resolved to the satisfaction of all.

In August 1942, it became obvious to General Kenney that he had to clean up the available air units and supporting organisations and produce a force capable of going on the offensive, and make possible an advance back across the huge distances taken so quickly by the Japanese since Pearl Harbor. Kenney had to do this at the end of a long logistics pipeline, with low priority, based in a large continent with a small population, which had been unprepared for war on its own doorstep.

One important step, which he took soon after assuming command, was to confront General Sutherland and have it understood once and for all just who was in charge of the Allied Air Forces in the SWPA. Kenney found that Sutherland was interfering in air war operations, ordering bombing attacks and giving other commands. To illustrate his point, Kenney drew a small dot on a sheet of paper and told Sutherland that the dot represented the General's knowledge and understanding of air power, and the rest of the expanse of paper represented his own. When Sutherland responded angrily, Kenney called his bluff and challenged him to let General MacArthur decide who was air commander. Kenney won, becoming the first person of senior rank not a member of the Bataan clique to achieve acceptance and support from MacArthur.

Kenney soon realised that Australia simply did not have the industrial base to support modern war. In 1942, Britain was too far away and unable to help. Washington was besieged by people from all the theaters of war demanding more of everything, each for his own area of responsibility. Kenney knew also that the Japanese could send reinforcements of all kinds to the South West Pacific in a matter of days, whereas his had first to be allocated and assigned shipping space, and then sent across the Pacific to southern Australia for shipment north.

The senior staff of the U.S. supply and maintenance organisation did little to improve the availability status of the aircraft, insisting on peacetime accounting procedures and on correct completion of the numerous forms and requests. Active squadrons took second place to ponderous paperwork. This had a cumulative bad effect on the morale of the squadrons tasked to fly missions. The major supply and maintenance base was at Tocumwal, 3,000 miles south of the combat zone in New Guinea. A modern base with comfortable quarters and a very good peacetime filing system had been installed there. The staff, who all had the maximum rank approved for the establishment, were startled when Kenney told them to halt all construction, mark all the materials for shipment to New Guinea, and prepare to move north. Two weeks later Kenney was confounded to find that the Tocumwal base was still as it had been when he left—they were waiting for his written orders to carry out his instructions.

The solutions were obvious. Acting decisively, Kenney removed those in command who were unable to understand that an Air Force at war must devote all its energies to providing the maximum number of flight-ready aircraft. He promoted to command positions those who could understand this essential requirement and who had the ability to function well in a war zone.

It should be pointed out here that it was not only the USAAC which suffered from a heavy peacetime oriented rear echelon. The RAAF 22 Squadron was equipped with Douglas A20s and in late 1942 it became known at headquarters in Melbourne— 2500 miles south—that the aircraft had been fitted with .50-calibre machineguns mounted in the nose for use in ground attack sorties. The headquarters 'viewed with concern' the fact that the A20s had been so modified without themselves giving the matter 'due consideration.' Investigations by the headquarters failed to identify who had approved the fitting of extra machineguns, though it was suspected either the squadron commander or senior RAAF officer in the area had done so, and so headquarters required that a letter 'in strong terms' be sent to the senior officer, informing him that he was held 'responsible for the breach of orders.' (1)

General Kenney also began a system of obvious rewards for performance for the men in the U.S. squadrons. He promoted the young and able, awarded medals, leave and rest, and removed the requirement to conform to certain regulations which interfered with the business of getting on with the war. Aware of the value of medals as a visible sign of courage rewarded, Kenney used awards as a means of raising the morale of an Air Force which had been severely battered by the enemy, had been in constant retreat for nine months, was operating in primitive conditions in a region which was barely touched by Western civilisation, and in which the flying weather, terrain and seas were greater enemies than the Japanese. Only days after taking command, he recommended Captain Harl Pease for the Congressional Medal of Honor, after a two-day series of bombing attacks on Rabaul during which Pease was shot down and lost with his entire crew. Some two months later, on the way to New Guinea, Kenney stopped at Mareeba and Townsville and awarded over 250 decorations to his units for recent actions against the Japanese.

Kenney also asked Washington for authority to organise the air units into a numbered air force, and was told he could use the number Five. At once, the U.S. air elements had a new identity to go with their new leader; a man who was seen to be trying to get things done and who gave credit and rewards where due.

The aircraft Kenney was receiving often needed modification, or even major rebuilding, before they could be sent up to the forward areas. The only fighter thought to be capable of asserting superiority over the vaunted Japanese Zero was the Lockheed P38 Lightning. Unfortunately these were shipped to Australia with leaking leakproof fuel tanks. Major work was also needed in the P38 wings. Such a program of repairs taxed an already strained maintenance system.

One minor bright spot was the performance against Japanese airfields of the 23-pound fragmentation bombs he had acquired in the United States. No one had wanted them, but George Kenney had them fitted with parachutes and used in low-level attacks against parked aircraft, gasoline trucks, and anti-aircraft crews. They were quite successful, and became a feature of U.S. strafer attacks in the SWPA.

The aerial torpedo was another weapon which rarely achieved better results for the Allies than it had for the Axis powers. The consistently poor performance of the torpedo was never really overcome to the end of the war. Washington asked why it was that, as of late December 1942, although 80 torpedoes had been delivered and 90 medium bombers were on hand to use against the 93 ships reported in the Rabaul area, they were not being used. MacArthur's headquarters replied that the torpedoes were allocated to the RAAF; three torpedo missions had been flown but with no hits; that there were only ten sights, but no trained crews; and anyway, Rabaul was out of range of medium bombers fitted with torpedoes. The reply to Washington also said that B17s and B24s were used to skip-bomb enemy ships in the Rabaul area, and reminded Washington of the small force of bombers provided to the 5th Air Force, a force which was already attacking numerous targets in the Wewak-Buna area, as well as around Kavieng, Rabaul, and the Shortlands. (2)

The fighters and some twin-engined aircraft were delivered by ship, but some others including the four-engined bombers were flown across the wide Pacific by newly graduated Lieutenants with less than 300 hours total flying time. The big bombers were barely out of the experimental and developmental stage. Only a few years before, highly experienced pilots and crews, notably Australian Charles Kingsford-Smith, became heroes after making pioneering flights from the United States to Australia. Now, in 1942–43, untried crews were flying new aircraft over those same routes in what was a mere first leg to combat. Few other examples show more clearly the speedy development of aviation in those years.

The attitude of some of the Australian labor unions was a problem about which the Australian and U.S. military could do little. The Australian continental rail network had been developed by individual state governments and this had resulted in different rail gauges in each state; so everything had to be transhipped at the borders. The unions refused to allow a single-gauge rail line to be built despite the national emergency, as it would affect the jobs of the transhippers at each border.

The Communist-controlled stevedores (longshoremen) came to work late, stopped frequently for breaks, enjoyed long lunches and left early; no work was done on weekends or public holidays. And all activity stopped completely at the first drop of rain. The same unions wrecked valuable aircraft and halted work until they were granted permission to enter and leave the wharf areas without being halted or searched by police or other authorities. This amounted to the freedom to loot cigarettes, liquor and such from cargoes. Only if the cargo was absolutely vital were Australian military used to unload the ships quickly. The Australian Labor government was controlled by trade unions. The rights and privileges of the union members were sancrosanct, in spite of the proximity of Japanese forces.

It was only after courageous parliamentary action by Prime Minister Curtin, and then only in a time of desperate need, that drafted military personnel were allowed to be sent outside Australia. All the army, navy and air force men who had gone overseas previously were volunteers for such service. The Labor Party denied that it suited the government to have only volunteers serve overseas. As these people generally disagreed with Labor Party policies and did not vote Labor at elections, if they were killed while fighting somewhere overseas, so much the better at election time. The Australian Labor Party was bare-faced enough to ask for young British and American men to be sent into combat close to Australia, but clung to its own doctrine of not requiring young non-volunteer Australians to be sent to battles outside Australia's boundaries. No amount of reasoning about fighting a capitalists' war can disguise the moral deficit in Australian Labor Party policy at that time.

In spite of a ponderous administrative and logistic tail, bad operating conditions and too few operational aircraft, the 5th Air Force and RAAF achieved some notable feats. Those already convinced of the advantages and power available from a good air force were pleased, and some of the pessimists and die-hards, whose concept of battlefield mobility had not expanded to grasp the machine age, were converted.

On 15 September 1942, General Kenney began a demonstration of air mobility which impressed General MacArthur and his senior staff. Kenney offered to fly the 126th Infantry Regiment, United States 32nd Infantry Division, from Amberley airbase, near Brisbane, to Port Moresby—in two days less than the time needed for a sea voyage. To do this, he needed every available transport plane, including Australian civilian aircraft and all bombers undergoing repairs or in transit on the ferry route across the Pacific. The mission was accomplished and Kenney gained MacArthur's support for air-lift operations.

U.S. and RAAF units had supported the Australian fighting retreat along the Kokoda Trail, over the unmapped Owen Stanley mountains, until the Japanese were halted only 32 miles from Port Moresby. The Australians went over to the offensive and the fighting surged north, back to the coastal plains around Buna, where the Japanese had landed in July. Air support continued as the Japanese were driven back, and the campaign ended with a U.S.–Australian victory, in January 1943. In the later stages of the campaign, reinforcements were flown in and casualties flown out; food, ammunition and even artillery pieces arrived by air; the Japanese were attacked by fighters, medium and heavy bombers; their own air units were incapable of influencing the operation as the

Allied Air Forces had done. 586 sorties were flown by Allied Air Forces in support of the ground forces. Captured Japanese diaries reveal the despair and anger of trapped but still resisting Japanese who could see no sign of their own air units.

Earlier, in August and September 1942, a Japanese sea-borne invasion of Milne Bay at the eastern tip of New Guinea, was held and then defeated by Australian Army and RAAF units. The Japanese were forced to retreat; it was the first time that this had happened to one of their landing forces. The Australian military forces are proud of three historical facts of World War II: They were first to defeat a full-scale attack by Rommel's German panzer division at Tobruk in North Africa in April 1941; they were first to defeat a Japanese land offensive on the Kokoda Trail, in August–September 1942; and they were first to defeat a Japanese invasion force, at Milne Bay, in August 1942.

Elsewhere in the world war, the U.S. Navy had won the decisive Battle of Midway in June, and in August the U.S. Marines had landed on Guadalcanal in the Solomons. The Japanese responded with air, sea and land forces. A series of savage battles followed with heavy losses to both sides, but by February 1943, the Japanese were defeated.

At the same time, in Russia, the German Sixth Army was fighting, freezing and dying, largely because the Luftwaffe was unable to carry out Reichsmarschall Hermann Goering's boast that the defenders of Stalingrad could be supplied by air. In North Africa, the armies commanded by German Field Marshal Rommel, retreating after the Battle of El Alamein, were constantly pounded by British air formations. U.S. General Dwight D. Eisenhower's Anglo-American force had also landed in Morocco and driven east to squeeze Rommel between themselves and British General Bernard Montgomery's advancing Eighth Army.

In New Guinea in January and February 1943, General Kenney's air transport service was crucial to the successful Australian defence of Wau. In a 16-day series of flights, mainly by the U.S. 374 Troop Carrier Group, the Australian force there was increased from 403 men to 3166, with arms, equipment, ammunition, food and other requirements all delivered by air. A total of 244 sorties were flown in the four days between 29 January and 1 February. The entire operation was co-ordinated by the RAAF 4 Fighter Sector at Port Moresby.

On 29 January, the day of crisis, there were 57 flights delivering a total of 814 men. Elements of the Japanese 51st Division, delivered to Lae by ship in early January, were decisively defeated in the actions at Wau. However, AAF attacks against the convoy had failed to prevent the Japanese from delivering a fresh force to the combat zone and battles on land had resulted. In addition to troop transports, there was considerable fighter and bomber support in the actions at Wau. RAAF Sergeants Downing and Box, a Beaufighter crew of 30 Squadron, were strafing an estimated 300 Japanese when an enormous explosion, which killed many Japanese, almost swallowed the Beaufighter. Sergeant Downing brought the plane back down to base at Ward's Strip, Port Moresby. There were 58 holes in the starboard wing alone. This same crew was to have another close call on 3 March, over the Bismarck Sea.

Although the Japanese in New Guinea had been defeated on the Kokoda Trail at Milne Bay, at Buna and at Wau, they remained a formidable enemy. But the war was far from over. The Japanese had succeeded in sending many convoys of various sizes from their major base at Rabaul to Lae and Salamaua in New Guinea. Between the 5th and 8th of January and under fire from the Allied Air Forces, the Japanese took a convoy of five transports and five destroyers from Rabaul to Lae. The convoy was halfway along a route on the south coast of New Britain before being discovered. AAF Squadrons began a series of attacks; one ship was sunk at sea and another at Lae, but the cargoes were delivered and eight of the ten ships returned to Rabaul. This obvious Japanese victory forced the Allied Air Force commanders and staffs in New Guinea to analyse the actions and determine just why the Japanese had been so successful. This had a direct bearing on the concept and methods of air attack used on the next convoy the Japanese would send through the Bismarck Sea.

Six single-plane sorties were flown against the convoy on the afternoon of 6 January, and an RAAF PBY Catalina from

Cairns located the ships and torpedoed *Nichiryu Maru* on the night of 6/7 January. On 7 January, a succession of attacks was made, as squadrons could be made ready: five B17s, twelve B25s, one B24, one B24, thirteen Beaufighters, twenty P40s, fifteen P38s, three B26s, five B26s, ten B25s, fourteen P40s, four B17s, and a single B24. A total of 104 sorties were flown, and because they were piecemeal, they were wasted. During the entire action against the convoy and its landing operation, the 416 sorties sank two and damaged three of the ten ships, although the cargoes had been delivered.

The AAF had located and shadowed the convoy for half its voyage. Communications were satisfactory and the P38s had performed well. What had been lacking were suitable tactics and the application of one of the Principles of War: Concentration. The gathering of an effective striking force was hampered by a lack of transportation; a lack of ordnance and bomb-handling equipment; a shortage of refuelling facilities; the failure of telephone lines; generally bad working conditions, such as mud, distance from bomb dumps to the aircraft; safety rules, such as no bomb-loading at night for fear of Japanese air attacks; and airfields in New Guinea at Dobodura-Buna that were not ready for use. As well as Allied short-comings and the weather, Japanese fighter and anti-aircraft defences combined to reduce effectiveness of the AAF attacks after the ships arrived at Lae. AAF staff realised that different tactics were essential for future success and that problems on the ground had to be solved to allow the strike force to assemble in the air.

An Australian officer on Kenney's staff had a positive effect on the future attacks. Group Captain, [Colonel] Bill Garing, came with air-sea experience that predated the war. He already had completed a tour of operations in the European theater and had won the D.F.C. by flying his Sunderland flying boat to break up attacks on a ship by five Luftwaffe Junkers Ju88s. Later he found a boat full of civilian survivors after a U-Boat sank the liner *City of Benares*. Since his return to Australia before Pearl Harbor, Garing had been busy preparing the northern aerial defence of Australia. With his long experience of air-sea operations, Garing persuaded Kenney and Whitehead that a massed but co-ordinated attack, from different heights and directions, was necessary to defeat future Japanese convoys.

High and medium-level bombing obviously was not very successful against ships. Despite bravery by crews in torpedo-bombers, the performance so far of Allied torpedoes in the war had been little short of scandalous. Kenney already had decided to modify some of his North American B25 Mitchell bombers to become what he called 'commerce destroyers.' Ever able to make good use of the talented men around him, he had designated Major Paul 'Pappy' Gunn to transform the B25 from a poorly armed medium-level bomber into a heavily armed low-level attack bomber. The story is now well known. Eventually the 90th Squadron, 3rd Attack Group, was equipped with B25s fitted with four .50-caliber machineguns inside the nose and another four in pairs below the pilot on the side of the fuselage. Each gun had 480 rounds, loaded against ships with two tracer, three incendiary and five armor-piercing. With eight .50-caliber machineguns firing ahead, plus the two in the top turret, the B25 could, and did, attack ships up to the size of a cruiser. In addition to the new armament, manoeuvrability was greatly increased by putting full boost on all servo trim tabs. A formidable fighting machine had been created in the field, despite opposition from the aircraft designers and makers and without the enemy becoming aware of it.

It was then decided to test low-level bombing against ships, and practise missions were flown against what was called 'the Moresby wreck.' Some squadron members assumed the target ship was the SS *Macdhui*, sunk by Japanese air attack near Moresby, but this was incorrect. Their target was the 4700-ton P&O Liner, the SS *Pruth*, which had been driven aground on Nateara Reef on 30 December 1923.

One technique, called 'skip-bombing,' had the aircraft attacking at 100–200 feet, a height at which the released bomb would skip along the water surface. If the skip-distances were correct, the fuzed nose of the bomb would hit the ship's hull or superstructure; if not, the bomb would skip right over the deck into the sea beyond. With mast-height bombing, the aircraft aimed the bombs directly at the hull, and at the waterline if possible. 'Skip-bombing' had already been used by RAF light bombers against German ships in European waters. In the SWPA, the first mast-height attack had been flown by three RAAF Hudsons against two Japanese ships at Gasmata on 11 February 1942. The ships had been attacked from normal height for two days, but with no observed result. Squadron commander J. Lerew, then took Flight Lieutenant W. Pedrina and Flying Officer G. Gibson in for a low-level attack and set both ships on fire with bomb hits and machinegun fire. But Lerew and Gibson were shot down by fighters and flak. Only Lerew himself made a safe return to Port Moresby nine days later. The defensive firepower of three Hudsons was inadequate.

Captain Ed Larner, of the 89th Squadron, 3rd Attack Group, had come to General Kenney's notice as a result of his bravery in ground attack missions in the A20. On one memorable occasion, Larner brought his A20 back from Buna after anti-aircraft fire had flipped the nose down; the airplane mowed its way through a hundred yards of palm tree tops. Larner was told by Kenney to become proficient at bombing and strafing the wreck in the modified B25. Kenney then placed newly promoted Major Ed Larner in command of the 90th Squadron, 3rd Attack Group, and told him to train the squadron in the new below-mast-height method of attack. Ed Larner was a bright star among the young combat leaders in the 5th Air Force. There are several tales told about him. One is that he sometimes dispensed with the usual military methods of justice and punishment, and took wrong-doers out of sight to settle the disagreement with fists. This may or may not be true, but Kenney described him as having 'fire, leadership and guts . . . a bit cocky, bragged some, and swaggered, too, but it was all right with me.'

It was obvious to all that the Japanese would be sending more reinforcements to New Guinea. Kenney had information from intercepted and translated Japanese radio messages—the now famous 'Ultra' system—that the rest of the Imperial Japanese Army 51st Division was to arrive in New Guinea by sea about 6 March, and that other units in the north were waiting. The only way to avoid another expensive and bloody series of battles at a time and place chosen by the enemy, was to inflict serious losses on the Japanese convoy then in the process of assembling. There was little time to perfect the new mast-height method of attack.

One B25 crew was lost during training when the tail of the airplane hit the mast of the wreck. Another B25's bomb exploded instantaneously on impact, badly damaging the aircraft and forcing the pilot to land on a reef, while a third aircraft was peppered with rust and small fragments when the bomb exploded almost instantaneously but inside the wreck. Five-second delay fuzes were combined with Australian detonators and pilots made 30 to 40 attacks on the wreck, using a selected point on the nose of the B25 as the aiming mark-bombsight.

A practise mission against the wreck was finally flown on 28 February 1943. All the elements of a co-ordinated attack were included. The B17s went in first, bombing from 8,000 feet, followed by medium-level B25s at 5,000 feet. RAAF 30 Squadron Beaufighters then went in firing their heavy armament of four 20mm cannon and six .303-inch machineguns, closely followed by Ed Larner's B25s with .50-caliber nose guns and 500-pound bombs.

One of the Australian Beaufighters was flown by George Drury, a pilot who had been in the theater since December 1942. Drury believed himself to be lucky, having been one of the first pilots selected for conversion to the new Beaufighter straight from training course. He had graduated from the Beaufighter training unit with 282 hours, loaded fresh fruit and vegetables into the new aircraft allocated to him and his navigator-observer, David Beasley, and set off for the war. The missions they had flown since their arrival at the squadron, attacking unseen ground targets in the jungles, had been frustrating, as no enemy were seen. However, an Army officer at the Wau battles had told the squadron of the good results they did achieve. Although the practise mission on the wreck was interesting, Drury did not realise 'the magnitude of what was ahead.' It was, after all, just a practise job.

Drury was impressed with 'the damned good bombing' from the U.S. 43rd Bomb Group B17s. The Beaufighters dived in as the 38th Group B25s were releasing their bombs, coming into range just as the bombs exploded, and strafed the ship, 'peeling off a few of the rusted plates.' They turned aside to watch four of Ed Larner's 90th Attack Squadron B25 strafers hose down the ship with a mass of .50-caliber gunfire, after which a formation of five came in and bombed. Drury witnessed one direct hit that sent a column of rusty smoke skyward.

J.W. 'Bill' Smallwood was a B25 pilot with the 90th. He had been aboard the SS *Holbrook*, in the first U.S. convoy to reach Australia on 22 December 1941, after the ships had been diverted from the Philippines. After time in the 27th Bomb Group, Air Transport Command and the 13th Squadron of the 3rd Attack, Smallwood had a total of about 556 hours, including 250 hours on B25s. He also had met, courted and married an Australian stewardess of Australian National Airlines. On a mission to Lae, on only his second flight in a B25, the Tainan Kokkutai Zeros attacked. The B25 leader took the 13th Squadron down to water-level for the fight back to the base. When his pilot was knocked out by a spent Japanese shell-case which crashed through the cockpit roof, Smallwood suddenly learned to fly a B25—in combat, in formation, at sea-level and under fighter attack. After 14 months in the SWPA, Bill Smallwood was quite experienced.

In the practise on the wreck, single P38s were present, each representing a flight. The pilots were not told why they were to do this, or that such a shipping strike was planned. Charlie King, a P38 pilot in the 39th Squadron, 'thought it very strange at the time. We were just told what to do, and not given a reason. Typical of how things were done at the time.'

Aware the Japanese convoy was assembling, General Kenney ordered an analysis of known sailing routes, north and south of New Britain, taken by all Rabaul–New Guinea ships and convoys during the previous four months. The result showed that whichever route was taken, the path used remained constant. The Japanese had three alternatives: go direct to Lae; split the convoy, with half to Lae and half to Madang; or go direct to Madang.

The weather forecast was—from the point of view of Allied Air Forces—for bad weather for the first three or four days of March, along the northern side of New Britain. Kenney believed that the convoy commander would use this weather to cloak his ships as far as possible, but until the convoy reached the Vitiaz

Strait it would not be in range of the closely timed co-ordinated attack he intended to unleash.

On 1 March, there were available to the 5th Air Force, 154 fighters: 34 light bombers, 41 mediums and 39 heavy bombers. General Whitehead, commanding the 5th's Advanced Echelon, 'Advon,' at Port Moresby, actually had for operational use 95 fighters, 49 light and medium bombers and 37 heavies. Kenney relied on General Ennis Whitehead as his deputy commander. Whitehead was tough, experienced, and what Kenney would call 'an operator.' He was widely respected and took great interest in checking all details of a mission; sloppy planning was forbidden.

At command levels below Whitehead, Kenney's actions had resulted in younger, able combat leaders taking command in flights and squadrons. By late February, crews were generally experienced, confident and eager to perform; staffs were beginning to work and function well; and aircraft had been modified and their roles altered to suit the theatre. With the new P38 able to demonstrate its ability to defeat the Japanese Zero, or Zeke, and increased proficiency in ground attack, the land-based 5th Air Force had yet to inflict a decisive defeat on ships, and so vindicate General Billy Mitchell. Of course, Billy Mitchell needed no further vindication. The German Luftwaffe, Italian Regia Aeronautica and Japanese Army and Navy Air Forces, flying from land bases, had been sinking aircraft carriers and Allied ships of all sizes since the Norwegian campaign of April 1940.

KENNEY'S SQUADRONS

The squadrons General Kenney used in the convoy battle had not reached the peak of efficiency they were to attain later in the war. Nonetheless, they had come through the bad period of retreat, lack of men, aircraft and parts, with the experience and confidence gained by the recent successful campaigns in New Guinea.

The 3rd Attack Group, consisting of the 8th, 13th, 89th and 90th Squadrons, had been chosen by Kenney to try his tactics of 'commerce destroying.' Commanded by Colonel Robert F. Strickland, it had been flying operations for almost a year. Five 8th Squadron Dauntless A24 dive-bombers, led by Lieutenant Bob Ruegg, had flown the first strike by the 3rd Attack, against Lae airfield on 1 April 1942. Apart from long-range B17 reconnaissance and bombing missions which mainly went to the Rabaul area, this was the first attack mission flown by U.S. forces in the New Guinea theatre, and the small force was escorted by six P40s of 75 Fighter Squadron RAAF. The 8th had flown its A24s from Townsville on 31 March, but the situation at Moresby was such that only two 500-pound bombs were available there, and the squadron was told to bring its own from Townsville or the refuelling stop on Horn Island. (3)

Another member of the 3rd Attack, Richard Launder, arrived in Australia on 22 December, aboard the SS *Willard A. Holbrook*. Of 21 pilots on the ship, only seven survived to return to the USA. Launder had taken part in the early missions and the debacle in Java.

As the premier strike group in the SWPA, the 3rd had a fund of hard-won experience with leaders who had gained position by way of their ability in combat. Since their arrival at Port Moresby, the 13th, 89th and 90th Squadrons had flown many missions during their detachments to New Guinea from Australia, and since arrival at Port Moresby. The 13th, with unmodified B25s, flew medium-level or low-level bombing missions and the 89th, with A20s, flew low-level attack missions. The 90th had just modified its B25s into 'commerce destroyers.' However, the 8th Squadron had been allowed to almost cease existence as a flying unit by Group Headquarters after a disastrous Buna mission on 29 July 1942. Only one A24, flown by Lieutenant Ray Wilkins, managed to get back to Moresby after Zekes intercepted the squadron. One other A24 made it to Milne Bay with a dying gunner. After that, the 8th became what amounted to a maintenance and repair depot for the 3rd, providing aircraft and crews for 89th Squadron missions. After Major James A. Downs assumed command in April 1943, the 8th began to function efficiently again, but the squadron was not to fly as a unit in the Bismarck Sea attacks.

AUSSIES IN THE 3RD GROUP SQUADRONS

Many Australians flew in the 13th and 90th Squadrons in all crew positions except aircraft commander. Suffering a shortage of flight crews from the early days of arrival, the U.S. groups had asked if Australians could be made available, and the RAAF responded by posting qualified airmen from all over the continent. The U.S. commanders did not have authority to place foreign nationals in command of U.S. aircraft, but the Australians were used in every other crew position. The RAAF supplied men to almost every U.S. bomber and transport unit, from early 1942 to mid-1943. Their contribution to the war effort has been largely ignored in official histories and publications.

Bob Guthrie, a pilot from West Australia, had applied to join the RAAF in 1940, but had to overcome a minor medical matter before being accepted for pilot training in June 1941. After graduation as a twin-engined pilot, he flew anti-submarine patrols and was a staff pilot in the southern part of Australia until February 1943. Then, along with a number of others, he was posted to Townsville, and allocated to the 90th Squadron. Others he knew went to bomber and transport squadrons. Bob Guthrie has good memories of his time with the 90th and recalls that the Aussies were welcomed 'and made to feel at home. We all seemed to get along very well with them.'

However, both sides found things to wonder at in the other. In the course of their anti-submarine patrols and staff flying, some of the Australian co-pilots had accumulated many more flying hours than their U.S. aircraft commanders, all of whom were commissioned officers. Bob Guthrie, a Sergeant, had a total of 855 hours, 708 of them as pilot in command of twin-engined aircraft, though none were in combat—the anti-submarine patrols were not counted as combat time. Guthrie was surprised to find a few enlisted Americans who could not read or write, and a ground staff Master Sergeant told him that he would read the letters of these men to them, then write their replies. (4)

Pilot Officer [2nd Lieutenant] Bill Blewett, a radio-operator gunner, arrived in the 90th but never flew in any of the practise missions. Having done his training in West Australia, he was waiting for a posting to an anti-submarine squadron in England, but after some disagreement with the CO of a station in southern Australia, he found himself in New Guinea with the American squadron.

RAAF co-pilot, Pilot Officer Royce Johnco, was born in England in 1913. Johnco's family immigrated to Australia when he was twelve. Drought drove his family off the land, and Johnco became a car salesman and then worked in the insurance business. In 1939, he tried to enlist, but was rejected by the Army because of flat feet; the Navy said he was too old, and the RAAF required better educational qualifications. Johnco studied, overcame the educational barriers, and joined the RAAF on 11 April 1942. He graduated as a commissioned Pilot Officer in November of that year, and went by sea to Port Moresby to be posted to the 90th Squadron. As an officer, he was included in operational planning, and knew Major Ed Larner and Captain Jock Henebry well. He regarded both as top-line fellows and was glad to serve with them. Of the 90th, Johnco recalled that 'they treated us wonderfully. We got on excellently with the Americans; most of us were sorry to leave.' Johnco flew with Lieutenant Bob Reed, and can well recall the training flights on the Moresby wreck: 'Great fun, but a deadly way of attacking ships; most effective. It was risky, but you were too busy to worry about that.'

THE BOMBERS

The 38th Bomb Group was commanded by Colonel J. O'Neill, and consisted of two squadrons, the 71st and 405th. When it first arrived in Australia, the 38th had no aircraft, and two of its squadrons had been held during the Pacific transit flight for use at Midway, then taken over by the 13th Air Force, and never actually made it to Australia. Less experienced than the 3rd at this stage, the 38th was to be used partly as medium-level bombers and partly as mast-height attackers, without the heavy nose armament of the 90th Squadron.

The 43rd Bomb Group, commanded by Colonel Roger Ramey, had B17 bombers. Kenney did not know for two weeks after arriving in Australia that this unit was under his command.

However, by February 1943, the 63rd, 64th, 65th and 403rd Squadrons were flying B17s against targets throughout the area of operations. In an attempt to get better bombing results, the 43rd pioneered the use of the big B17 in mast-height night attacks on Japanese ships. For a time, the 43rd was General Kenney's only heavy bombardment unit and it was expected to cover the entire SWPA. By the end of February 1943, the 43rd was a confident outfit, proud of its record and title—'Ken's Men'— after the great low-level bomber pilot, Ken McCullar.

There was great competition between the 43rd and Kenney's second heavy bomber group, the 90th, commanded by Colonel Ralph E. Koon. The rivalry lasted throughout the war and beyond. Of the 90th's four squadrons, only the 320th and 321st would be used in the Bismarck Sea actions. A few early B24s had operated with the 435th Squadron, 19th Bomb Group, but from early 1942, the 90th was the first formed Consolidated B24 Group in the SWPA. The 90th struggled against low serviceability rates, lack of parts, insufficient training, and poor flying conditions. Bill Moran, a photographer-gunner, said that 'we were still learning to fly the B24, and our friends were being killed in them.'

THE FIGHTERS

The 35th and 49th Fighter Groups had come through the time when the Japanese A6M Zero had reigned supreme. The inferior P39s had been outflown due to a combination of lack of experience, maintenance, and in some cases, leadership. Now the excellent P38 Lightning was available in the 9th and 39th Squadrons, and with P40s, the 7th and 8th Squadrons had learned to make use of its strong points. The P38 was first in combat over Buna on 27 December 1942, when twelve Japanese planes were destroyed and another four were claimed as probably destroyed. The pilots knew they had a superior fighter, and as one pilot said, 'It was love at first sight.'

Already there were several P38 aces, notably Tommy Lynch, Ken Sparks, Hoyt Eason and Dick Bong. Lynch was regarded by some who knew him as the best fighter leader in the theater. He already had eight victories to his credit, including three claimed over Moresby in the P400, an export version of the Bell P39. These P400 victories, on 20 May 1942, were the first for the 39th Squadron. Sparks, who was not amenable to discipline, had begun to score with the P38 and had seven victories claimed since 27 December 1942. Hoyt Eason also began to score on 27 December, and claimed six victories in three combats between 27 December and 8 January. Dick Bong had come to the attention of General Kenney for his unauthorized low-flying over San Francisco. Although he had been reprimanded at the time, Kenney had remembered the cherubic pilot and asked that he be assigned to the SWPA. On the flight over, in a B24, another pilot had studied the bunch of 2nd Lieutenants and made his assessments of their potential. He placed the quiet, innocent-looking Bong last in the group. In a P38, Dick Bong was exceptional, and since 27 December had five destroyed Japanese to his credit.

THE RAAF SQUADRONS

Two RAAF squadrons would play a significant part in the Bismark Sea actions, though aircraft from other Australian squadrons would be used in surveillance and night attack. 30 Squadron RAAF was commanded by Wing Commander (Lieutenant Colonel) Brian 'Blackjack' Walker, a very experienced airman. The 30th was the first unit in the SWPA to employ the British Bristol Beaufighter, a heavy, twin-engined attack aircraft which had been successful as a nightfighter over England and the Mediterranean theater. In early 1943, the two seater Beaufighter was the most heavily armed fighter in the world. With four 20mm cannon firing ahead from under the nose, and six .303-inch (7.7mm) machineguns in the wings, it could deliver a formidable amount of firepower onto its target. It was soon modified to carry a bomb under each wing, and later fitted with rocket racks. In Europe, rocket-firing Beaufighters created havoc in German convoys.

The first Beaufighters in the SWPA were supplied from Britain, but Australia built her own from plans taken from microfilm. 30 Squadron was formed on 9 March 1942, and its first Beaufighter arrived on 2 June. Walker took command on 4 June.

He had commanded a Wirraway unit at Darwin during which the Japanese attacked the town, harbor and airfield and inflicted heavy casualties. On 17 August 1942, the squadron moved to Bohle River, near Townsville, and on 6 September the first three Beaufighters arrived at Fall River, Milne Bay, at the eastern end of New Guinea. The next day they flew their first operational mission against Japanese shipping off Normanby Island.

Many 30 Squadron pilots were experienced on the Beaufighter. Many had flown it in England, others were experienced twin-engine pilots, and some had been instructors. The 'backseaters' were a special class of men, all well-qualified and some with extensive flying experience. At least two of the observers had logged 1,000 hours. Observers kept a general lookout, particularly for enemy aircraft, navigated, operated the radio and a camera (if necessary) and loaded the cannon and rear machinegun (fitted later).

Fred Cassidy, observer for Mos Morgan, finished his training as a gunner, radio operator, navigator and bombardier in June 1942. He had arrived at the squadron with 131 hours of flying time. By the time the squadron arrived in New Guinea on 9 September 1942, he had 186 hours, and up to the time of the Bismarck Sea battle had flown 30 low-level attack strafing missions, in support of bombers.

Another experienced 30 Squadron navigator, Sergeant Alf Nelson, joined the RAAF in December of 1939, and went on to join 21 Squadron at Singapore. After their Wirraways were annihilated, Nelson and others made their way through the Netherlands East Indies (Indonesia), took over a merchant ship which had only the captain and a Chinese crew member aboard, and sailed it to Fremantle, West Australia. He joined the newly formed 30 Squadron when it formed, and was impressed by the big aircraft. 'To see those Beaufighters, that was a marvellous experience. I thought, "I'm going to get my own back on these buggers now," ' he recalled. Nelson had 441 flying hours when he joined 30 Squadron, and by the time of the Bismarck Sea battle had flown 27 operational missions in the Beaufighter. His pilot was Len Vial, brother of the famous Coastwatcher, Leigh

Vial, who had reported Japanese activity around Salamaua and sent warning of Japanese air formations heading for Port Moresby. Because of the dangerous lonely job, Leigh Vial was known as 'Golden Voice,' and became something of a legend in his own time, but was killed in a crash in April 1943.

Blackjack Walker and Ed Larner of the U.S. 90th Attack Squadron were friendly rivals. The Australian Beaufighters used to 'beat up,' or buzz, the 90th camp, and would 'whistle up the valley at tree-top height and shake the devil out of Larner's tent on the top of the hill.' Larner even moved his tent, to a position where he thought no one could fly low over it, but Walker flew as close as possible, then turned away and used the prop-blast and slipstream churning back from the Beaufighter to buffet the tent. (5)

Late February 1943 was a crucial point in the SWPA campaign. Japanese command of the sea allowed them to reinforce and resupply their own formations in New Guinea to take the offensive again. Australian and U.S. land forces were exhausted after the Buna battles. Out of a population of only 7 million, Australia had 820,000 men in the army. Since July 1942, in New Guinea the Australian Army had 2800 killed and 3600 wounded, plus 14,000 hospitalized with malaria, typhus and other serious diseases. In the October–November 1942 Battle of El Alamein, in North Africa, another 5800 men had been killed or wounded. U.S. casualties in New Guinea numbered 671 killed and 2,172 wounded, with another 1,592 killed on Guadalcanal, in the Solomons.

The available Australian and U.S. divisions were not fit for battle. It had been learned the hard way what happened to partly trained Australian and U.S. units which attacked the formidable Japanese defensive positions. Japanese losses in New Guinea and the Solomons were estimated at 36,000 killed or dead of disease. Nevertheless, they had far more men and units along with the ships to bring them to the battle zone. All the factors save one were in favor of the Japanese—that single factor was the air strike force being assembled by Generals Kenney and Whitehead.

THE SHIPS, THE MEN

After the Japanese retreat across the Owen Stanley mountains and destruction of their force in the Buna-Gona area, Japanese headquarters at Rabaul decided to send a strong force to the Lae area of New Guinea. Japanese convoys had made the journey with relatively light losses from air attack. There was no Allied naval presence north of New Guinea, as it was fully occupied in the Solomons campaign. In addition to the successful convoy to Lae in January 1943, the Japanese had managed a brilliant series of destroyer operations and removed most of their surviving forces from Guadalcanal. The Imperial Japanese Navy was confident of its ability to engage and defeat Allied naval forces in the region, and believed that with adequate Army and Navy air support another successful operation could be launched to reinforce Japanese Army formations on New Guinea.

An intercepted Japanese message of 8 February, received at MacArthur's General Headquarters (GHQ), referred to landings of 20 and 41 Divisions at Wewak and Madang. Allied translators had problems deciphering the addresses in the message but Allied Intelligence believed that an accurate text of the message had been passed to Allied headquarters in the Pacific theaters. (6)

MacArthur and Kenney knew the Japanese would reinforce New Guinea, and now they had been given a small scrap of information about the enemy units involved. It was obvious to both men that the SWPA air forces presented the primary means of attack and prevention of these Japanese forces from arriving in New Guinea.

On 22 February 1943, Lieutenant General Adachi, commander of the Japanese 18th Army, issued the order for the next reinforcement operation. Operation Order A 157 stated that the Japanese intended to send fresh reinforcements to the Lae area, and to 'establish quickly a strong strategic disposition in the vicinity of Lae, Salamaua and the Markham Valley areas.' The Army and Navy planned to force a landing in that area and prepare for future operations. As soon as possible after landing, the troops were to co-operate with the existing anti-aircraft force in defence of the anchorage and airfield at Lae. Then they were to capture

Markham Point, secure the Lae–Salamaua road and reconnoitre the enemy position and the terrain on the south bank of the Markham River. The Japanese were aware of the need for radio silence. A paragraph of the operation order stated that no radio transmissions would be made during the voyage, except by the Shipping Engineer Regiment, a unit which was to assist in the unloading and debarkation phase of the operation. Lieutenant General Adachi was to sail with the convoy and land in the first wave, to establish his headquarters at Lae. (7)

Allied radio monitors, however, had already picked up more transmissions indicating the assembly of a convoy on 19 February and on 21 February two more messages from the Japanese Naval Air Force's 11 Air Fleet Headquarters were intercepted and deciphered. The first 11 Air Fleet message was only partially translated, but enough was deciphered to know that it was addressed to the Combined Fleet, (the 4th Fleet and 1st Naval General Staff) and that it referred to the arrival of the Japanese Army 51 Division at Lae on about 6 March, and the subsequent move of 20 Division to Madang. This message was included in the USN CinCPAC Bulletin #347 on 26 February.

The second message, sent at 08.14 on 21 February, went from 11 Fleet to Combined Fleet and 1st Naval General Staff, and was a general report on the intended landing operation. Six ships were to transport 51 Division to Lae, on about 5 March, depending on the readiness of the Japanese Army Air Force to assist with air cover for the ships. About a week later, 12 March, the landing operation at Madang was to take place. (8)

General Kenney now knew the basic details of the next convoy operation, but he did not know one important detail— the route. Commander of the 3rd Destroyer Flotilla, convoy commander Admiral Kimura, decided to take the route out of Rabaul along the north coast of New Britain and then south through the Vitiaz Strait to Lae. As convoy speed was only seven knots, Kimura decided to move to and from Lae by the shortest route and as quickly as possible. Kimura accepted that he would be found by Allied aircraft, but hoped the northern route would make the Allies think he was going to Wewak. (9)

After campaigns in New Guinea and the Solomons, the

Japanese were well aware of the danger from Allied air power, but believed that it could be countered. They accepted that this landing would be carried out under Allied air attack, so that it could be done successfully in the shortest possible time. They decided on the following important aspects of the operation:

- the Transport Commander had to exercise complete control of all units and detachments aboard ships from beginning to end of the voyage;
- shipment of non-essential articles or luxuries 'will on no account be permitted;'
- all loading of cargo was to be done from consideration of the actual unloading operation, and position of cargo was to be made with the unloading in mind as the first essential;
- all personnel of units and detachments 'must therefore apply themselves to the task and make best use of the unloading craft. Organisation and distribution must be perfected in order to eliminate all idle time.'
- order of unloading was to be personnel and necessary equipment first, then munitions, rations and anti-malaria medicines, then the most important equipment of each unit, then baggage.

The Japanese assessed that the Allied aircraft were most likely to interfere with the operation during the unloading phase off the beaches at Lae. Thus they emphasised the need for speedy but efficient activity by all concerned in this period. In some previous operations of this type, personnel eager to avoid bombing had gone ashore as quickly as possible. In some cases this had resulted in a shortage of people to help unload cargo, and on a few occasions there was nothing unloaded and no one left to direct operations. But this operation was carefully planned, with a chain of command and clear priorities that included a set of instructions for all units and detachments involved.

At Kabakaul, near Rabaul, the Japanese 51 Division issued Order A 59, stating that with the Navy's co-operation it would 'make a vigorous landing in the vicinity of Lae,' and that the Division Commander, Lieutenant General Hidemitsu Nakano, would be aboard destroyer *Arashio* from 27 February. Its Order A 60 stated that 'the division will make a landing at all costs in the vicinity of Lae on the night of 3 March.'

On 22 February 1943, the reinforcement forces sent to the Lae-Salamaua area were composed of the 51st Division and the following attached artillery and AA units:

> Divisional Headquarters
> 115 Infantry Regiment
> 14 Artillery Regiment (less two battalions and ammunition train)
> 51 Engineer Regiment (main strength)
> Divisional Signals (main strength)
> Attached units:
> 21 Independent Mixed Artillery Brigade
> 50 Field AA Battalion (less one company).

Debarkation of the force at Lae would be facilitated by:

> 3 Debarkation Unit
> 3 Company 5 Shipping Engineer Regiment
> 8 Shipping Engineer Regiment.

The convoy would also have Army Command Station (part of the 15 Independent Engineer Regiment), an Army Signals unit, 22 Airfield Battalion, 209 Airfield Battalion, and 5 Air Signals Regiment. The units which accompanied 51 Division came under command at 07.00 on 25 February. This force was distributed aboard the ships in such a way that if a ship was lost, any one unit would lose only a fraction of its men and equipment. The Japanese had assembled a balanced force, some of which would be used to help unload subsequent convoys.

In addition to the *Nojima*, a Naval Special Service ship of 8251 tons, seven transport ships were assembled for the important convoy: They were:

Aiyo Maru	(2746 gross tons)
Kembu Maru	(953 GT)
Kyokusei Maru	(5493 GT)
Oigawa Maru	(6493 GT)
Taimei Maru	(2883 GT)
Teiyo Maru	(6869 GT)
Shin-Ai Maru	(3793 GT)

The seven ships carried a total of 6004 men destined for the Lae-Salamaua area. Many Japanese documents give the total as 5954, and do not include the *Kembu Maru*, which transported 50 men from 51 Division units and 221 Airfield Battalion. Unit weapons included 12 anti-aircraft guns, 21 artillery pieces, seven mortars, and 138 motor vehicles. The ships carried 38 large motorised landing craft (MLC) and 8250 cubic metres of fuel and ammunition. The six larger ships carried 750 drums of fuel, and the *Kembu Maru* held another 1650 drums. Because the fuel and ammunition was to be unloaded as soon as it got to Lae, it was stored where it was readily accessible. This aspect of planning would have special significance in the upcoming battle.

The ships carried the usual anti-aircraft defenses: anti-aircraft guns, pom-poms, machineguns and army unit field guns. The break down is as follows:

Aiyo Maru had two anti-aircraft guns, two pom-poms and a fieldgun,
Kembu Maru—two machineguns,
Kyokusei Maru—four anti-aircraft guns and a field gun,
Oigawa Maru—two anti-aircraft guns and a field gun,
Taimei Maru—two pom-poms, two machineguns and one field gun,
Teiyo Maru—two anti-aircraft guns, two pom-poms and a field gun.

The destroyers also carried MLC, collapsible boats, and members of Army units. *Uranami* and *Shikinami* carried one small MLC and nine collapsible boats; the others each had two small MLC and six collapsible boats. Army personnel on the destroyers were detachments of from six to 60 men, from 18 Army Headquarters, 51 Division Headquarters, 51 Division Signals, 115 Infantry Regiment, 14 Field Artillery Regiment, 51 Engineer Regiment and 8 Shipping Engineer Regiment. 150 men were to be carried on each of *Tokitsukaze, Arashio, Yukikaze, Asashio, Uranami*, and *Shikinami*, with 29 on each of *Shirayuki* and *Asagumo*. The convoy was commanded from *Shirayuki* by the commander of 3rd Destroyer Flotilla, Rear Admiral Shofuku Kimura. Lieutenant General Hidemitsu Nakano, commander of 51 Division, was to sail on *Arashio*, but he and his group were put aboard *Yukikaze* instead. Lieutenant General Adachi, commander of 18th Army, was to travel aboard *Tokitsukaze*.

The convoy divided into two Divisions. Each ship was numbered by division and carried an additional number by which it was usually known.

No. 1 Division	I	*Shin-Ai*	324
	II	*Teiyo*	842
	III	*Aiyo*	947
	—	*Kembu*	(nil)
No. 2 Division	IV	*Kyokusei*	776
	V	*Oigawa*	480
	VI	*Taimei*	967
	VII	*Nojima*	(nil)

The destroyer escort had orders to cover contingencies which might arise—such as attack by enemy surface ships or air attack. Under air or submarine attack, the convoy was instructed to take evasive action on order from the escort commander or the leading warship, but if the attacker was discovered at short range, a ship was permitted to take evasive action as long as it did not endanger any other ship. Paragraph 8.b. of the landing plan stated that on discovery of enemy planes, the escort was to make a smoke screen, and 'attacks will be directed towards enemy planes.'

Paragraph 9 of the plan included an air-escort time-table and explained that the Army and Navy would each provide half a day of air cover from sailing on 1 March until their return to Rabaul on the 7th. Air cover would be provided from 05.00 daily until 18.00, during the voyage, unloading at Lae, and on the way back. It was expected that the cover would be provided by 40 Navy and 60 Army fighters. In addition, Japanese Navy air units planned to attack Port Moresby and Milne Bay, and Army air units would attack Wau and Buna during the period of the convoy, its unloading and return to Rabaul. Allocation of times was:

1 March	all day	Army aircraft
2 March	05.00–12.00	Navy
	11.00–18.00	Army
3 March	05.00–12.00	Navy
	11.00–18.00	Army
4 March	05.00–12.00	Army
	11.00–18.00	Navy
5 March	05.00–12.00	Navy
	11.00–18.00	Army
6 March	05.00–12.00	Army
	11.00–12.00	Navy
7 March	all day	Navy

Daylight cruising formation of the convoy was to be:

DD *Shikinami*   DD *Uranami*

DD *Arashio*   DD *Tokitsukaze*

Kyokusei Maru   *Shin-Ai Maru*

Oigawa Maru   *Teiyo Maru*

Taimei Maru   *Aiyo Maru*

DD *Asashio*   DD *Yukikaze*

Nojima   *Kembu*

DD *Shirayuki*   DD *Asagumo*
rescue ship for aircraft forced down

There were other formations for night or times of close visibility, but generally the destroyers were some two kilometres from the convoy ships, which were 800 metres from each other.

Loading the cargoes into the merchant ships began on 22 February, with munitions being loaded on all ships first, followed by some of the materials belonging to the units which would embark, then more munitions, unit freight, and finally on 28 February, the personnel. All ships were carrying munitions, with the exception of the *Kembu Maru*, which was fully loaded with gasoline—1000 drums of aviation gasoline and 650 drums of lower-grade. This gasoline was intended to allow increased Japanese air attacks from bases in New Guinea.

The commander of 115 Infantry Regiment, Colonel Torahei Endo, issued a mimeographed speech to his unit on 25 February:

Our regiment is about to enter the decisive battle area of the Great Asia War. From the first, this has been the inspiring deed for all officers and men. There is no greater feat than this. It has been observed that this task is extremely serious and at the same time important. It is our objective to bring the Great East Asia War to a close by suppressing New Guinea and then subjugating Australia, which is our appointed task, thus sealing the fate of our enemy. One cannot refrain from saying that the result of this decisive battle will decide the destiny of the Great East Asia War. Therefore, all officers and men, advance vigorously, fight bravely, and plunge into the jaws of death. Exalt the brilliancy of our regimental colors. Display the traditional spirit of Joshu boys. You must be determined to accomplish this important task. Study the following poem by Nanko:
      "Divorce yourself from life and death
        and let Heaven guide your sword"
Give your special attention to the following instructions. I want brave and prompt action.
1. Always be loyal. Display your aggressive spirit and annihilate the strong stubborn enemy.
2. Display the power of unity and collaboration. Advance

vigorously with the Company Commander as the backbone of a strong impetuous charge.

3. Staff must always have absolute control over men. No matter what difficulties you face, don't be terrified. Lead your men boldly, fight wisely and bravely.

Instructions concerning conduct aboard ship were issued to all units. One duty for officers was to take turns leading a daily half-hour of singing war-songs. The emergency orders stated that on hearing an air-raid or submarine alarm, all personnel were to prepare to abandon ship. If bomb hits caused fires, the bridge was to be informed at once, while the fire was fought, and those men in the holds went on deck. The abandon-ship order would only be given by the transport commander, and the order was to be carried out in a 'speedy and orderly manner. It is strictly forbidden to try to rush out first, causing general confusion.' Rope ladders and nets were prepared and held ready in the holds in case the ship had to be abandoned. After boarding the ships and settling into their quarters on 28 February, all units carried out abandon-ship practise at 17.00 hours.

Some of the men going aboard had considerable military service, some had little. Going aboard *Aiyo Maru* as a member of 8 Shipping Engineer Regiment was Private Akio Fujiwara. Fujiwara had been working on a fishing boat before being inducted in Korea on 1 December 1940, and joined 23 Engineer Regiment there. On 8 January 1942, he landed in Malaya and participated in the capture of Singapore. On 24 March he landed at Lingayen and took part in the fighting on Bataan and Corregidor. From there he went to Manchuria, back to Japan and on to Rabaul, where he took part in the evacuation operations from Guadalcanal. On 11 February 1943, he went to Kokopo, and from there his unit was detailed for the convoy to Lae. He was 22 years old. (10)

Also on *Aiyo Maru* was Private Juichi Okamoto, a 23 year old in Captain Koike's motor transport battalion. Okamoto was called to service in Hiroshima in August 1940. Trained in Manchuria, he served in Korea, before arriving in the South Sea and Rabaul on 14 January 1943. (11)

A civilian deckhand on the small *Kembu Maru* was Higari Shimomida. He had been aboard *Shiki Maru* when it was torpedoed on 8 September 1942. He joined *Kembu* on 20 December. Another man on *Kembu* who had been torpedoed was Sergeant Masaji Sasaki, member of an AA pom-pom unit. Inducted in January 1939, Sasaki was wounded in China in June 1940 and once again in February 1941. Army service had taken him to China, the Philippines, Ambon, Timor, Indochina, the Midway expedition, Singapore, Rangoon, and to the ship *Zenyo Maru*, which was torpedoed on 2 August 1942. After a tour of duty in Japan, he arrived in Rabaul on 19 February. (12)

At 27, Tatsue Machida had been a railway clerk before the military called him for a second time. When he was called in August 1941, he had already done military training. After garrison duty and light clashes with the Chinese at Whampoa and Chung-sheng, in December 1942 he sailed for Rabaul, and after about two months training, his unit, 115 Infantry Regiment, began loading for the voyage to New Guinea. (13)

2nd Lieutenant Goichi Hikozaka had been conscripted into 1 AA Regiment in 1928, and had been soldiering ever since. He served in Manchuria and China and was Adjutant of 50 AA Battalion for a year. The battalion sailed from Korea to Rabaul in December 1942, and Hikozaka boarded *Oigawa Maru* with a detachment from his unit. (14)

On *Teiyo Maru* was a member of 51 Division Signals, 24-year-old Private Mikiwo Omiya. He had gone into the Army in January 1940, seen service in China, and arrived in Rabaul on 13 December 1942. Also on *Teiyo Maru* was 39-year-old Warrant Officer Shichi-Hei Matsushima, 115 Regiment, who volunteered for military service in 1919, at the age of 17. He had seen war service in Manchuria and China, and was discharged in 1939. He had joined the Nissan Automobile Company, but in July 1941 was called back to active service, going back to China, and then to Rabaul, arriving 21 December. (15)

On *Shin-Ai Maru* was another older man, 38-year-old Private Seiji Kojo, in 3 Debarkation Unit. He had been an apple farmer until called to service in August 1942, arriving in Rabaul in December. (16)

An oiler on *Taimei Maru* was 29-year-old Eiki Kiyo, a Korean. His primary education had been at Kobe, Japan, but he had studied agriculture for two years in Korea, before being forced to leave for taking part in student riots. He joined the Nippon Yusen Kaisha Line, and from 1935 to 1940 had been aboard *Tenzan Maru*, and made several voyages to the South Seas. He joined *Taimei Maru* on 24 November 1942, and arrived in Rabaul on 29 December. After a voyage to Wewak the ship then traveled to Erventa and in the last week of February began preparing for the Lae Convoy. (17)

Thirty-seven-year-old Private Yokichi Kitamura, 8 Shipping Engineer Regiment, was on DD *Uranami*. He had worked for nine years in a color type company, and for ten years as a taxi and truck driver. He was called to service in July 1941. (18)

As they had no access to information which was not provided by their homeland propaganda service, until they reached the frontlines, few Japanese had any idea of the real situation there. It was true that Japan had won some smashing victories over the Americans, Dutch and British, not to mention the Chinese, and the French, who had meekly allowed Japanese forces to occupy French Indochina. The borders of the Empire had rolled south at an astonishing rate in the first months of 1942. But then Allied resistance hardened, and the long supply lines from Japan proved inadequate. From mid-1942 there had been few victories, only intense fighting, and the defeats at Midway, New Guinea (Kokoda-Milne Bay-Buna-Gona) and the Solomons.

Imperial Headquarters provided victory claims of even greater achievements, as for the Solomons battles from 7 August 1942 to 30 January 1943. The Japanese people were told Allied losses had been: Battleships 20; Cruisers 40; Aircraft-carriers 8; Destroyers 36; Submarines 10; Transports 23; and Aircraft 910. Japanese losses were said to amount to only 1 Battleship, 41 other ships and 224 aircraft. (19)

These ludicrous figures could only be presented to people in ignorance of the true situation. No Japanese appears to have questioned the enormous U.S. construction program needed to create that many ships in the first year of the Pacific War, or the training effort required to produce crews to man the ships being sunk in these battles. The Japanese on the Lae convoy were to see for themselves the accuracy of the Imperial Headquarters claims.

By late afternoon of 28 February, both sides in the coming battle had prepared themselves as best they could. That day, the Allied Air Force practised putting a strike force across a target in finely co-ordinated attacks at all heights, and reorganised its staff and logistics system to fully support the attacking squadrons. For their part, the Japanese had arranged air attacks on the Allied air bases, agreed on air cover for the convoy, distributed and loaded the Army units throughout the ships to minimize losses if one ship was sunk, detailed everything necessary for defence of the convoy when it arrived at Lae and planned to unload quickly. The escorting destroyer crews were experienced. Out in the Bismarck Sea was the expected bad weather which would shield them from Allied reconnaissance aircraft. With a little good fortune, the Imperial Japanese Navy would complete another successful convoy operation and deliver the Imperial Army formation to Lae.

TWO

FIRST
CLASH

1–2 MARCH 1943

At midnight 28 February 1943, the Japanese convoy assembled outside Rabaul harbor, and early on 1 March set course along the northern coast of New Britain, north-west from Rabaul, before turning west and then south. Plodding along at seven knots, the ships saw no sign of enemy activity and the dark hours passed. The weather favored the Japanese with a gale, mist and rain. 1 March passed, the steady thumping of the ships' engines drawing them on to New Guinea.

But at 16.00 hours, B24 Liberator #1-24070 of the 321st Squadron, 90th Bomb Group, popped out of the cloud. The mission of Lieutenant Walter Higgins' crew had originally been to search the south coast of New Britain, turn north and cross the island near Rabaul, and then fly home along the north coast. However, the bad weather forced the B24 back along the south coast until a break was found, which they followed, and so came out over the ocean farther west than planned. The navigator, George Sellmer, first sighted the ships. Higgins' crew counted and reported a 14-ship convoy at 04.30 degrees South, 150.45

degrees East—six destroyers, one 7000-ton AK, one 5000-ton AK, and the remainder 1500 to 2000-tons. The sighting report from the B24 and the acknowledgement from Port Moresby was intercepted by the Japanese ships, and DD *Tokitsukaze* informed Rabaul and the convoy commander. General Adachi passed the message on to Army units on the ships.

As the weather was still very bad discovery did not mean attack was to follow. Admiral Mikawa had promised to attack Allied air bases in New Guinea, but did not do so. The bad weather which covered the convoy also blocked Japanese attack on the Allied air bases. If the bad weather persisted, however, the convoy might be able to complete the voyage to Lae without interference. Mikawa also had underestimated the number of aircraft available to RAAF and USAAF units.

The Japanese troops aboard ship had no cause for alarm, although some were told the convoy had been sighted by Allied aircraft. Yasuhira Yamazaki noted that the first night aboard ship was without incident, but when he was told of the aircraft sighting, his comment shows that he expected air raids to follow: 'Security and black-out orders were more rigid. All individuals arranged their belongings in order.' A soldier on *Teiyo Maru* was able to see the north coast of New Britain as they steamed west and noted in his diary that there were eight transports 'in two close columns escorted by eight destroyers.'

But as in all military organisations, some did not get the correct information, and were told that a submarine had found them. As the day faded into dusk, and dusk into night, the convoy moved on without difficulty, and the troops began to think of the battles they would fight in New Guinea. One wrote in his diary that 'the day for landing in New Guinea, our foremost battle line of the Greater East Asia War, is drawing nearer.'

Generals Kenney and Whitehead alerted their strike force, and the long-range heavy bombers set off for the area of the ships. Another B24 from the 321st Squadron, flown by Lieutenant George Shaffer, arrived over the area of the convoy at 20.40 hours, and at a height of 1500 feet, received some anti-aircraft fire. Four 500-pound bombs were dropped, but there was no more fire, and no sighting of the convoy. Seven B17s of the 63rd

Squadron, 43rd Bomb Group, attacked the airfield at Gasmata with sixteen 500-pound instantaneous fuzed demolition bombs within an hour after 21.42. Twelve flares were released over the estimated position of the convoy, but the bomber crew did not sight it, nor any activity from it. Below the bombers, the Japanese watched the flares falling to starboard of *Kyokusei Maru* as the ships steamed on under the clouds. (1)

Next day, 2 March, the weather was still bad, but had eased somewhat. The USAAF formations had to contend with overcast skies, low broken clouds down to 1000 feet, and intermittent thundershowers. At 07.30, a single B17 of the 65th Squadron, 43rd Bomb Group, arrived in the area where the convoy was expected, but did not sight it. One 6–7000 ton ship on course for Lae was seen at 06.40 degrees South, 147.35 degrees East. Meanwhile, at 06.30, six A20s attacked Lae airfield and dropped twelve 500-pounders and twelve 250-pound bombs, fitted with instantaneous and 11-second delay fuzes, claiming fifteen hits on the strip. The attack was intended to prevent use of Lae airstrip by enemy airplanes for air cover over the ships. A B24 of the 320th Squadron, 90th Bomb Group, found the convoy at 08.15 hours, counted seven warships and seven merchantmen at 05.05S, 148.30E, and circled until the approaching bombing formations arrived.

Next to report action in the convoy area were sixteen P38s of the 39th Fighter Squadron. At 9000 feet, they flew on through the weather, and at 09.30 engaged three fighters, identified as Japanese Army Nakajima Ki-43 Oscars 50 miles north–north-west of Arawe. The Japanese were flying along after a formation of B17s about to attack the convoy. According to the Japanese time-table for air cover, these should have been Navy fighters, Mitsubishi Zekes. Captain Charles King, who had flown on the practice mission two days earlier, and wondered at the purpose of the flight, was one of the P38 pilots. The P38 formation had surprise and fired on one enemy fighter, scoring hits; the Japanese fighters turned. Lieutenant Wilmot Marlatt fired on one from the left front, sending it down and out of control, with heavy smoke streaming behind. Charlie King dived on another from behind and shot it down. Captain Curran Jones claimed another, identified as a Zero, as a probable. The P38s did not sight the convoy. Japanese 18 Army Headquarters recorded a total of three JNAF aircraft destroyed over the convoy during the day. There was to be more combat between U.S. bombers and Japanese fighters later. (2)

At 09.50, seven B17s of the 63rd Squadron, 43rd Bomb Group, arrived. Leading, in *Talisman*, was Major Ed Scott, with Captain Harry Staley on his right, and Lieutenant Francis Denault on his left in *Lulu Belle*. The formation had flown north from New Guinea, passed just east of Rooke Island, circled south of Sakar Island, and then flew east to Cape Gloucester. From there, Scott went north-west, passed over the convoy, and counted seven ships through the clouds—two destroyers and five transports. Scott turned starboard at 7000 feet to go in and bomb.

Scott and his wingmen stayed together and attacked, while the other B17s split up and went after ships as individuals. Scott held his formation of three at 6,500 feet and began a run on one large transport. Although it was still raining, the clouds had cleared somewhat, and the ships could be seen below. As they began the bomb run, eight Japanese fighters attacked with co-ordinated passes from high and low.

Ignoring the fighters and anti-aircraft from the destroyers, Scott's bombardier released their four bombs. The bomb run had been made to cross the line of ships, going over the target at the ten o'clock position. It was believed that three bombs hit near the funnel and the fourth exploded in the water close by. The last of Staley's four bombs hit the bows of the ship. The first of Denault's exploded on the stern and the others fell into the water nearby. A huge cloud of smoke and spray flew up, hiding the ship, and then what were thought to be internal explosions were seen.

This ship was *Kyokusei Maru*. Japanese on board later described a succession of hits: a group of three, and two on No. 1 hold, or two on No. 2 hold. The 2,000 cubic metres of munitions on board were the probable cause of the secondary explosions. On board were 1,200 Army troops, including the 3rd Battalion 115 Infantry Regiment.

The battalion diary records that twelve bombers attacked

and that the ship's guns fired at them, adding to the anti-aircraft fire from the destroyer escorts. The diarist thought that ten bombs were aimed at the ship:

> Two hit No. 1 Hold and two other bombs scored a direct hit on No. 2 Hold, thus starting large fires. While we were engaged in extinguishing the fires and saving the wounded, the ammunition and gasoline caught fire and exploded. We were then forced to stop work. The fire was getting worse and worse, and finally spread to the bridge. At 10.30 the transport commander ordered all personnel to abandon ship. Through the co-operation of the ship's crew and men of other units, the wounded of Headquarters, No. 9 Company, were taken out of the ship. Their position had received so direct a hit that almost all of them were badly wounded. They were unable to get out of the fire and only a few were saved. The rest, who were either unconscious or unable to walk could not get to the deck. Finally, after all the survivors had abandoned ship, the flaming ship exploded and sank at 09.22 (Tokyo time). (3)

A soldier in the unit commanded by 1st Lieutenant Ogawa wrote that at 07.30 (Tokyo time) they were 'sailing peacefully, escorted by planes and destroyers, when discovered by four enemy Boeings. The convoy's anti-aircraft guns went into action. The enemy dropped eight bombs, and six of them made direct hits. The ship was soon on fire, and at 09.27 hours she sank.' (4)

Only four boats or rafts had survived the explosions, but the destroyers came to rescue as many as possible. DD *Asagumo* saved many, including the diarist in Ogawa's unit, while *Tokitsukaze*, with Lieutenant General Nakano aboard, stood by. Lieutenant Ohara, 14 Artillery Regiment, reported his endeavours:

> Working with all our might, we were able to salvage two mountain artillery guns from the burning transport *Kyokusei Maru* and successfully set them afloat on the sea. This evidence of the spirit of the artillerymen greatly moved the captain and men of the destroyer *Asagumo*. Regardless of

the effort, the destroyer made every effort to raise the guns. The guns were rusted and some parts were lost, but they could be fired. (5)

Overhead, the air battles continued. Barely able to see through the heavy rain, Lieutenant Jim Murphy took B17 #381 *Panama Hattie* in after Scott's formation. He selected a destroyer as a target, but the agile ship dodged the bombs while sending up accurate fire at the bomber, and after a second run through the close explosions, Murphy decided to try for a transport ship. He attacked one, and the single bomb was reported to have hit and blown out the side of the ship. Crew members said the ship broke completely in two, with the bow and stern sinking separately within minutes. This may have been *Kyokusei Maru*, as no other transport was sunk in the attacks that day.

Despite heavy and accurate anti-aircraft fire, Captain Sogaard attacked a ship with two bombs exploding some 25 feet from it, causing smoke and flame to shoot out of the ship's hold. This was reported as a small ship, 5–800 tons, presumably *Kembu Maru*, which survived the day. Survivors do not mention such damage on board. More bomb runs were made, but the bomb sight failed, and Sogaard had to turn away, with two bombs left. Captain DeWolf attacked two ships, but bomb-rack malfunctions caused his bombs to miss, and Lieutenant Moore leveled all his bombs at another ship, but without success. Lieutenant Dieffenderfer made two runs on the same ship. Attacked by fighters, he dove the big bomber at them and then escaped into the cloud cover.

Bombardier Lieutenant Fred Blair had watched their eight 500-pounders miss a transport, but thought the ship was slowing from concussion damage to the hull. Sitting in the nose of the diving B17, Blair watched the air speed indicator show 200 mph, then 250, then 280. He remembered the times they had seen 20-foot long sharks in the waters below, and was not pleased at the possibility of meeting them face to face. Dieffenderfer and co-pilot Jack Campbell braced themselves with feet on the crossbars under the instrument panel and hauled back on the wheel, dragging the big bomber out of the dive and into level flight at about

1,000 feet. The dive had loosened fabric on the elevators, making control difficult, but Dieffenderfer got it back to base. A Boeing representative from Seattle was waiting at the revetment when they taxied *Old Baldy* back in. He congratulated the pilots, telling them that he was surprised that the B17 had been able to stay in the air, let alone cross the mountains. (6)

As they left the ships, the B17 crews believed they could see two ships burning, and one other high out of the water and on fire. They reported attacks by up to twelve fighters, claiming three probably destroyed, with four B17s holed by enemy fire. A few minutes after Scott's squadron, the 65th arrived with six B17s. These crews claimed three hits on a 5-7000-ton transport, with results unseen due to the weather, and the placement of one bomb within 40 feet of a light cruiser. As no cruisers were present, this must have been one of the larger destroyers. About twelve enemy fighters attacked, inflicting damage on one aircraft, but none were claimed in return. As crews left, they reported two ships of 5–8000 tons burning, with destroyers trying to assist. This may have been a duplicate sighting of *Kyokusei Maru*.

Bombs fell astern of *Oigawa Maru*, and Corporal Rihei Koido saw no damage inflicted on the ship. Private Nobuo Yamada, Signals Company 115 Infantry Regiment, saw one bomb explode only 100 meters away. With the exception of a few on duty top deck and those manning the AA guns, the infantry had been ordered below decks. Later on they were told a ship had been sunk. A Warrant Officer of 2 Battery 50 AA Battalion was one of 65 men of the unit on *Oigawa Maru*, saw four bombs hit *Kyokusei Maru* and watched it burn and begin to sink. Five B17s later attacked but did no damage, flying on through the AA fire, and two came in again, but one was hit and set on fire. Still it came in, dropping a bomb which hit 50 meters from the ship's after well deck, and a second which hit only ten meters from the port quarter. (7)

This B17 was from the 64th Squadron, during an attack at 18.20 hours. From 4500 feet, two more B17s of the 65th Squadron attacked separately at 10.15, claiming a hit and two near misses on a 6–7000 ton transport, and sighting a large ship, the *Kyokusei Maru*, burning and smoking amidships. Six fighters, identified as Oscars, had attacked them at 09.35, putting holes in one B17.

The 64th Squadron had eleven B17s, including several from the 403rd attached for the mission, over the convoy at 10.20, bombing from 4700 to 5600 feet. The pilots were Major Mc-Cullar, Captains Salisbury, Giddings, Holsey and Nelson, with Lieutenants Schultz, Humrichouse, McMullen, Olsen and Gowdy. McCullar had been one of the leading enthusiasts in using the B17 for low-level night attacks on Japanese shipping in the theater, and was another of the young able leaders noted by General Kenney. The formation claimed a direct hit and two near misses on a 6000-ton ship and a near miss on another of the same size. Some twenty fighters had attacked, holing one B17, but the gunners claimed three Japanese destroyed and five as probables. Crews reported seeing a 7000-ton ship explode, an 8000-tonner 'in sinking condition' and another 5000-ton ship on fire and smoking, plus a destroyer thought to be on fire. In the prevailing weather conditions, with formations entering the convoy area at short intervals and criss-crossing the scene, there was considerable repetition of reports of damaged shipping.

Entering the combat area at the same time as the 64th, but at 7000 feet, two B24s of the 321st tried to drop their twelve bombs on a cruiser and a 4000-ton ship, but with no hits or other damage. Fifteen Zekes attacked but were driven away by P38s. The B24 crews sighted five warships and what they believed to be nine transports, and reported that the B17 attacks had sunk one transport and set another on fire.

Meanwhile, at 10.42, Lieutenant Archie Browning, in B24 #42-24108, *The Butcher Boy* of the 320th Squadron, 90th Bomb Group, had taken off and flown to the convoy area. He slipped down out of the clouds long enough for the crew to count the scattered ships and give their figures. They reported the numbers by radio to Port Moresby: three cruisers, four destroyers and seven transports.

Beginning at 11.30, there was a break of about two and a half hours before a B17 from the 63rd Squadron returned and remained for the next six hours. During the pause in attacks, the destroyers began picking up survivors from *Kyokusei Maru*, and one diarist from 115 Regiment recorded that all were saved by 13.00. He noted that of one unit, 80 out of 200 men had been killed, of another, 130 were wounded, 50 of 80 artillerymen were killed, 50 percent of company headquarters were killed, and there were no machineguns or battalion guns left.

The next attack was at 17.40. A lone B17 from the 403rd Squadron, 43rd Bomb Group, missed with two 1000-pound bombs, and for its trouble was attacked at 7,500 feet, by twelve Zekes who shot holes in the bomber.

Forty minutes later, from heights between 4500 and 7800 feet, nine B17s of the 64th and 403rd Squadrons attacked despite interference from Japanese fighters. The bombers were flown by Major McCullar, Captains Giddings and Holsey, and Lieutenants Humrichouse, Schultz and McMullen of the 64th and Captains Smith and Brecht, with Lieutenant Gowdy of the 403rd. The B17s claimed two direct hits amidships on a 6000-ton ship, two near misses on another, which stopped, and two more near the stern of a 5000-ton ship which had its stern lifted out of the water. This ship was probably *Teiyo Maru*, as described below. The crews reported sighting six warships and ten transports, with two of them on fire.

Captain Holsey's B17 of the 64th was struck in the bomb bay by a heavy-caliber shell, and fire flared. Seven crew were injured, but Lieutenant Reeves and Technical Sergeant Young fought the flames for twenty-five minutes. At one point, it seemed that the fire was out of control and Holsey was thinking of a forced landing. He radioed this to Captain Giddings, who replied, 'Hold on, Ray, and I'll be right down.' Giddings' instant and calm reply went into squadron lore. He took his B17 down and circled Holsey, adding his own firepower to that of the damaged bomber. A Japanese voice broke into the conversation with relevant remarks, but Holsey's answer is unprintable. He took the B17 back to base safely. An estimated eighteen Zekes and Oscars attacked before the formation arrived at the convoy, persisted until after they left, damaged four B17s and wounded seven crewmen, though one Zeke was claimed as destroyed and one as a probable.

The convoy was last seen at 18.45 hours, at 05.40 degrees

South, 147.30 degrees East. There were only six warships remaining. *Asagumo* and *Yukikaze* had pushed on to Lae with the survivors from *Kyokusei Maru*, unloaded them there, and returned at high speed to the convoy that night. By the end of the day's attacks, the convoy had lost *Kyokusei Maru* (sunk) with *Teiyo Maru* and *Nojima* damaged.

Captured Japanese documents and prisoner interrogations showed that *Teiyo Maru* had been damaged by a near miss to the bows, buckling plates, but damage was not heavy. Private Tadashi Tsurume, of 50 AA Battalion, thought that *Teiyo Maru* was bombed and strafed and hit on the stern, with about fifty men killed or wounded. Also aboard, Sergeant Chikui of 115 Regiment, noted that although four men of the unit died and about twenty or thirty were wounded, the ship remained with the convoy. (8)

Private Yoshio Watanabe, of 1 Battalion of Shipping Engineers, also believed that the ship was damaged aft by two bombs, and that 2nd Lieutenant Sakai, commanding 2nd Platoon of his unit, was killed. The ship kept on with no reduction in speed. The near misses made dents and small holes in the ship that were seen by Probationary Officer Ryuji Sakieda of 51 Division Signals unit. He knew bullets had hit the ship, but his own unit had no casualties. (9)

On *Shin-Ai Maru*, Private Akimoto of 115 Regiment noted that five bombs fell 200 meters from the starboard side of the ship. However, most of the other troops on board were ordered below decks, and saw little of the action. (10)

Private Juichi Okamoto, a member of a motor transport unit on *Aiyo Maru*, watched the B17s attacking through the clouds and rain, and thought them 'terrible, fearful.' He saw *Kyokusei Maru* hit and sink, but did not know the name of the ship. Private Akio Fujiwara watched the air attacks, and saw ten Japanese fighters attack nine B17s at low altitude, only about 3–4000 feet, and watched as one B17 (Holsey) flew off on fire. (11)

Another B17 from the 65th Squadron had searched the Dampier and Vitiaz Straits for some nine hours from 18.15, but sighted nothing.

After unloading from the destroyers at Lae, the survivors

from *Kyokusei Maru* began the task of checking losses and preparing for future duty. Lieutenant Ohara, who had saved two mountain guns, was given 'the heavy responsibility of guarding Markham Point. The guns became rusty, but to me they were more important, just as regimental colors, of which only the pole is left. I would like to die beside my mountain guns.' His battalion commander, Major Kiyotaka Sakaba, had been drowned in the sinking. Sakaba had been ceaseless in his training of the unit, and on the morning of their departure from Rabaul had drunk a toast with the officers, saying, 'I pray for our success.' The few words gave Ohara confidence. His diary was captured five months later, at Bobdubi, New Guinea. (12)

The survivors of 115 Infantry Regiment were marched six km to a bivouac area. First Lieutenant Ogawa and the remnants of his unit were landed at 23.00 hours (01.00 local Tokyo time) and made the march. A count showed that there were 32 present, with 13 others known to be safe, 37 wounded, and 52 dead including three officers and eight NCOs. Of the leaders, only two officers, including Ogawa, and the Sergeant Major remained with the survivors; they had suffered losses of two-thirds. Other companies suffered even more, and the company was later combined with the 31 survivors of the 11th and 12th Companies to form 9 Mixed Company, with a total of 107 men by the end of March. (13)

Meanwhile, the convoy had turned south, to pass through Vitiaz Strait between New Guinea and New Britain. Admiral Kimura decided to circle for a while during darkness, and time his arrival off the coast at Lae for next morning. This decision doomed the Lae convoy.

At Port Moresby, preparations for the strike by the massed squadrons went on. In the Australian Beaufighter squadron, George Drury wrote the following in his diary: 'Pandemonium. A Jap convoy of 7 transports, 4 destroyers and three cruisers with about 40 Zekes as top cover was sighted on the north coast of New Britain heading thisaway evidently. This morning the whole squadron was briefed to do a co-ordinated attack beginning as soon as the convoy came within safe range.' The Beaufighters, as practised, were to go in ahead of the B25 strafers and attack the gun crews. The squadron took off for Dobodura, but was ordered back to Ward's Strip. The weather had closed on Dobodura and they just got back to Ward's before it too was closed. The feeling of excitement in the squadron was growing with each report of the convoy battles.

An RAAF PBY Catalina from 11 Squadron, A24-14, piloted by Flight Lieutenant (Captain) Terry Duigan with Squadron Leader (Major) Geoff Coventry as co-pilot, took off from Milne Bay to search for and shadow the ships. Coventry was with the squadron to gain experience, and left a few weeks later to do the formal training course to qualify as a Catalina crew commander. Duigan was a very experienced Catalina pilot, on his 31st mission of the tour. He already had 1872 hours flying time, 775 of them as aircraft captain by day, and 453 by night. The Catalina, based at Cairns, Australia, was to refuel at Milne before actually beginning the search. It does not seem as if Coventry had flown to Milne Bay before, as Duigan recalls.

When approaching Milne Bay from the south, the mountains appear as a continuous line, but just west of the head of the bay, at Mullins Harbor the coast makes a little 'zig-zag,' allowing low-level entry into the anchorage. The usual thick weather disguised this short cut, but the old hands knew it, and used it to watch the effect on new co-pilots. With solid cloud down to 400 feet, to the uninitiated, the coast seemed to be a wall of mountains.

At the correct moment, Duigan turned the big 'Cat' right at the coast and flew for it. To Coventry, it seemed they were flying straight into the hillside. 'As we approached eternity,' recalled Duigan, 'from the corner of my eye I could see white knuckles gripping his wheel, perhaps contemplating a Caine Mutiny. Then we slid through a saddle and popped into the clear, floats down, throttles back, and alighted, to drop off the step just short of our mooring buoy.'

The actual mission was not to be flown until after dark, so the Catalina crew had the afternoon to spend in Milne Bay. Terry Duigan had cause to go to the latrine. An American officer was also there, and seeing the verdigris on Duigan's cap badge, asked if he was with the Catalina moored offshore. Duigan acknowledged he was. The U.S. officer was Lieutenant Walter Higgins of the 321st Squadron, 90th Bomb Group. He told Duigan that he had been forced to ditch his B24 (#41-23750) when flak set a No.1 engine afire during an attack on the January convoy. Higgins put down the B24, 'Cowtown's Revenge,' in the water off Islet Island, and the crew struggled ashore. Sergeant Gaudet was killed or drowned in the ditching, and Sergeant Satterfield died next day of injuries. The remainder were sighted by a searching B24, and rescued by an 11 Squadron Catalina, piloted by a namesake, Flight Lieutenant B. H. 'Tubby' Higgins. Lieutenant Higgins told Duigan that he'd been out on reconnaissance the day before and seen ships off the northwest coast of New Britain.

Duigan took the Catalina north into the search area, and quite early in the flight, at 22.00 hours, the Anti-Surface Vessel (ASV) radar clearly picked up the convoy in the open sea. There was no confusion caused by radar returns from the many small islands south of Rooke Island. It was realised that if the convoy was heading for Finschafen, it was making a wide swing. Duigan put the Catalina into a run across the ships in order to release a flare for making a visual vessel count that was then reported to Port Moresby.

In the darkness of the Catalina fuselage, Bill Clough took a flare and prepared it for dropping on command from Duigan, but felt something happening inside the tube. He reacted instantly, flinging the potentially dangerous thing out the open blister hatch, and almost at once it ignited. Duigan was surprised, but assumed something had gone wrong behind him, and got on with the job of reconnaissance, even though the early ignition and flood of light illuminated the Catalina in the sky rather than the ships below.

The first thing the Catalina crew saw was a ship's wake, heading south-east, and as the flare blossomed they counted six large ships, with what Duigan described as, 'hints of more beyond the illumination, all quickly adopting a disturbed ants' nest configuration.' Knowing from experience that Japanese night-fighter activity was rare, and then mostly on moonlight nights, Duigan circled the convoy and reported that they could see five ships, including one cruiser, and a 10–12,000 ton transport, on course

180-degrees, at 05.45 S, 147.35 E. This placed the convoy west of Umboi Island, between it and the New Guinea coastline. The Japanese monitored this sighting report, sent at 22.40 hours. (14)

Port Moresby told Duigan to remain with the ships 'until dawn,' which Duigan translated with a private codicil out of respect for flak and fighters—'well before dawn!' He realised that they were expected to try to slow down the convoy while a proper reception was being organised for it. He did not think his single aircraft could demolish the convoy single-handedly, and was 'in no hurry to do anything desperate.'

The night was what Terry Duigan termed '10/10th dark,' and the ships were visible only from 2000 feet directly overhead, as black blobs against white wakes. Once the convoy had re-formed, the Catalina crew released another flare and watched the ships scatter again. This went on several times, and twice single bombs were dropped at unidentified ships, with no visible results. Eventually, the ships did not bother to take any action as the slow-flying Catalina approached through the night and clouds. It was only after this mission, when they reported the almost instantaneous ignition of the flare, that defective aerial flares were presumed to have caused the destruction or loss of three other Catalinas which had signaled radio alarms 'on fire!' received at base.

During the night, Port Moresby instructed Duigan to continue to remain with the ships and guide torpedo-carrying RAAF Beauforts from 100 Squadron at Milne Bay's Gurney Field to the scene. This sort of operational co-ordination had never been discussed, let alone practised, and thus was ignored.

As dawn and the time to depart approached, Duigan decided to use the remaining four 250-pound bombs to stir up the ships. After several passes over the convoy, he selected a warship recognisable by its slim hull, which he estimated to be a cruiser. It was later acknowledged to be a large destroyer. At 2000 feet, he brought the Catalina up on the bow of the ship, popped out a flare ahead and to one side of it, passed overhead and down the wake, turned as tightly as possible and came back on its trail, with the flare still illuminating the destroyer. Bob Burne, the navigator and bombardier, took over the bomb run, giving corrections to Duigan, then called, 'Bombs gone.' Duigan swung off to starboard and made a circle to port as they all watched the bomb bursts walk up the wake of the destroyer—1,2,3, and the fourth just shaved the fantail. Bob Burne had set the bombsight to 'stationary,' mainly due to fatigue and the many different ship's speeds and courses they had encountered during the numerous runs across the convoy; if the sight had been set to '20 knots,' Duigan believes those four bombs would have hit.

The sole remaining striking power remaining with the Catalina was the .30-caliber (.303-inch) machineguns fitted for defence. Duigan did not intend strafing anyone with them, so they remained above the ships until it was time to put some distance between themselves, the convoy, and the expected Zeke fighter cover which would arrive at dawn. Duigan finally turned away at 02.40, reporting the convoy at 06.13S, 148.02E. The Japanese also picked up this message. The ships were well south of Umboi Island, north-east of Finschafen and steaming south; obviously not intending to go to Madang.

As the Catalina went on home to Cairns, another aircraft with navigation lights on passed under them, flying west. They did not know if it was a Beaufort or a B17 tasked to replace them, or even if it was a Japanese heading for Lae. Hours later, they arrived, and Duigan caught a taxi home from the wharf. Mrs. Duigan had made her own assessment of the strategic military situation and moved from Melbourne to Cairns, so Terry lived a relatively normal home life, going out to fly and then returning on home. The taxidriver guessed Duigan had returned from a mission and asked if he'd been a long way, 'like up past Cooktown?' Cooktown is less than 150 miles from Cairns; Duigan had been airborne 15.5 hours by the end of the mission Milne Bay–Cairns.

At 04.00 hours, the Japanese radio monitors picked up yet another report, giving the convoy's position as 6.45E, 148.45E, almost due east of Finschafen. As they had not turned west there, the Allied commanders could presume that the ships would be going on to Lae.

At Port Moresby, plans were made for a concentrated daylight attack at about 10.00 A.M. The ships would be within striking range of the twin-engined bombers and strafers from the Moresby bases and within fighter range of the P40s. Apart from the tactical necessity of successfully attacking the ships, there was also the higher need to demonstrate the capability of air power.

From the assembled reports of the B17 attacks, it seemed that considerable damage had been done already. Apparently no hard-nosed assessment of claims had been made by anyone at 5th Air Force that took into account the abominable weather and bombing conditions, with B17s under attack, and the past record of such attacks in the SWPA. By the end of the first day's strikes, 5th AF accepted the following: at *08.25* a 14-ship convoy, including seven destroyers, had been counted by the 320th Squadron. In the first attack by the B17s one large ship had split in two, rolled over and sunk; two others were badly damaged and on fire, one was sinking. When the B17s left the scene, the two burning ships had been left behind by the convoy; leaving only eleven.

At 14.05, a 63rd Squadron reconnaissance B17 reported six warships and nine merchant vessels, with two more unidentified ships appearing to join after 15.30 hours, plus the sighting of two warships leaving the convoy at 17.30 hours, on course 185-degrees.

In the second attack, sixteen ships were counted at 17.45 hours. Of them a medium-sized vessel had been hit twice and was sinking, a large ship was stopped after two near misses, and a medium-sized ship was badly damaged by two near misses.

In his report of 6 April, General Whitehead summed up the effects of the B17 attacks on 2 March as follows: one very large transport and three of 6,000-tons sunk, and one 6,000-ton and one 800-ton ship gutted by fire.

At 18.20, the convoy was last seen in daylight and counted as 16 ships. However, late the day before and again early this same morning, 14 ships had been counted. If four ships had been sunk and two burned out, it seemed a second convoy must have joined the first. In fairness to the Intelligence and Operations staffs, they had a very difficult task trying to accurately assess bombing results, and had been confronted with the large number of 22 reports describing attacks and bombing results and sightings filled with multiple references to hits, fires, near misses, sinkings, capsizings and similar descriptions. The lack of good reconnaissance or strike photography showing the entire convoy added to the difficulty of post-mission analysis. In addition, no useful information coming from the 'Ultra' radio intercept service.

Nevertheless, the enemy also was disturbed by the air attacks and though aware that only one ship had been sunk, some of the Japanese were beginning to worry over the increasing strength and expertise of their enemy. Despite air attacks, the January convoy got through and attacks continued after the ships arrived at Lae. There was some reluctance among middle-ranking and senior officers about sending this convoy in March, but theatre command decided to do so, even at potential losses of fifty percent; the Army in New Guinea had to be reinforced.

Thus far the weather had been to the advantage of the Japanese and the American heavy bombers had not been very effective. One transport out of eight was an acceptable loss, the same as that suffered at sea by the January convoy.

By noon next day, 3 March, the convoy would be anchored off Lae and unloading of 51 Division would be in full swing. The combined defensive fire from eight destroyers, convoy ships, and guns on shore would be formidable, while strong fighter defence from nearby Lae would be quite effective. In another 24 hours the operation could be deemed a success.

THREE

ONSLAUGHT

After Terry Duigan left the convoy, there was a short period of quiet for the ships, although pressure was to be maintained in spite of the bad flying weather. 100 Squadron RAAF had sent off seven Beaufort torpedo bombers to attack, but the weather was so bad that only two crews found the ships. At 03.23 (local time), Squadron Leader J.A. Smibert, the Beaufort squadron CO, took off from Milne Bay. Behind him, the other aircraft rolled out for take-off. Bill Ewing was navigator for Pilot Officer Ken Waters in A9-193, and they began the mission at 03.55. The rain-storms were right down on the surface of the sea, and cumulo-nimbus were dotted through-out the area. The pilots had to change course to avoid the worst of the weather, which made things more complicated for the navigators. Ewing suspects that the combination of the local weather and need for emergency procedures to fly through such weather resulted in the loss of some crews. Individually, the Beauforts struggled through the night weather towards the convoy location.

At 06.15, Smibert found the convoy, and counted ten ships

at 06.45S, 148.05E. He dropped flares to guide the following aircraft, and at 06.25 Ken Waters arrived. In the nose of the Beaufort, Bill Ewing realised that the rain and clouds had lifted a little, and the grey half-light was just enough to dimly see some of the ships. He went back to sit next to Waters as the attack began: rock-steady at 150 knots, 100 feet, running in to 1,000 yards (metres), using the Dibbs Director—a system of lights to assist in getting the best angle on the bow of the target.

Waters made a torpedo attack from 45-degrees on the bow of what was thought to be a cruiser, watched the torpedo run to within 100 yards of the ship, but saw no results. He made the standard flat skidding turn to avoid gunfire, and in the turret, watching the torpedo wake, Stan Webber could see it running straight and true for the target, and firmly believed it would hit, then the Beaufort was in cloud and zig-zagging for home. Destroyers *Asahio* and *Shikinami* reported a total of three attacks in the early morning hours, but no damage.

Thirty minutes later, Flying Officer (1st Lieutenant) Lew Hall attacked an 8,000-ton ship, but the torpedo would not release. The Beaufort was built to accommodate the British torpedo, and the different size U.S.-made version presented a problem. Allied torpedoes, in general, never did function at an acceptable operational standard. Determined to do some damage, he went in at the ship and fired 1000 rounds at it. *Shin-Ai Maru* reported being strafed at 05.00 (07.00 local time). The Japanese thought a B25 had attacked. Hall and his crew saw the rounds hitting the superstructure of the ship, and turned away into the night.

The RAAF crews had counted 13 to 15 ships, believed to be stationary, in the flare light. All three crews returned to base after a mission lasting 4½ to 5 hours, much of it through very bad weather. Alan James and his crew saw distant flares, but could not locate any ships near that spot when they arrived, in spite of spending almost an hour in the target area chasing the three sighted flares. Eventually they arrived back at Milne Bay after a 4 hour 15 minute search under exhausting conditions. (1)

The Australian torpedo attacks had failed. The convoy moved steadily on to Lae. As dawn came closer, Kane Yoshiwara, a staff officer from Rabaul, went up on deck aboard

Tokitsukaze and looked around. Far off to the west was the thin dark line of New Guinea, and as he watched he saw an enemy reconnaissance plane flying north, faintly visible against the sky. Suddenly Yoshiwara felt a strong premonition of danger. The distant plane had been checking the convoy route, and it was obvious the ships were going to Lae. To fool the enemy, the Japanese should change course. Then, to calm himself, Yoshiwara remembered the skill of the ships in dodging bombs the previous day, and told himself that even if a thousand aircraft attacked, the convoy would get through with slight losses. He went below for breakfast. (2)

At Port Moresby, the Japanese ships were now known to be going to Lae, and the Allied air headquarters could activate the plan to apply concentrated air power onto the convoy. At the air bases around Port Moresby, there was a gathering feeling of anticipation. As always, some people seemed not to have gotten 'the word,' and did not know what was being planned. Others did, and the sense of excitement grew. There was a certain amount of competition to get onto the list for the mission.

As practised, the Beaufighters of 30 Squadron RAAF were to go ahead of Ed Larner's 90th Squadron, and strafe the Japanese ship decks and guncrews in order to force them to take cover and gain the crucial few seconds needed by the low-flying B25s and A20s as they sped onto their targets. Thirteen Beaufighters were tasked for the mission. Wing Commander Blackjack Walker's navigator-observer had been classified as unfit for operational flying, but Walker decided to go along, taking a newly arrived navigator, to observe and control his squadron from higher altitude. For some time, he had been thinking of positioning the formation leader in the second or third flight so that he could observe the beginning of an attack and manoeuvre the force to take advantage of opportunities as the attack developed, rather than be first across the target and have little control over the following aircraft in the formation. Squadron Leader Ross Little led the actual strike force of twelve aircraft; no one knew Walker intended going along.

They were to rendezvous at Cape Ward Hunt with the U.S. force of B17s, A20s, and B25s, plus the P38 escort, and then go on from there to the convoy. The transports were first priority, then warships, and third Lae airfield. The bomber radio callsign was 'Peanuts,' and the fighters were called 'Popcorn.' As there was no teletype connection with Moresby operations, there was no written order. All mission instructions were verbal, and the actual form was not received by 30 Squadron until after the squadron had taken off, at 08.46.

During the briefing, Walker bluntly told the crews to attack the ships' bridges and thus cause maximum destruction and confusion at the location where the ship was controlled. He emphasised that as much damage as possible was to be inflicted in order to assist the strafers that would follow. The Japanese had to be destroyed before they landed and began offensive land operations in New Guinea.

The Aussie groundcrews gathered to wave goodbye to the Beaufighters. There were grins, thumbs-up and waves as the big green attack aircraft taxied out. 30 Squadron had flown numerous strike missions, but had rarely seen a Japanese below the green carpet of trees. Alf Nelson, the navigator who had escaped from the Singapore debacle in a merchant ship, among others, was looking forward to this strike. This time they knew that the target would be easily visible. According to Nelson: 'This time, we were going to see some Japs. This time, we really knew. The blokes were excited about it.' (3)

With 30 Squadron was the Australian combat cameraman Damien Parer, already famous for the way in which he filmed from the most dangerous locations. He had sent back dramatic footage from the Mediterranean theatre, from the Kokoda campaign, and continued to get right into combat for the best possible results. Parer bunked with George Drury and Dave Beasley, but flew almost non-stop with all the units, sometimes climbing out of one aircraft and going directly to a different squadron for another mission. 'Parer was the most incredible person,' said Drury. 'With the greatest respect, he had to get killed. No one could do the things he did and expect to live out the war.' On this mission, Parer would fly with 'Torchy' Uren, standing behind him and filming through Uren's windshield. Parer's film would show the results of the attack in a way which could not be refuted.

At the 90th Squadron, 3rd Attack Group, Major Ed Larner gave a short briefing. Usually he defined individual tasks in an attack, but on this day, as with the RAAF squadron, there was no teletype connection. It was 5 minutes to 9 when Larner was informed that the squadron was to rendezvous 160 miles away on the far coast of New Guinea at 09.30. He called out, 'Cape Ward Hunt! Let's go!' and walked out to the aircraft.

Royce Johnco, the English migrant who had been refused by the Australian Army and Navy because of his age and flat feet, was flying with Bob Reed in Larner's squadron, and recalls that the B25 crews did not quite know what the mission was until they were quickly briefed, but apart from that and some excitement, things seemed to be normal. However, as the B25s and A20s of the 3rd Attack Group roared off, non-flying personnel lined the strip, waving goodbye. Some in the departing bombers did not expect to survive a low-level attack up to and over muzzles of guns on a convoy protected by warships. Many groundcrew agreed, and gathered to bid farewell. Bill Smallwood, who had arrived in Australia 22 December 1941, and had since married an Australian airline stewardess, found out after the mission that most pilots had anticipated 50 percent losses.

For the mission, Ed Larner was leading, and behind him were Captains Chatt and Henebry, and Lieutenants Howe, McCoun, McKee, McNutt, Moore, Bob Reed and Harlan Reid, Sbisa and Smallwood. Gordon McCoun flew on Larner's left wing, Bill Smallwood on his right, with Chuck Howe as fourth man.

The 89th Squadron, 3rd Attack Group, commanded by the respected Glen Clark, would be taking its fast Douglas A20s on the mission, along with three crews from the Group's 8th Squadron. Ed Chudoba was Operations Officer for the 8th, and had been fully informed of the mission from the start. Glen Clark, whose initials G.W. had been shortened to 'Geedub,' had been with the squadron from the beginning. He had gradually worked his way up to become squadron commander, and was described as having a calmness from which others took confidence.

One of the new 89th Squadron pilots, Charles Mayo, finally talked Clark into placing him on the mission list as a standby for the 13th A20. If someone had mechanical problems, Mayo would take his place in the 12-plane formation.

Mayo and the rest were keen, despite having seen a well-known photo of the crews of the Navy Torpedo Squadron 8, taken before the Battle of Midway. An 'X' marked Ensign George Gay, sole survivor after the slow U.S. torpedo formation was massacred by anti-aircraft fire and Zeros. All knew that in a low-level attack against Japanese ships, their A20 tactics allowed variations in direction of attack, height, speed and evasive action, none of which could be used by torpedo bombers making a run-up to drop their torpedoes.

Clark called a briefing for those on the mission, and at 08.30 they gathered in and around the small room. Clark's voice carried to those outside, where everyone who could do so gathered to listen. Clark went over the information on the strike order. He then added that the squadron was the clean-up squad in the attack, but that he could not give detailed instructions on how the attack would be made. After the ships were sighted, he would pick one. Other pilots were to do the same, but also watch that they did not all attack the same ship. With a grin, Clark then told the assembly that there would be 40 Lockheed P38s overhead. Rendezvous was to be 09.30 over Cape Ward Hunt. He concluded with a time-hack, and wished everyone good luck. The 13th man, Chuck Mayo, was in luck. Captain Osterreicher's engines gave trouble, and he had to leave the line. Mayo took his place on the mission.

The 89th Squadron had not actually practised the new mast-height attacks, and after briefing, 'the thought of attacking warships at mast height did not thrill the hell out of us,' recalled 1st Lieutenant Jack Taylor. His A20, #40–162, was named *Kentucky Red*, in honor of his red-haired wife, Dottie.

Captain Bill Beck, 89th Squadron, had wondered if the A20s would be able to reach the convoy, attack, and get back to an airfield before running out of fuel. Captain Roger 'Dixie' Dunbar took off and began climbing as fast as possible, leaving the others behind. Beck found Lieutenant Neel, leading the third element in the flight, formating on him, and the four A20s went for height while climbing the slopes of the Owen Stanleys and cleared the crests by what Beck later estimated to be 20 feet; 'no circling for elevation that morning,' he said. The squadron joined up and moved into formation.

The 89th Squadron formation as they set course was:

Clark

Chudoba   **Richardson**

Mayo   **Beck**

Ruby

Dunbar

Neel   **Taylor**

Montagano   **Conn**

Messick

First at the rendezvous point, the 71st Squadron, 38th Bomb Group began a wide, lazy circle at 5,300 feet as they waited for the armada to follow. The crews then saw a procession of air power greater than anything the Allied Air Forces had concentrated before in New Guinea. Captain W.S. Royalty described it as 'an almost unbelievable number of planes.' B17s were moving into formation above the 71st; below came three separate flights of B25s; in formation and beginning to circle were Beaufighters and A20s; the highest up were the P38s.

Charlie King, who had scored his first victory in the rain clouds over the convoy the previous day, was leading an element in Major George Prentice's 39th Squadron of P38s. He looked down and was impressed by the sight of so many Allied aircraft. 'It was a first for all of us,' King said. The 64th Bomb Squadron, with three 403rd aircraft attached, slid into formation. The B17s were piloted by Major McCullar, Captains Nelson and Salisbury, and Lieutenant Schauweker, with Captain Hocutt and Lieutenants Glyer and Piccard of the 403rd.

It was a bright sunny morning, and the first squadrons circled slowly while watching the others coming over the mountain ranges. There had not been a sight to equal it in the New Guinea theater. Everyone in the aircraft was impressed by the gathering might. Any earlier feelings of unease or lack of confidence began to dissipate. Then two flights of three B17s set off, followed by the 71st's B25s, and the strike force moved north to the convoy.

Several crews in the lower squadrons reported seeing some bombs from B17s falling into the sea well before the convoy was reached, but it is not known if this was accidental, or someone lightening their load. There was minor disagreement as to whether the splashes were caused by P38 drop-tanks or bombs, but most witnesses believed they were bombs. Bill Beck of the 89th Squadron thought that perhaps a B17 was under attack by Zeros.

The Beaufighter crews noticed a dark-green twin-engined plane up above with the P38s, identified it as another Beaufighter, and wondered briefly who it could be before realising it was Blackjack Walker, determined to be in on the event, if only as an observer. The Beaufighters moved into formation, with each flight of six aircraft in vics of two and the flights in line astern. The rendezvous height was 6,000 feet, and the Beaufighters began a shallow dive towards the convoy, with zero boost and 2000 revs. Ed Larner's 90th Squadron B25s, with eight .50-calibers in the nose, were in an echelon right formation behind the Beaufighters.

Aboard destroyer *Tokitsukaze*, Kane Yoshiwara had finished breakfast and gone on deck again. It was full daylight. He looked around for enemy aircraft, but saw none. As the ships had now passed the narrowest part of the strait between New Britain and New Guinea—the logical place for an air attack—and the convoy was still untouched, he believed they were safe. He went below to his cabin, and then next door to talk to another staff officer about matters concerning plans for after the landing at Lae. It was 09.45 A.M. (4)

South of Yoshiwara, in the 90th Squadron's #946 *Margaret*, with 'Seabiscuit' Sbisa, Australian Bob Guthrie heard a radio call, 'that the convoy was in sight; and the game was on!'

The following diagram of the convoy formation at 10.00 hours, 3 March 1943 is compiled from Japanese documents captured after the battle, prisoner interrogations and Japanese reports after the battle. None agrees entirely with any other, and a * after the name of a ship indicates its position has been given as such by two or more sources. For example, DD *Uranami** shows that the ship is referred to in at least two documents as being in the right flank leading position.

DD *Uranami*   **DD *Asashio***   **DD *Asagumo***

DD *Shirayuki* *Shin-ai** *Teiyo** *Aiyo** *Kembu*

DD *Shikinami* *Oigawa** *Taimei** *Nojima**

DD *Tokitsukaze*   **DD *Arashio***   **DD *Yukikaze***

The description of the action which follows is based on study of offical reports from the Allied squadrons, personal recollections and records of participants, translations of captured Japanese documents, interrogation reports on Japanese captured after the battle, and photographs. Even at the time, it was not certain which aircraft and crew attacked which ship, and now that so many years have passed, the author does not claim one hundred percent accuracy. However, by collecting and analysing information from the sources above, it is believed that what follows is reasonably correct.

Captain W. S. Royalty of the 71st Squadron, in their unmodified B25s which bombed 'normally' from medium level, described the first sight of the convoy, as he saw it then: 'Nearest to us, as we came closer, were what seemed to be two cruisers and three destroyers. These ships were making violent maneuvers and wakes were streaming out ten or twelve times their lengths. I counted six transports and cargo vessels on the other side of these warships, and at least two warships further on. The warships were moving fast, but the cargo ships seemed to be almost at a standstill.' (5)

Bill Beck, in the 89th Squadron, was staring ahead at an empty sea, clear to the horizon, when he first noticed two wakes and then the destroyers making them. The 89th Squadron formation swung left, and there ahead of him were the ships.

Aboard the convoy, preparations were beginning for the landing and the quick efficient unloading operation desired by the planners. Troops were being assembled to hear instructions. On *Oigawa-Maru*, Private Tatsue Machida, in the Signals Company of HQ 115 Regiment, had just joined the group on deck. The briefing officer, Lieutenant Hashimoto, told them that Japanese air units had flown in force to Moresby and attacked the airfields there, and thus the threat of Allied air attack was now gone—there would be no air raids. While he was speaking, the troops saw two formations of Allied aircraft appear—B17s at height and the twin-engined bombers lower down. The officer kept on talking heedlessly, and Machida wished he would stop. Finally, when the attackers were close, he did so, and the men fled below to follow orders about preparing to abandon ship if necessary. Private Noburo Yamada, of the same unit, recalled that no sooner had the officer said the convoy was close to Lae and there was no further fear of bombing, than the Allied aircraft appeared out of the clouds.

Suddenly Army bugles blared the air-raid signal, and those assigned gun stations with their unit weapons of 50 AA Battalion hurried to their positions. An anti-aircraft gunner on one of the ships had first seen eight B17s. Then the gunners saw more aircraft lower down. 'Together they numbered fifty planes and swarmed over our heads. Everyone had a feeling of helplessness. There were none of our planes.' (6)

On small *Kembu Maru*, with its cargo of dangerous gasoline drums, the AA defence consisted of two 20mm cannon mounted on the bridge. The guns were from the AA Company of 23 Artillery Regiment, and were commanded by Sergeant Masaji Sasaki. He and the six other men in his section would have a good but short view of the beginning of the attack. Private Tagayasu Kawachida was a loader on one of the guns, and he was watching the oncoming Allied aircraft very carefully.

On *Taimei Maru*, the watch was changing, and the bridge was crowded with those coming off and those going on duty. Admiral Kimura's decision to circle during the night and arrive off Lae in mid-morning was now to result in destruction of the convoy. If he had continued during the night and slowed, halted, or circled close to Lae, so that at dawn he was able to move into the allotted unloading positions, the convoy would already have been disembarking men and supplies, under the protection of guns aboard ships and those ashore, only one minute flying time for Japanese fighters from Lae and Malahang airstrips. But the ships were still on the high seas.

The Japanese would have seen the approaching squadrons beginning to spread out, before coming at them from all sides. B17s and some smaller bombers—B25s—swung to the east; other B17s flew towards the western end of the convoy; more twin-engined aircraft descended directly at the ships; and still more came on behind those. The four-engined bombers were high against the clouds, closing more slowly than the diving twin-engined bombers. The Japanese Navy commanders decided to concentrate the heaviest guns on the four-engined bombers and use the smaller guns, plus the ships' manoeuvring, to defeat the twin-engined aircraft and avoid the torpedoes which the smaller bombers were quite sure to drop at 1,000 or 2,000 meters distance. After fifteen months of war, the captains and crews were experienced and confident of their ability to cope.

As the destroyers fired their main armament, great sheets of flame were clearly visible to the approaching aircrews. It was agreed later that the destroyers' fire control was excellent. No fire was opened on the aircraft until they were in position for cross-fire, and then the warships fired together. Admiral Kimura's crews were experts. Even at six miles, the shells burst within 100 yards of the Beaufighters, and it was noticed that the bursts were in patterns of three, with the first at about 50 feet and the other two stepped down to sea level.

Some of the Allied air units enforced radio discipline, but the 3rd Attack was noted for the loose chatter among its pilots. Now the air waves resounded to the yells and calls: 'Look at that! Go, boy! Atta boy! Yippee!' RAAF Beaufighter Pilot George Drury felt that this increased excitement and got the adrenaline flowing, but made it almost impossible to send a message of importance.

When the Beaufighters were within range of the destroyers' guns they were at 500 feet, but the pilots went down rapidly and attacked at 220 knots, in line abreast. Their course would have taken them from south to north over a line of four destroyers. Both flights turned starboard to avoid the warships, but the destroyers, thinking they were about to be attacked by torpedoes, and obeying the orders issued before sailing, turned towards the approaching planes.

Captain Royalty, watching from medium height in his 71st Squadron B25, recalled that 'we followed along behind the B17s as they flew parallel to the line of warships, and the nearest cruiser [Tokitsukaze] threw three broadsides at us—as we got opposite this ship, the B17s turned off to go over the convoy.'

As the B17s approached to attack, Japanese fighters appeared overhead at a height of about 3,000 feet. Major George Prentice, leader of the 39th Fighter Squadron, decided on simple tactics—lead the formation of sixteen P38s into the middle of the largest group of Japanese. There were an estimated twenty or thirty Japanese fighters, in groups of eight. Prentice went left after them and the combat began. The shower of released long-range tanks from the P38s fluttered down towards the approaching low-level squadrons. Some of the Japanese fighters engaged, but three or four remained above. Charlie King kept on climbing up through the clouds to get at them. But they'd gone. Looking down, he saw a P38 with a Zeke behind it, and dove to get near—that was where the fight was going on.

To the south, diving to mast height, Captain Ed Chudoba was flying A20 #40–89 Adam La Zonga of the 89th Squadron. He saw the convoy from 6,000 feet; the transports were still in a regular formation, but the escorting destroyers were turning hard towards the aircraft, and leaving long curving wakes as they did so. (7)

As the RAAF Beaufighters were dodging the destroyers, suddenly they found themselves passing through a shower of large tumbling drop tanks from the P38s. Alf Nelson, the Singapore escaper, was in the back of Len Vial's Beaufighter and at first wondered what they were, then hoped that they would not hit one—the result would be disastrous. Now at very low level, 30 Squadron passed the destroyers, turned back to port, and on to the merchant ships. As no great amount of fire was coming from them, the Beaufighters climbed, to then make a diving attack and cover the decks with fire from the 20mm cannon and .303 machineguns. Some of the Beaufighters went to port, going past the sterns of the destroyers in order to attack the leading ships in the convoy, while others passed ahead of the warships and took the rear of the convoy.

In the 405th Squadron, 38th Group, Captain Williston Cox saw the tumbling P38 tanks leaving veils of unused gasoline, and told his crew that the P38s had spotted Zeros and so they had better be ready. (8) It was 10.00 o'clock, 3 March 1943; a decisive moment for Allied Air Forces in the South West Pacific.

The destroyer manoeuvre of turning towards the attacking planes, designed to interfere with torpedo attacks, left the other ships unprotected, and by the time the destroyers reversed course and moved back, the first wave of strafers had flown over. However, heavy fire from the warships was still being directed at the Beaufighters, particularly when they climbed.

George Drury saw the leading transport [*Oigawa*] was too far to the left, but the second one [*Taimei*] was in line for him to attack, so he put his sights on the bridge and fired, holding course until he was so close he had to bank on pull-up to go between the masts. The ship's watch had been changing, overcrowding the bridge, and survivors recalled the hail of 20mm cannon shells which created havoc among the assembled officers and crewmen. Smoke can clearly be seen flowing back from the bridge in the photograph taken as a Beaufighter flew past. The same was happening on other vessels.

The Beaufighters roared among the merchant ships, cannon and machineguns flailing bridges, sweeping the decks and guncrews. The deck cargo of what was estimated to be a 10,000-ton ship burst into flames under Pilot Officer Dick Roe's 20mm cannon fire and exploded into a ball of fire which turned into a large smoke ring. This was seen by many crews; photographed and reported. The ship may well have been *Teiyo-Maru*. Other ships were well strafed and many guncrews annihilated. On one ship, the gunners were clearly visible, pointing up at the B17s, gun barrels elevated, before the blast of 20mm and .303-inch from an approaching Beaufighter flung them aside. On another, a large

■ 73

Red Cross marking was painted on the rear hatch cover, but next to it was a 3-inch gun in a circular mounting. Flying Officer J.T. Sandford saw a guncrew turning to fire on a B25, brought the Beaufighter nose onto them and mowed the crew down.

Behind the Beaufighters came Major Ed Larner's 90th Attack Squadron in their modified B25s, and this below-mast-height attack was just what they had practised. Ahead of the B25s splashes flicked up, as the drop tanks from the P38s overhead reached the sea. Larner broke away to port to go for a large destroyer, and the other three in his flight, McCoun, Smallwood and Howe, followed. Larner told them to get away and find their own boats, and the attack was on in earnest. Larner's aircraft attacked from the front; the second flight, led by Captain Jock Henebry, went on to the north a little, then came in from that side; and the third flight of four went on the original approach line, more or less parallel to the ships, before turning in onto those not bombed by the first eight B25s. In a post-battle public relations film of the action, Blackjack Walker made reference to the B25s coming in behind his Beaufighters. Ed Larner quickly replied, 'With you, Blackjack, with you. Not behind you!' Some B25s were indeed right up with the strafing Beaufighters.

1st Lieutenant Harlan Reid was flying fourth in the third element of the 90th's twelve plane formation. Reid, quite accurately, counted seven transports and eight warships, and noticed the large volume of fire going up at the B17s, with little aimed at the low-level attackers. He went down to water level, dodging and weaving, with engines at 2,400 revs, 38 inches of manifold pressure, mixture full and rich, cowl flaps closed, looking for a target.

The 20mm cannon fire of the Beaufighters had kept down the heads of the ships' guncrews, and now massed .50-caliber machineguns in the noses of the B25s maintained the pressure. The ammunition was belted in the following sequence: one tracer, two armor-piercing, and then two incendiary rounds. The impressive volume of flame from the eight muzzles in the aircrafts' noses had not been seen by the Japanese, and some of them thought the approaching aircraft were on fire.

Larner began 'butterflying' violently as he approached, then at 500 feet and 1500 yards from the selected warship he straightened out, fired an aiming burst, and at 1200 yards fired continuously, tapping the rudder to spray the whole ship. He went down to below mast height before releasing two bombs and pulling up over the Japanese ship. Larner scored a direct hit and a near miss, rolling the destroyer on its side. He passed on to the flank of the convoy, swung back, and then started a fire with his machineguns and scored a bomb hit on a transport. He then turned to port and on to the last destroyer in the formation, where his fourth bomb exploded close astern. Zeros attacked as Larner was leaving the combat area, but fire from Sergeant Timberlake, in the top turret, drove them off and they turned away.

DD *Shirayuki*, Rear Admiral Kimura's flagship, was hit early, if not first, according to Lieutenant Commander Handa, of Kimura's staff. He had watched the aircraft coming in, strafing and bombing. Most of the men on the bridge were killed or wounded, and when the bomb hit aft, at the turret, a fire started, the magazine exploded and the stern section broke off, flooded, and sank. (9)

A member of 115 Infantry Regiment, aboard a destroyer he did not identify, wrote that it was hit aft and those on deck were strafed. DD *Shirayuki*, a *Fubuki*-class destroyer, was a 1,750-ton ship. Ed Larner probably hit this destroyer, then *Shin-ai-Maru* and attacked DD *Asagumo*. (10)

Lieutenant Charles 'Chuck' Howe, in B25 #980, went for a ship estimated to be 5,000-tons, camouflaged grey and white, directly behind the row of destroyers. The ship was *Teiyo-Maru*. Howe's run forced Jock Henebry away to starboard. He then passed between what he thought was a cruiser and a destroyer, their heavy anti-aircraft fire forcing him to fly violent evasive manoeuvres 'to an extreme never contemplated' by Howe. He opened fire with machineguns at 300 yards, continued to 40 yards, when he released two bombs, and then shot up and over the ship and back down to the water; no one saw the results of these bombs.

Howe spent three or four seconds charging his noseguns to clear them, and then turned 90 degrees starboard to attack *Aiyo-Maru*. He described the ship as a 4–5,000-tonner, dark brown

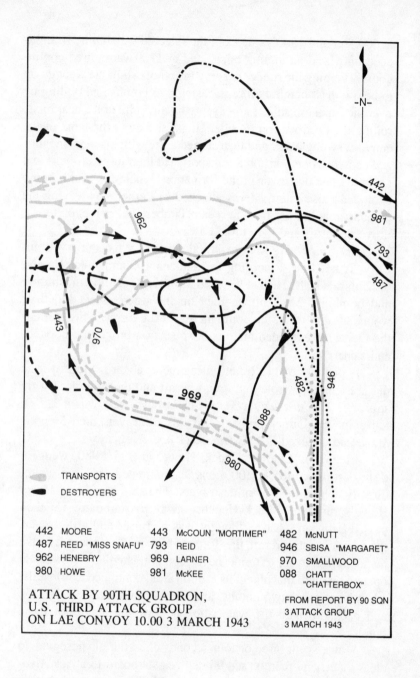

-N-

442
981
793
487
962
443
970
969
482
946
088
980

TRANSPORTS
DESTROYERS

442	MOORE	443	McCOUN "MORTIMER"	482	McNUTT
487	REED "MISS SNAFU"	793	REID	946	SBISA "MARGARET"
962	HENEBRY	969	LARNER	970	SMALLWOOD
980	HOWE	981	McKEE	088	CHATT "CHATTERBOX"

ATTACK BY 90TH SQUADRON,
U.S. THIRD ATTACK GROUP
ON LAE CONVOY 10.00 3 MARCH 1943

FROM REPORT BY 90 SQN
3 ATTACK GROUP
3 MARCH 1943

in color, with considerable loading equipment on its decks. He opened fire at 500 yards. On this attack, the gunner saw their bombs land as a near miss and then as a direct hit amidships. The hit set off a 'terrific explosion which all but cut the vessel in two. This vessel was left obviously in a sinking condition.' Then, only 900 yards away was another vessel, either *Nojima* or *Taimei-Maru*. Howe immediately began machinegunning it and saw his incendiaries going into the cabin and superstructure. He then passed over it, turned onto 180 degrees and, at a height of twenty feet, left the convoy.

Survivors from *Aiyo-Maru* said that they were hit by the first bomb between the bridge and funnel. The explosion was followed by fire before another bomb hit aft and the boiler exploded. Then munitions and gasoline in the No. 3 hold were ignited by the bomb hit there and the flames were impossible to control. Troops who went up to the deck suffered heavy casualties from the strafing aircraft. (11)

Captain Jock Henebry, in #962, was leading the second flight of the 90th Squadron B25s when he looked over through the ack-ack and noticed the Beaufighters on his right and, farther back, the approaching A20s. His co-pilot was 2nd Lieutenant Walter Lee. Henebry was forced away by other aircraft going for his first target [*Teiyo*], and so swung on to another, probably *Oigawa-Maru*. He machinegunned the transport ship, but as his .50-caliber rounds spattered over it, there was already fire on the decks, probably caused by Beaufighter strafing. Henebry pulled up to avoid the mast, and Lee released two bombs. One hit on the starboard waterline amidships, and the other missed by about fifteen feet. Henebry swung on to the *Shin-ai-Maru*, last ship on the northern side. He passed the *Aiyo-Maru*, and attacked the stern of *Shin-ai-Maru*, starting a fire there with his machineguns; the 500-pounder was a near miss. He flew out of the convoy, turning south for New Guinea.

Oigawa-Maru had increased speed as the planes approached, but was hit amidships by a bomb which smashed all the landing craft and killed many of the troops there. Fire broke out. Private Machida, who had wished the officer would stop talking as the planes came closer, began with other soldiers, to assemble a collapsible boat. (12) Flames burst from the portholes, and there was some panic among the officers and men. Seiichi Hagihara, a code specialist in Artillery headquarters, was told the bomb had penetrated the engine room, severing steam mains and damaging the boilers. He thought that the damage was not bad enough to cause the ship to be abandoned, and believed that if the fire had been fought, the ship might have been saved. (13)

Sergeant Jun Sasayama and others from 50 AA Battalion had taken cover as the Beaufighters strafed and B25s attacked. The strafing and exploding bomb killed seven from Sasayama's section, but he and others fought the fire for 20 minutes in an effort to keep it from reaching the ammunition and causing a terrible explosion. (14)

Also aboard were thirty men of the 23rd Independent Infantry Battalion, men in the 35-year old group, of poor physical condition. They were below decks when the bomb hit, and tried to scramble outside. A cook in 50 AA Battalion, Sergeant Masao Kojima, lost consciousness from the strafing and was wounded in the head and legs. (15)

Flying Officer George Drury turned his Beaufighter onto two of the ships in the far line, but his manoeuvre brought him close behind a B25, and he followed it, watching two bombs drop very close to its target. As he flashed over, he saw the deck was already smoking and on fire. His sight bulb had burned out, so he resorted to more basic methods of sighting—aiming at the next ship, firing, then as the splashes appear on the water, gently lifting the nose until the rounds were striking and sparking among the barges and crates on deck. Fires were starting as he passed overhead.

Soldiers in full equipment could be seen on the deck of Lieutenant Gordon McCoun's target, *Teiyo-Maru*. As he flew #443 *Mortimer* over it, he put one bomb at the waterline, another on the deck, and a third over into the sea, but the ship began to burn. He banked to port, away from the convoy, and out to sea.

On McCoun's left wing was Lieutenant John W. 'Bill' Smallwood in #978, with Bill Blewett RAAF as radio-operator/gunner, and Sergeant Martin in the top turret. Martin was so excited by what he could see from the turret that he climbed down and yelled to Blewett, 'You ought to see what's going on out there!' Blewett replied, 'Get back in that *#+%#* turret!' Seeing McCoun had selected the ship he was about to attack, Smallwood swung right, behind *Mortimer*, going for *Teiyo Maru*. But this took him between destroyers *Shirayuki* and *Shikinami*, which were firing at a Beaufighter flying across Smallwood's nose. Fire from one of them hit the B25. Smallwood kept on, opened the bomb-bay doors in case he had to jettison the bombs, attacked, put two bombs into *Teiyo Maru*, pulled up over it, claimed two direct hits, and went down again, dropping a third bomb at the bows of the next ship in column, the *Aiyo Maru*, which rolled as the explosions flung up a column of water.

Survivors from *Teiyo Maru* recalled the hits, saying that the second caused the ship to blow up, though she was last to sink. The day before, about 50 men were believed killed and many wounded during the strafing attack by B17s. (16)

Smallwood turned north away from the scene in the same direction as Larner, Henebry, and McCoun. To jettison weight, Bill Blewett began throwing all loose items out, the B25 had its hydraulics shot out, and the bomb doors were hanging down. Smallwood set course for Port Moresby, relieved that the aircraft seemed OK, but thinking ahead to a landing without hydraulic pressure. Later, he tagged onto a flight of Beaufighters and returned to the coast with them.

Beaufighters and B25s, now mixed, hammered ships all along the convoy. The 90th Attack pilots were right up with the Australians and took advantage of the effect of the 20mm cannon. Looking out of the Beaufighter cupola behind Mos Morgan, Fred Cassidy became aware of something in the air at the same height. He looked over, saw a 500-pound bomb sailing along with them, flying after its 'skip' on the water, and heading for a Japanese ship. As Dick Roe, with Peter Fisken in the back seat of his Beaufighter, attacked another ship, they flew into the blast of a bomb dropped by a B25 also going for the same ship. The Beaufighter was flicked upwards and given a dent in the fuselage belly. He fell away to the sea, but then managed to recover from the shock and straighten out. Fisken said he saw little of the action, as he was busy in the fuselage replacing the cannon magazine. (17)

Flight Lieutenant G. Gibson was attacking a 6,000-tonner, its decks covered with cargo and barges, when a bomb exploded amidships. Gibson flew on between the masts and out the far side. George Drury and Flying Officer R. Brazenor had close escapes from debris hurled out by bomb explosions, but dodged around and continued. Two more direct hits were confirmed by Flying Officer R.C. Bennett. All around ships were being strafed and hit by bombs. Vivid impressions of the attack, which they would remember for the rest of their lives, were imprinted on the minds of the airplane crews.

In the cabin on DD *Tokitsukaze*, Kane Yoshiwara, who had a premonition when he saw the distant dawn reconnaissance aircraft, now heard the siren signal air attack. Even while it was still sounding the ship began receiving automatic weapons fire, the rounds smashing into the metal, pinning Yoshiwara and the others in the cabin away from the door. Later, Yoshiwara recalled counting 122 hits in the walls and that, at the time, he had relied on Heaven to protect him. Suddenly there was a shock, as though the ship had run onto a rock, and Yoshiwara realised that it was the end. He waited for the final explosion, but nothing happened, and the ship kept right on going, the guns still firing. Then he noticed that the engine vibration was gone; the creaking and groaning of the hull as it wheeled and rolled in evasive manoeuvres died away, and the destroyer came to a halt.

Yoshiwara went to the bridge, noticed casualties scattered around, and asked the captain what had happened. The reply was brief: 'We've had it.' The captain explained that they had been torpedoed. Yoshiwara asked why there was no explosion, and was told that the missile had passed through the hull and exploded on the far side. Yoshiwara looked around at the battle scene, appalled to see smoke and flames coming from about half the ships in sight. He then suggested transferring to a ship which was not damaged, and pointed to one close by. *Tokitsukaze* had taken a direct hit in the engine room. All twenty staff there were dead, and those on deck were appalled to see the water alongside turning red with blood flowing from the holes in the hull.

Close behind Larner's 90th Attack B25s were two formations of six fast Douglas A20s from Gee-dub Clark's 89th Squadron of the 3rd Attack. Ahead, the 89th pilots could see the developing chaos in the convoy. As he passed through 4,000 feet in the diving approach, Ed Chudoba saw a large explosion, with flames shooting 2,000 feet into the air, followed by a huge column of smoke. He noticed a destroyer appear from close to this smoke, which was coming from a small ship—almost certainly *Teiyo-Maru* and its exploding stern cargo of aviation fuel, or the stern magazine of *Shirayuki* detonating.

At this time, the only anti-aircraft fire seen by Chudoba was at 8,000 feet. Jack Taylor, on the wing of Captain Roger 'Dixie' Dunbar, saw 'a truly breath-taking sight. There were Japanese ships everywhere, and there were Allied planes everywhere, also.' Bill Beck, leading the right-hand element in the flight, saw an enormous explosion where a destroyer had been, and then watched as the ship came out of the smoke, apparently unharmed. He presumed that a tanker alongside the warship had disappeared in the blast. This was probably the effect of Larner's bombs on the stern of *Shirayuki*.

Ahead of the 89th, the third flight of the 90th was also busy. In *Chatterbox*, Captain Robert Chatt had Australian Maurice Carse as co-pilot. Chatt went down to water level some three miles out and decided on a 1,500-ton destroyer as his target. He weaved towards it until he was 1,500 yards away, and then straightened up and fired the nose guns. The destroyer turned towards him, and his attack went in on the bows rather than the beam. He sped over the water, so low that fire from the destroyer was seen by a crew of another B25 to be passing over *Chatterbox*. He released all four bombs, scored two direct hits on the bows, and what appeared to be two more hits or near misses on the deck, blowing most of the superstructure away.

Chatt probably hit DD *Arashio*, which was reported by the Japanese to have taken three hits at the beginning of the attack. Below deck on *Arashio*, Sub-Lieutenant Reiji Masuda felt the speeding ship seem to jump several times and felt large shocks through the hull. Then the lights went out and the power supply failed. He called to the bridge, but there was no answer. Masuda sent a messenger to the bridge, but could hardly believe what the man said on return—there was no bridge and the bows were on fire. He ran up to see for himself. The bridge had been blown away by a direct hit, and also gone were the captain and all the officers, all the Army officers and the newspaper men who had been there. All that remained was the front window frame—and a grisly sight. The body of the navigator, Lieutenant Itamoto, was impaled on the remains of the window. Another direct hit had penetrated No. 2 gun turret and the bomb had exploded in the aft machine room. But with no one at the helm the destroyer was still rushing on at full speed.

With its rudder out of action, the destroyer veered off course and rammed the Naval Supply ship *Nojima*, inflicting fatal damage. *Nojima* had been brought close by her Captain, Matsumoto, to assist his fellow Navy men. (18)

Aboard DD *Arashio*, the survivors staggered as the hull received another shock. They had collided with *Nojima*. The Chief Engineer of *Arashio* came up on deck and took command. The bows of the destroyer had been forced back by the collision. Reiji Masuda looked up at the damaged *Nojima*. Its bridge was a mass of flames, the mast was broken and burning ammunition aboard the supply ship was exploding. Masuda looked around and saw that all seven transports were hit and burning.

1st Lieutenant Harlan Reid selected what he estimated to be a 7–8,000 tonner, moving on a straight course at eight knots. Reid climbed quickly to 500 feet, then dove steeply to port, about 2500 yards from the ship, still jinking the B25. At 1800 yards, he fired the nose guns, saw splashes as the rounds fell short, and then at 1200 yards came into range. By tapping the rudders, he moved the nose from side to side, sweeping the decks with .50-calibre fire. At 260 m.p.h., and at twenty feet, Reid levelled off. His RAAF co-pilot, Flight Sergeant Langley, opened the bomb doors, Reid ceased firing the guns, released all four 500-pound bombs and pulled up steeply to clear the masts; diving to port again as he passed.

The B25 hurdled the target, and Reid could see the decks covered with supplies, equipment and troops. He looked back, seeing one hit and a near miss on the ship's portside and two misses to starboard. He had flicked the last two bombs over the ship as he pulled up over it.

Still in the midst of the convoy, Reid pulled up to 100 feet, passing another ship, and was looking for the best way out of the chaos when suddenly, at the head of the convoy, he saw that he was about to fly across the bows of a large destroyer, which was firing at him. Hauling the B25 around to starboard, and away from the Japanese, he passed in front of the transport he had just flown by. He passed another, and then swung to port and flew back over those two transports and yet another, strafing all three. Reid may have bombed *Nojima*, avoided DD *Uranami*, and strafed *Taimei*, *Oigawa*, and *Teiyo Maru*.

Nojima had suffered little damage from the first planes, but a bomb hit near the officers' quarters, then there was a second hit. The damage was in addition to that caused by being rammed by the destroyer, and meant the end. The 24-year old ship began to sink quickly.

From their Beaufighter, Alf Nelson and Len Vial were enthralled. 'It was fantastic, really. There was smoke, and things flying in every direction, bomb splashes everywhere. I saw one destroyer going in circles, with smoke pouring out of it.'

In B25 #487, *Miss Snafu*, was 1st Lieutenant Robert Reed, with Pilot Officer Royce Johnco RAAF. They first saw the convoy on their left, through thin cloud, and Johnco wondered if the Japanese could actually see them. After Ed Larner led the peel-off, Reed had to 'S' back to his original heading and the ship he had selected—a transport in the center of the convoy.

Reed jinked the B25 every few seconds, taking the bomber between a large destroyer and another smaller one, and heading for the portside of the ship ahead. Reed described it as about 8,000 tons, with two high masts with radio antennae on them. As they approached, he saw other B25s scoring direct hits on it. The detail of the masts probably identifies the IJN ship *Nojima*. Reed pulled up to 100 feet, dived slightly, and began machine-gunning the decks—short bursts at 1500 yards, and continuous fire from 1,000 yards to 400 yards. Then he concentrated on bombing. At 260 mph, at deck level, Johnco opened the bomb doors as the machineguns opened fire. Reed dropped their three

500-pound bombs and lifted the B25 over the masts. As they sped over, Private John Boggs, upper gunner, sprayed the decks with his twin .50s. Reed pushed the nose down again, they went to sea level, and looked back.

'We were able to see the result,' said Royce Johnco. 'Most satisfactory. A badly crippled ship.' Reed saw two direct hits amidships. He turned port to avoid warships ahead, then strafed another destroyer from bow to stern, but the ship swung away from them and the B25 passed down its portside. Johnco was able to see the 'marked effect on the personnel' from the B25's massed machineguns. 'I have a very clear recollection of a gun-crew with a deck-mounted gun having a crack at us,' he said, 'but we were fast and low, a difficult target, and they only succeeded in peppering our tail. We got a few holes, but no casualties. I think they suffered quite a few.'

Reed jinked right, then circled port, passing and then turning onto the stern of a second destroyer, machinegunning it while noting that the transport was burning. He swept over the destroyer, turned to port, and headed out to the open sea. At the rendezvous point he met Ed Larner and Harlan Reid, formated on them, and returned to base. It seems that Reed had attacked *Nojima* or possibly *Taimei*, and had strafed DD *Tokitsukaze* and DD *Arashio*.

Meanwhile, at medium level, the 38th Group B25s were still skirting the southern flank of the convoy, turning north before coming in to bomb. Captain Royalty, 71st Squadron, saw, as he said, 'an almost endless stream of planes strafing and skip-bombing every ship in the convoy. A B25 scored a direct hit on a large transport and the whole stern blew up and burned fiercely.'

Ahead of Royalty, among the ships, Lieutenant John 'Sea-biscuit' Sbisa flew the 90th Squadron's #946. He had flown along the original line of approach, past some of the destroyers, then swung port between two of them, and lined up on a ship that was described as having 'two masts and one funnel'—probably *Taimei Maru*. As they sped to it at 230 mph, jinking moderately, Bob Guthrie noticed the puffs of smoke from exploding ack-ack shells. He was poised to open bomb-bay doors and release their bombs.

84 ■

Sbisa went down lower and the massed .50s were fired, 'blasted well and truly into the superstructure,' the bomb-bay flicked open, the ship was at the right distance, Guthrie pressed the toggle switch, and it was thought all three bombs released, but none did. Sbisa hauled the B25 up and over, between the masts, turning tightly to go back, but they were surprised to see it 'going up in smoke, big black puffs of smoke. . . . An A20 had come lengthways down the ship and hit it!' said Guthrie. (19)

Sergeant Redus Harrell, the gunner, had reported all bombs had dropped and one direct hit had been scored, but later it was realised that the release mechanism failed. The A20 was probably either Clark, Chudoba or Richardson, of the 89th. Obeying orders to go in once, attack, and get out, Sbisa climbed away and turned back to New Guinea. Sbisa reported that about half the machineguns jammed and that the aircraft was 'rather slow.'

On *Taimei Maru*, the radio operators were Mr. Kawakami and Mr. Suzuki. The preliminary strafing which had hammered through the bridge and superstructure had driven them to the floor. When the hail had finished they got up and Kawakami urged Suzuki to get below decks quickly. They began to run to a ladder, but as they reached the front of the saloon there was a huge deafening explosion. The intense flash of light was so vivid Suzuki thought it would pierce his body. Simultaneously he realised he was still alive, but thought he was bound to die in a moment. The explosion blew a large hole in the bridge. Kawakami, Purser Mitsuyashi, and Assistant Purser Kawaguchi all fell into it, disappearing into the chaos below. Survivors believed a burning plane had crashed between the bridge and the funnel. None had, but the massed muzzle flash of the .50-calibers from the very low-flying attackers, pulling up as they did at the very last moment to avoid hitting the ship had created that impression in the minds of the Japanese. (20)

By this time, the mast-height attackers were all over the convoy area. Beaufighters, B25s and A20s were going in all directions. Overhead were more B25s and B17s. The attacking formations overlapped and the entire action was over in less time than it takes to describe.

1st Lieutenant Roy Moore, with co-pilot Flight Sergeant J.S. Stephens RAAF, had also flown along the southern side of the convoy and turned up past the rear of the ships, searching for a target which had not been attacked. He picked a transport, estimated to be a 5,000-tonner, probably *Shin-ai-Maru*, swung away from the destroyer [*Yukikaze*] which was obstructing his run, and then turned back. He dived on the merchant ship, turning parallel to it, then swinging in again directly at it as he went to full power, corkscrewing, jinking, and when in range began hosing down the deck with his eight .50s. Moore had the firing button on the control wheel, with the bomb release button on the console between the pilots. The assembled Japanese were on deck, firing rifles at him, before the big machinegun rounds smashed among them, mowing them down, sending some over the side into the sea. Moore began to pull up over the ship as Stephens released two bombs which skipped over the water and flew home against the hull as the B25 soared over, climbing left away from one of the destroyers on the far side.

Shin-ai-Maru was hit on the bridge, where the explosion had killed the captain, and at the No.3 hatch. Fire started, and the steam pipes were damaged. B25s screamed so low overhead that crewmen thought the planes would hit the bridge. The damage was fatal, and at 10.20 the order was given to abandon ship. (21)

The gunner who had watched the first eight B17s appear and felt helpless at the sight of so many Allied aircraft saw '. . . the Boeings bombing, the North Americans strafing, and the fighters were watching the sky. I saw our convoy burn. Our ship began to list, and we were still on the bridge. Our group of eight ships was completely destroyed.'

The scene over the convoy was something never before seen by Allied crews. No one person was able to sit and watch the entire scene. The Beaufighters and 90th Squadron B25 strafers had been overtaken by 89th Squadron A20s and the higher-level B25s of the 38th Group. Overhead the 43rd Group B17s were on their bomb-runs, despite the Zeros, and P38s were diving and climbing through the Japanese fighters. The ships were being attacked from almost every direction, frantically trying to defend themselves as bomb after bomb struck home and the deadly whip-lash of the massed .50-caliber machineguns flailed hulls, decks and superstructures, smashing deck cargo to splinters.

Lieutenant Don McNutt, in B25 #482 of the 90th Squadron, went for a destroyer on the southern flank. This may have been *Arashio*. He strafed into bombing range, passing over it from bows to stern, hauling the B25 into a port turn, and went back at the warship, guns hammering again as he flew over the forward part of the ship, continuing on the course out of the battle area. Behind them, the destroyer had taken two hits and a near miss. This swift attack on a warship by a single aircraft left the ship burning and sinking and made a vivid impression on one of the AA gunners watching from the bridge of *Kembu Maru*.

2nd Lieutenant Keith McKee, in the 90th's B25 #981, attacked a 5,000-tonner at the east end of the convoy. This ship was making only 5–6 knots, following ships McKee thought were a cruiser and a destroyer. The ship swung its bows to McKee, making his attack easier; he noticed it strafed by Beaufighters as he approached at 75 to 100 feet, with 2,400 rpm, and 38 pounds of manifold pressure. At first McKee intended attacking a 'large troop transport near the middle of the convoy,' but saw it was the target for other aircraft, so he flew on past, altering height by 25 or 30 feet. McKee noticed that while both warships were firing at him, most fire was going behind the B25. He headed down till he was 25 feet off the water. As he attacked, he ignored the anti-aircraft fire and went for the ship. Beaufighters were strafing from the beam, so McKee went in on the bows; after Beaufighters came B25Ds [38th Bomb Group], bombing from 300 feet, but missing completely. As soon as the Beaufighters were clear, McKee began firing his .50s, until it was necessary to pull up over the ship.

Co-pilot 2nd Lieutenant Rosebush operated the bomb doors and dropped all three bombs in quick succession. He intended to drop them so as to get one in the water and one on deck, but as they dropped a little late, the first hit the waterline and the second went off under the rear deck. The third hit about 20 yards from the stern. The bombs went off together, and the gunner, Staff Sergeant Bennie Estep, only had time to fire six rounds at the Bofors type gun on the stern.

As soon as they had passed over, McKee went down to water level, but when Estep said the ship's had its deck blown up and was no longer able to shoot, he banked around to starboard to survey the damage. He reported seeing 'considerable smoke and some debris still sailing through the air.' McKee later stated that the A20s and Beaufighters were doing a 'superb job.' In his opinion, the most significant factor in the success of the attack was its superb co-ordination with attacks from high and low under an effective fighter umbrella.

Larner's squadron had dropped 37 bombs on eleven ships and claimed seventeen hits—eight merchantmen and three destroyers. One B25—Smallwood's #978—had been hit heavily and was on the way back to Moresby. Along with DD *Shirayuki*, various Japanese reports indicate that *Arashio* and *Tokitsukaze* were hit. *Arashio* was stopped, and *Tokitsukaze* received four hits. One of these bombs from the starboard side hit the engine-room, and the destroyer came to a halt; there were three other hits. As *Arashio* slid to a stop, *Teiyo-Maru* came alongside to pick up as many as possible of those aboard. But the attacks were far from over. (22)

Mixed with Larner's B25s, the Beaufighters had finished their first run. About eight Zekes were seen overhead, and they began to attack. George Drury had climbed a little to dive onto another ship when from the rear cockpit Dave Beasley yelled, 'Zeros, and the bastards are firing at us!' Drury 'opened the taps' and took *Malola Two* down to sea-level, where she registered 263 knots, leaving the Zeros behind. The Japanese pulled up and dived onto Sergeant Bob Bennett, but could not catch him. One Japanese then swung onto Ron Downing in A19-53. Downing had almost had his Beaufighter destroyed by an enormous explosion while strafing at Wau, and now was to have another close shave. The Japanese pilot opened fire at 1,000 yards and hit with his first burst of 20mm cannon, wounding Downing in the shoulder and his navigator-observer, Sergeant Box, in the thigh and wrist. Downing skidded and jinked the Beaufighter, avoiding the Japanese as he made further attempts to bring his sights onto the RAAF aircraft. The Japanese closed to 100 feet, then pulled up into an almost vertical climb. The Beaufighter had its port engine stopped, port elevator shot away, holes in the fuselage and damage to the starboard engine. Downing swung away from the battle area and headed for New Guinea.

Leading the Beaufighter attacks, Squadron Leader Ross Little saw a Zeke on the tail of a B25 on his left, swung the Beaufighter and fired at a range of 600 yards. He was too far away, but intended to make the Zeke break off. The Zeke climbed, then as the Beaufighter passed below, dived on its tail, firing from 500 yards, closing to 300. Little's observer, Spooner, had designed and installed a rear gun mounting in his observer's cockpit. After he fired 120 rounds at the attacking plane, the Zeke fell back out of range and ceased to bother them.

Meanwhile, overhead, the P38s were tangling with Zekes, trying to keep them away from the B17s. It was a free-for-all, with pilots' attention concentrated on their own battle, and little time to watch the convoy action. Charlie King, who had scored his first victory the day before, noticed three P38s dive below after the Zekes, and later realised that it was Ed Faurot, along with Eason and Shifflet.

Leading six A20s of the 89th Squadron in three two-ship elements, Captain Glen 'Gee-dub' Clark flew east along the southern flank of the convoy, passing in front of DDs *Arashio* and *Yukikaze*, before swinging north-west to attack. Clark began diving onto the convoy. He intended each element of two aircraft to attack separate ships, but four planes went for the same one. Chudoba, in *Adam LaZonga*, was second plane from the right in the six-plane formation, with Lieutenant Charles Mayo, the 13th and reserve pilot who was able to fly the mission, in A20 #40-094 *Rebel Rocket*. Chudoba selected a ship ahead but to the left, and dived more steeply to pass under Clark and Richardson. He then saw other A20s going for the same ship, and to avoid concentrating on it, swung back to the one ahead, *Taimei-Maru*. But

Clark and Richardson were also attacking it. Realising there was crowding, Mayo broke formation and went to starboard for another ship. 'I'm going off to get me a fat one,' he called.

Chudoba, with Clark now behind him, flew for the target ahead, firing machineguns, aware of the cordite fumes swirling up into the cockpit, of the tracers flicking back at him from the ship, of Clark passing ahead and bombing, then he released his own two bombs as a small bullet clacked through the plexiglass and pulled up just a little too late, clipping the top of the ship's radio mast with his right wing, and the A20 shook at the impact. No wonder survivors from the ship thought a burning plane had hit them behind the bridge.

'Seabiscuit' Sbisa and Bob Guthrie, in their 90th Squadron B25, had just left the ship, and were looking back in vain for the results of their own hung-up bombs. Guthrie saw the A20s passing over their intended target as the Japanese radio operators began their dash to safety below decks.

As Chudoba flashed away, the explosion of Clark's bombs belted into the rear of the A20. The photographs taken with Clark's camera showed Chudoba's bombs exploding on a ship whose name, they could read, was *Taimei-Maru*. As the A20s passed beyond the convoy, Chudoba flew sharp evasive patterns to avoid the fire from one of the destroyers ahead and to the left, but was not hit. He strafed another transport, made for the rendezvous point, Cape Ward Hunt, and then nursed the slowed-up A20 back to base.

Chudoba's gunner, Felix Larronde, observed the convoy and the attack from his rear hatch. He felt both bombs release and looked back to see them in the air; one bounced off the sea in a wobble and headed for the bows of the ship, the other skipped straight into the hull, amidships. Five seconds later both exploded in quick succession, but Chudoba had quickly swung the A20 to port and Larronde could no longer see the ship. As they left for home, Larronde counted five separate large columns of smoke rising from burning ships. Larronde had been with the 8th Squadron from the beginning and was one of the gunners in the first formation of A24s to fly up to Port Moresby on 31 March 1942.

Captain Clark selected a 5–7,000-tonner; there was no fire

General George C. Kenney, commander of Allied Air Forces in the South West Pacific Area, architect of the longest-ranging tactical air force of World War II. (USAF)

Major General Ennis Whitehead, bomber commander in General Kenney's U.S. 5th Air Force at the time of the Battle of the Bismarck Sea, March 1943. (USAF)

Lieutenant Colonel George Prentice, commander 39 Fighter Squadron, led its P38s over the Japanese convoy during the battle. (Dennis Glen Cooper)

Left: **Captain Tommy Lynch, 39 Fighter Squadron. Already an 8-victory ace before the battle, he added to his score during the convoy. (RAAF)**

Captain Charles W. King, 39 Fighter Squadron, scored his first victory in the battle. (Charles King)

Lieutenant Curran Jones, 39 Fighter Squadron, claimed his fourth victory. (RAAF)

Lieutenant Bob Vaught, 9 Fighter Squadron, 49th Fighter Group, became an ace over the Japanese base at Lae. (49th FG)

Port Moresby
· APPROX. SCALE OF MILES ·
(·)
· 8th photo sqdn · 5 dec '42 ·

Above: A photo mosaic of Port Moresby and the vital airfields built around it in 1942. At bottom right is Kila-Kila (3-Mile); center is Ward's (5-Mile); center right is Jackson's (7-Mile); top left is Durand; top center is Schwimmer and top right is Berry. "3-Mile", "5-Mile" was the distance from Port Moresby. (RAAF)

Right: The well-known sign of the third attack Group, "The Grim Reapers." The premier attack formation in the South West Pacific Area. (W. H. Garing)

North American B25 #946 "Margaret" having eight .50-caliber machineguns installed in the nose. Note the ammunition feed chutes on the floor, left of the nose wheel. (RAAF Museum)

The "Moresby Wreck," where the convoy attack was practised. The S.S. *Pruth* ran aground in 1923. Here it is with many Papuan *lakatois* (canoes). (R. K. Piper)

Boeing B17 "Flying Fortress" in the Port Moresby area. The sunny weather in this photo is how crews would have liked it; in reality they had to battle through dangerous tropical storms to reach their destination. (Bob Peterson via Kev Ginnane)

Consolidated B24 "Liberator" after bombing Lae airfield, which can be seen running inland from the water's edge at left. This stretch of coast was the destination of the convoy. (Kev Ginnane)

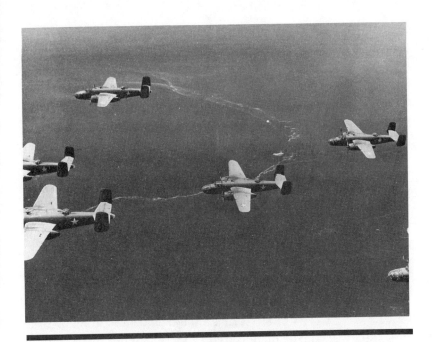

North American Aviation B25 "Mitchells" of 71 Squadron, 38th Bomb Group, near Townsville, Australia. The "glass nose" for the bombardier is clearly visible. (USAF)

Lockheed P38 "Lightning" over the Port Moresby area. The "84" indicates that it belongs to the 9th Squadron, 49th Fighter Group. The P38 was the outstanding Allied fighter in New Guinea 1942-44, and most of the leading aces flew it. (Steve Birdsall)

Crews of 89 Attack Squadron who flew against the Japanese convoy on 3 March 1943. The pilots are, standing from left to right, Ed Chudoba, Bill Beck, Ed Richardson, Rodger "Dixie" Dunbar, Glen "Gee-dub" Clark, Charles "Chuck" Mayo, Ed Montagano, Bill Neel, Jack Taylor and Gordon Ruby. (Jack Taylor)

Right: Major Ed Larner, CO of 9 Squadron, 3rd Attack Group, led the devastating mast-height attack in the heavily armed B25 strafers on 3 March 1943. He sank destroyer *Shirayuki* in his first pass by detonating her magazine with a bomb, then attacked a transport and another destroyer. (RAAF)

aimed at him during the actual time of the attack. Approaching at about 200 feet, he descended to mast height from a distance of about 1,000 yards, and fired the nose guns at the ship's decks. At 300 yards and a speed of 260 mph, Clark released both bombs, then went into a series of dives and zooms to throw off any anti-aircraft fire. He dodged the other ships, flew out of the convoy on a north-west heading, and then swung back south, passing west of the scene. One of his bombs hit *Taimei-Maru*, and another was a near miss. Clark took note of the other ships on fire and the destroyers manoeuvring at high speed, firing at the aircraft.

Lieutenant Richardson, on Clark's wing, made an attack very similar to Clark's and claimed one hit and one near miss. He also saw a DD take a direct hit from a B25.

Survivors from the *Taimei-Maru* agreed that she was hit many times. Private Yoshio Sukita knew of three hits—one forward, one amidships and one aft. The order to abandon ship came in about 20 minutes. Nobukatsu Ishida was a stoker on the ship, and was told there were four hits, at Nos. 1, 2 and 3 hatches and aft of the bridge, followed by fire. The first hit stunned Sergeant Tsuneo Aoki, of the medical unit of 8 Shipping Engineers. The second blew him overboard minus most of his clothes.

Sergeant Tetsuo Hosoda, formerly with 2 Artillery Regiment, now with the Shipping Engineers, was on guncrew duty when the attackers hit twice at No. 2 hatch, twice on the bridge and once at No. 3 hatch, smashing all the boats and rafts on deck. The engine room was smashed, then flooded; lights and power failed. The steering gear was destroyed, and when troops came out onto the deck they had to jump over the side, as the MLCs could not be launched. (23)

The rapid succession of hits and near misses rocked the hull wildly from side to side. Inside *Teimei Maru*, the intermingled dead and wounded were rolling back and forth, flung around by the tremendous explosions. Waves of blood were said to be literally sloshing across the decks, while panic-stricken members of the crew and passengers ran screaming to and fro in the shambles. A witness described the scene as 'a painting from hell.' (24)

Charles Mayo, fourth in the formation with Clark, Chudoba, and Richardson, realised that he would not be able to attack the ship they all were going for. He broke away to starboard to pass in front of *Nojima* and attack what was probably the *Shin-ai-Maru*. Running up at mast height at an air speed of 260 mph, he first machinegunned the decks and went down to deck height to release both bombs at 300 yards. He then began altering altitude to avoid any anti-aircraft fire. Both bombs hit the ship. Mayo also saw explosions on *Taimei-Maru* after the other three A20s passed, as well as a hit on one of the destroyers he had flown past. He saw a B25 attack a destroyer east of the transport he bombed, and watched the B25 circle back for a second run, scoring a direct hit. This was, possibly, Don McNutt of the 90th.

Captain Bill Beck, leading the second element in the second six-ship flight of the 89th Squadron, with Lieutenant Ruby on his wing, turned port from the A20 formation, and went through the leading part of the convoy. He continually changed altitude, but remained below 200 feet, at 230 mph. He saw Clark's formation scoring hits and a ship burning in front of him. He then turned left to a third ship, a 3–5,000-tonner. Opening the bomb-bay doors and unlocking the racks, he aimed his A20 nose at the funnel. He passed over it, machineguns firing throughout the run, but his bombs failed to release. Staff Sergeant Joseph Fox, the gunner, told Beck that the bombs had not dropped, and visually checked on Beck's order. Two 500-pound bombs were still with them. 'I just couldn't believe it,' said Beck. Around them were burning ships and destroyers firing at them.

By now, Beck was to the far side of the convoy looking for another ship to bomb, when he saw DD *Uranami*. He went for it, while the destroyer captain tried to bring his ship around to allow all guns to fire broadside, but the A20 was more agile, and Beck was able turn left, faster, to attack from the bows, passing over the ship. The rear guns on the destroyer fired, but the shell bursts blossomed behind the dodging A20. As Beck aimed for the destroyer's bows, he could see it slicing through the waves, throwing off a creaming pattern to either side. Swiftly, in the few seconds remaining, Beck opened the bomb-bay doors, checked the switch to be sure it was on 'Demolition,' not 'Fragmentation,' the bomb release switch was on 'Individual Release,' and that the racks were unlocked. He held the sharp angle on the bows of the onrushing destroyer, and, in his own words, 'flicked the bomb release with a vengeance. I was still flicking it as I passed over the ship at a sharp angle from bow to stern. This time I took a look back to see my bombs explode. I saw a large explosion at the far end of the ship.'

But again his bombs had failed to release. Sergeant Fox reported that the bombs were still there, and again climbed back to look into the bomb-bay and confirm it. They could only assume that the explosion was a depth charge detonated by the machine-gun fire from the A20. During all this, Beck saw four other merchant ships either sinking or on fire, and a destroyer hit by what appeared to be high-level bombing.

Lieutenant Richard Ruby, 8th Squadron, in A20 #40-139 *Maid In Japan* of the 89th, flew with Captain Beck, but his bombs also failed to release. Ruby first saw the convoy when he was approaching at 3,000 feet and the ships already were under attack by B25s. By the time the A20s attacked, Ruby thought the action 'appeared to be more or less a rout already.' He followed Beck, describing the ship they attacked as having two funnels and a white superstructure on a black hull; it appeared to be a passenger vessel and it did not fire back. Ruby followed Beck as he attacked the destroyer, and watched Beck's tracer hitting the bridge. After they had passed, Ruby's gunner, Corporal Allport, saw a great plume of black smoke coming from the ship, but could not see anything which might have caused such an explosion. As he thought he had hit the ship, Ruby did not try to drop his bombs on the destroyer. Allport did not tell him as the intercom was faulty. Beck and Ruby identified the destroyer as *Fubuki* class, and reported that it had two white stripes on the aft funnel.

Beck brought back a vivid photograph of the destroyer, one which became a classic of low-level attack photography. Many details of the deck, funnels and anti-aircraft crews are clearly visible. Beck was so low that he thought he might have hit the mast, and tried to avoid looking at the wing until he was over the New Guinea shore, when the damage was seen to be caused by one of Lieutenant Ruby's machinegun bullets. At the coast, the Neel element joined them, and the four A20s returned to Moresby.

After Captain Dixie Dunbar also attacked across the convoy, being forced off the other ships he intended to attack by eager A20s and B25s, with Jack Taylor on his wing, they tried for a couple of ships. Taylor strafed what was probably *Nojima* from 600 feet. Then, as Taylor recalled, they 'finally spotted what must have been the smallest ship in the convoy, later estimated at about 800 to 1000 tons. One of our 'buddies' claimed it had outriggers on it, a blatant lie if ever I heard one.' *Kembu-Maru* was a smaller type of ship not yet encountered by the Allies, and prisoners were later questioned about it. The Japanese had decided to build large numbers of small ships to move freight and personnel, and called them 'sea trucks.'

Going at 275 mph, the two A20s swung around on to the *Kembu-Maru*, Duncan going for the midships, and Taylor, on his starboard, lined up on the stern. The small ship was passing from their right to the left; Taylor moved out slightly, and as they flashed over he released his two 500-pound bombs. They pulled up to pass over the top. Duncan kept on climbing, hauling the A20 into a type of Immelmann turn, with Taylor following.

Taylor knew that this was not a good idea, as it made things easier for enemy gunners. 'We both wanted to see the damage we had done. As she came into view over our left shoulders, her entire stern blew off, lifting her out of the water by the aft section. She sank almost immediately. Roger claimed his bombs had missed.'

Dunbar claimed two near misses. He flew a circle to port, which allowed him to strafe two other ships, then saw a destroyer hit by high-level bombing, and other ships taking hits from B25s and being strafed by Beaufighters.

Japanese survivors recall that the *Kembu-Maru* was the first to be lost. Japanese accounts record the loss ten minutes into the attack. The anti-aircraft gunners on the bridge watched the first waves flying at them, noses sparkling as they fired. Tagayasu Kawachida, loader on one of the guns, was amazed at the performance of a B25. He watched one approach and strafe a destroyer, circle and sweep in low despite the anti-aircraft fire, bomb it, and leave it sinking. This was probably McNutt in #482,

90th Squadron, attacking *Arashio*. Kawachida was very impressed that just one such plane could sink a destroyer. (25)

Sergeant Sasaki, commander of the AA detachment on *Kembu-Maru*, said she was hit, exploded in flames and sunk all within five minutes. Higari Shimomida, a civilian deckhand, who knew a bomb had hit aft, flew over the side into the water as the fire exploded. He expected to be rescued. Takashi Nagao, a member of 221 Airfield Battalion, thought two bombs had exploded aft, creating fires and explosions. He had his lifebelt and went overboard, grabbing a piece of the ship's timber to keep him afloat. More Allied aircraft passed overhead with guns hammering, and the shock waves of exploding bombs pummelling them under the water. (26)

Taylor pulled around into another starboard circuit, passing the *Taimei-Maru* and swinging back to strafe her. He turned to starboard and passed over and strafed a ship he estimated at 10,000-tons, probably *Nojima*. He also saw a destroyer hit by high-level bombing, and what was probably *Shin-ai-Maru* burning after an attack by Beaufighters and B25s. By this time, *Taimei-Maru* was stopped or making very little progress.

A Japanese fighter made a pass at Dixie Dunbar, but his inexperienced gunner did not fire. Taylor's gunner, Staff Sergeant Marion, was firing away, and Taylor warned Dunbar 'what was NOT happening from his gunner. He must have chewed on him, because he started firing on the Jap soon after.' The fighter broke away, apparently unharmed, and neither A20 was damaged.

Lieutenant Messick of the 89th flew into the western section of the convoy over a destroyer which had been hit by a B25, and bombed what he described as a 8 to 10,000-ton ship centered between three transports. He then swung south in a wide circle to port, coming back south past a stationary destroyer at the head of the convoy. One of his bombs hit the ship and exploded. Given the dislocation of the ships by this time, Messick may have attacked *Oigawa-Maru*.

Lieutenant Montagano approached at 250 mph, strafed his way up to a ship estimated at 5–6,000 tons, passed over it, and then swung starboard to bomb what seemed to be a 4,000-ton tanker. He then turned starboard and left the area, counting one hit on his target. He may have strafed *Oigawa* and bombed *Teiyo*. He also saw two other ships hit, a destroyer burning amidships, and Lieutenant Neel attacked by a single seat fighter.

Many survivors said that *Teiyo-Maru* was hit twice, first on the deck, causing many casualties, and then in the engine room, after which the ship listed. Warrant Officer Matsushima, 115 Regiment, felt the explosion of both bombs, then a third when part of the cargo detonated. (27)

Another man aboard, Yoshio Aoki, 50 AA Battalion, was below deck, so ill from attacks of malaria that he did not know at first that they were under attack, and did not care. The first fires were put out, and work began on keeping the ship afloat. This was soon to be made impossible by the arrival of more bombers. (28)

Sergeant Chikui, 115 Regiment, kept a notebook in which he wrote a recollection of the events. Chikui was below decks. . . . 'inside the ship became a living hell. Our ship rolled two or three times and listed to port. The burst of bombs and rattling of machineguns could be heard simultaneously.' (29)

Lieutenant William W. Neel was hit several times by anti-aircraft fire as he was attacking a ship on the eastern side of the convoy. He dove from 2,000 yards and at a height of 3,000 feet firing the A20's noseguns as he went in. Neel believed that the strafing should be done from this height and angle in order to cover the decks with machinegun fire. He strafed three ships and saw others burning. Both bombs were dropped simultaneously. They were attacked by a Japanese fighter. Staff Sergeant Sorenson, Neel's gunner, identified it as a silver Hap, with clipped wings, silver in color. After several bursts from the fighter, the A20's left engine began smoking, and the Hap pulled up into the clouds. Neel brought the A20 back to base.

Lieutenant Conn of the 89th Squadron, with Corporal G. J. Hall as gunner, approached from the south, passing between the third and fourth destroyers on the southern flank—probably *Arashio* and *Yukikaze*—and attacked an 8–10,000-ton transport. Light, inaccurate anti-aircraft fire came from the bridge of the ship, probably *Nojima*. However, he may have passed between

Tokitsukaze and *Arashio*, and bombed *Oigawa-Maru*. He flew at the ship's side, dropped his bombs and passed overhead, confining his evasive action to shallow dives and zooms. He did not strafe at all, but saw hits on three other ships, and thought that another one, behind their target to the east, was out of control.

Oigawa Maru was hit in the engine room, and fire broke out in holds Numbers 3 and 4. Colonel Endo, commander of 115 Infantry Regiment, realised the ship was beyond saving, and began giving the necessary orders to his officers. Aboard the ship were the regimental colors, with the honor guard, and these had to be saved. Lieutenant Kondo was designated as standard bearer, with Sergeant Namiki in charge of the six-man color escort party. (30)

Twenty bombs had been dropped by the 89th, who claimed eleven hits on seven ships. Two of the 500-pounders were claimed to have hit a 150-foot vessel which exploded—certainly the gasoline-laden *Kembu-Maru*. While the 90th and 89th Squadrons were bombing and strafing, the 38th Bomb Group's B25s began their attacks. Overhead, the B17s of the 43rd Group were making the first of their bomb runs. The Japanese were swamped by attacks from all angles and heights, making defence of the entire convoy impossible; each ship was on its own, whether destroyer or transport.

At 10.05, from 7,000 feet, six B17s of the 65th Squadron, 43rd Bomb Group, attacked with twenty-four 1,000-pounders, claiming a hit on a 5,000-ton ship which caught fire, and two hits on a 4,000-tonner which exploded and sank. Some sixteen Japanese fighters attacked for 30 minutes, causing major damage to two aircraft. Five Zekes were claimed destroyed and one as a probable. The crews also reported fifteen ships in the convoy, including eight warships. They saw the A20s hit two ships, the B25s hit a destroyer, and other B17s hit a destroyer, as well as two smoking ships.

At the same time, the B17s of the 64th and 403rd Squadrons, 43rd Bomb Group, led by Ken McCullar the low-level B17 pioneer, dropped twenty-four 1,000-pounders, claiming a direct hit on a 5–6,000-ton ship already hit by a B25, and another hit on a 6,000-ton ship. For half an hour, between twelve and nineteen

Zekes attacked and injured two men. Seven Zekes were claimed as destroyed and one as probably destroyed. The squadron counted 15 ships, and saw a destroyer sink, two hits scored by B25s on other ships, and also saw two others smoking and one more sinking.

The Zekes, attacking head-on, scored hits on the cockpit of Captain Hocutt's B17, wounding Hocutt in the head, and hitting the co-pilot, Lieutenant Evans, with flying plexiglass. Evans wheeled the aircraft out of formation in order to get Hocutt back to medical attention. He survived.

The 13th Bomb Squadron, 3rd Attack Group, and the 71st Squadron, 38th Bomb Group, were approaching to make medium-level attacks. Another low-level attack was coming in by unmodified B25s, without the eight .50s in the nose. At 200 feet, from the north-east, six B25s of the 405th Squadron, 38th Bomb Group, went through the smoke and growing disaster among the ships, dropped 35 bombs, claiming four direct hits on three ships, one of which exploded. The 405th had approached from the south, swung east around the convoy in a counter-clockwise path, and then turned back to attack from the north-east, or rear.

In the lead B25, #903 *Damn Yankee*, were eight men, with the Group CO, Lieutenant Colonel B. O'Neill, and Squadron CO, Major Ralph Cheli, as well as the normal crew. The Engineer, Staff Sergeant C. Murphree, was to fly with Cheli on the strafer mission to Dagua on 18 August, when Cheli was to win the Medal of Honor. Murphree and the rest of that crew were to die in the crash of the B25 off the beach at Dagua, or, soon after, be murdered by their Japanese captors. Cheli also died, or was murdered, at Rabaul in March 1944. But, on this March day of 1943, the 405th was about to play its part in the attack on the Japanese convoy.

In #903, from a distance of fourteen miles and at 4,000 feet, fourteen ships were counted in the convoy. Initially, the 405th came in above and behind the Beaufighters, then swung away to go around to the rear of the ships and attack. The six B25s broke into twos for the bombing runs, each element taking a target. A destroyer, probably *Yukikaze*, fired at them, but the planes swung out to evade her fire. They then dived to almost water level, and Cheli made his bomb run at the same time the ship was strafed by two Beaufighters. From 150 feet, the bombardier, 1st Lieutenant I. Johnson, dropped five 500-pounder GPs fitted with five-second delay fuzes. From his position in the nose, Johnson could see Japanese sailors on the decks, running for cover from the strafing Beaufighters. (31)

As they turned port, the destroyer was hit on the stern and beginning to settle. Johnson looked down to see their 500-pounders exploding into the side of the ship they had attacked. Other ships were hit, burning, sinking, or escaping near misses. Three columns of smoke, probably burning aircraft, fell to the water; the P38s were busy above them. As #903 left the area, columns of smoke from four burning ships could be seen. Johnson could see balls of fire marking burning Zekes going down into the sea.

2nd Lieutenant Pavlich, in #899 *Filthy Lil*, also counted fourteen ships as he flew on Cheli's wing in the wide approach to the ships. Pavlich saw what seemed to be an aircraft broken in six pieces, falling into the water. He attacked a 5,000-ton ship, following the Beaufighters, and as they passed it, he began strafing the decks. Then 2nd Lieutenant Thomas, the bombardier, released five 500-pound bombs. One direct hit and one near miss were observed by the top gunner, Staff Sergeant Morgan. The ship lurched violently, throwing men and supplies overboard, and the gunners machinegunned the decks as Pavlich flew past. Cheli and Pavlich had probably attacked *Shin-ai-Maru*.

Ralph Cheli made two more passes through the battle area, taking the B25 past what was thought to be a tanker with red flames and thick smoke billowing from it. As all ships were carrying gasoline in drums, it could have been any one of them; there was no tanker in the convoy.

Captain Williston M. Cox was flying #998 *Tugboat Annie*, for a run leading the second element, on a 650–1,000-ton ship, almost certainly *Kembu-Maru*. However, his bombardier, Lieutenant Sheerer, did not release the safety, and the bombs failed to drop. Cox hauled the B25 around in a turn to port, circled round to make another run and dropped three 500-pounders from mast height on a 3,000-ton ship, probably *Aiyo-Maru*, scoring one hit which started a fire. Then Cox turned starboard onto a camouflaged 10,000-tonner, dropping two bombs, one so close as a near miss that the column of water thrown up shot out at an angle to the ship's hull. This may have been *Oigawa-Maru*. Cox saw a ship with burning fuel pouring overboard collide with a destroyer. These last two ships almost certainly were *Nojima* and DD *Arashio*. Cox's navigator, Charles Mclean, believed that the first three bombs missed, falling short, and one of the next two made a hit on an unidentified transport.

1st Lieutenant Mondelli, in his #907 *Scat*, flew on Cox's wing, but made his run on the destroyer which had fired at them as they swung around the stern of the ships. From 150 feet, 1st Lieutenant Mussman dropped five 500-pounders on the destroyer, probably *Yukikaze*. Mussman, Sergeant Amos and Staff Sergeant Bressi saw one direct hit and a near miss that rolled the destroyer to port, and then back to starboard. Mondelli aborted another run on a transport—no bombs remained. As they left, Bressi reported seeing two ships ram each other; probably *Nojima* and *Arashio*. Mondelli joined Pavlich and Cheli, and they returned to base.

The third element of the 405th, B25s #971 *Dirty Dora* flown by 1st Lieutenant Ruark, and #908 *The Scoto Kid* flown by 1st Lieutenant McCartney, swung into the attack after the other two elements. Ruark began running in on a destroyer, possibly *Asagumo*, but the volume of anti-aircraft fire turned him away. Ruark saw Beaufighters strafe a 5,000-tonner so well that anti-aircraft fire from it stopped. He promptly swung onto this ship, possibly *Shinai-Maru*. One hit and two near misses resulted, but as about ten Zeros were seen above, Ruark went to water level and left the area. Smoke was rising to 1,000 feet above the ship they had bombed, and three other columns of smoke were seen. McCartney, on Ruark's wing, also bombed, and his crew saw Pavlich score a hit and a Zero fall into the sea. Anti-aircraft fire burst below them as they flew through the convoy at 200 feet.

After the B17s had turned port to attack, the B25s of the 71st Squadron continued for about a minute along a course parallel to the convoy. They then turned to make their own bombing run. As they were banking, Captain Royalty saw a B17 bomb strike the leading cruiser or destroyer amidships. A cloud of smoke billowed; he was then too busy to watch anything outside the activities of the 71st.

The Squadron was attacking from the north-east, along the line of advance of the convoy. They lined up on three transports, and selected the centre as the target—probably *Taimei-Maru*, with *Oigawa-Maru* ahead and *Nojima* astern. Riding in the nose behind the bombardier, Captain Royalty saw a formation of Zeros ahead, but as he saw them, P38s dived and combats began. Royalty had to concentrate again on what the 71st was doing.

The Squadron bombed from 5300 feet, claiming one direct hit and several near misses on the target, probably *Taimei-Maru*. As the B25s turned south after reaching the head of the convoy, Royalty saw three ships burning and two others smoking. Below, B25s, A20s, B17s and Beaufighters were strafing and skip-bombing every ship in sight. He climbed back from the nose position, and watched the scene behind from the navigator's dome. From about 30 miles away, he saw a ship explode, spreading what Royalty described as a tremendous volume of smoke and flame over half the ocean. Three other ships were burning, and bombs were still exploding around the ships. 'It was a bird-seye view of a show that was almost unbelievable,' said Royalty. On the way back to New Guinea, they dropped a life raft to a P38 pilot at 07.30S, 148.30E.

By 10.15, fifteen minutes after the attack began, all seven transports were hit and sinking, and three destroyers were badly damaged or sinking. Still the attacks came in, and at 10.15, at heights between 3,000 and 6,000 feet, six B25s of the 13th Squadron, in two three-plane elements, made runs from north to south, but only two bombs from the first element fell as planned and the squadron made one claim for a hit, on a 6–8,000-ton ship, leaving it sinking. The first element pilots were Lieutenants Small, Hutchinson and Hearn, while the second three were flown by Lieutenants Hamilton, Martin and Tabb. Several other bombs fell very close to a 2,000-ton ship. Two of the B25s were hit by AA, and one Zeke was claimed as damaged. The 13th crews also witnessed a B17 score hits on a large destroyer.

Five B17s of the 65th Squadron, 43rd Group, had taken off

from Jackson Field at 08.50, and began their attacks at 10.15, splitting into a flight of three and another of two, at 7,000 feet. The formation of three B17s had flown to the west of the convoy, then attacked along its line of advance, generally to the north-east. They bombed with twelve 1,000-pounders what seemed to the B17 leader to be the largest ship in the convoy—probably *Oigawa-Maru*. The B17 claimed a hit and a near miss, before being attacked by fighters, identified as Oscars. The Navy was responsible for cover during the morning, so it is more likely that these were Zekes. The attacks were described as feeble and lasted only two minutes, during which time the B17s went down to 5,000 feet, and returned to Jackson Field.

The flight of two had veered away to the east, going to the rear of the convoy, then attacked on a generally south-west run, aiming at what was thought to be a 4,000-ton ship, possibly *Shin-ai Maru*, dropping twelve 1,000-pound bombs on it, claiming two hits, two near misses, and another explosion on the ship, which was reported to have sunk as the formation left the scene. As the B17s came up to bomb-release point, they were attacked by six fighters. These were not a great problem and the bombers claimed 1-1-0, losing the fighters when the B17s went into cloud. One B17 was slightly damaged by the fighter attacks.

Survivors from *Shin-ai Maru* confirmed two hits by a formation of B17s, one by No.2 hatch and one on the bridge, killing the Captain. The ship was also pounded by B25s and A20s.

At 10.10, a formation of four B17s from the 63rd Squadron were west of the convoy. The squadron had hit *Kyokusei Maru* the day before. Three B17s were in V-formation, with the fourth some 1,000 feet higher to the rear. Captain Thompson, in #381 *Panama Hattie*, was leading, with Lieutenant Woodrow Moore in #356 on his right wing and Lieutenant Denault in #358 *Lulu Belle* on the left. Lieutenant Kirby flew the high rear B17, #574 *Tuffy*. The formation began a dive from 9,000 feet, turned 90 degrees left, then 90 degrees right, levelled off at 7,500 feet, and bombed at 10.22. They passed diagonally across the ships, bombing first a small, then a larger one, probably *Aiyo-Maru* and then *Nojima*. Two 1,000-pound bombs went down at the first ship, and ten at the second; all missed, except four near misses claimed 25 feet from the second ship. Kirby also dropped his four 1,000-pounders on this one, straddling it with three bombs on one side and the fourth on the other.

As the B17s were running up on the second ship, Lieutenant Woodrow Moore's B17, on the right, was hit by a Zero. As ten or so Zekes came in, Thompson's crew claimed three Japanese destroyed. Francis Denault, in *Lulu Belle*, claimed two more Japanese before a Hamp zoomed up below Moore's B17 #1356 from the 10 o'clock position, got home a telling burst, rolled over and dived away. A fire started in mid-fuselage, Moore pulled away from the formation, salvoed his bombs, then the tail section bent up, broke off, and the B17 started down to the Bismarck Sea. Seven men were seen to bale out, but one slipped from his harness. Three Japanese fighters—clipped wing model Hamps—dived on the parachutes, machinegunning them. To the other B17 crewmen, it seemed no one survived; an extra gunner had gone on the mission, making a total of eleven men in Moore's aircraft. The parachutes landed in the center of the convoy. To the Japanese, with the 'Bushido' tradition, no mercy was due an enemy who happened to have left his disabled aircraft. Many other Japanese in the convoy below were to reap the results of this act by the fighter pilots.

It is thought that Captain Bob Faurot, 39th Fighter Squadron, saw a B17 being attacked by the fighters and took his two wingmen, Hoyt Eason and Shifflett, down to assist in their P38s. All three were shot down. Other members of the 39th believed that Faurot was too tired to function properly after an intense operational tour of duty. Charlie King knew him well, describing Faurot as 'the type to want to get into a fight, and to heck with any Zeros that might be just above.'

On *Taimei Maru*, radio operator Suzuki had been knocked unconscious, but was brought back to reality by the pain inflicted by numerous soldiers running on and over his body. He looked groggily around and stagged out on deck by No. 2 hold. The ship was burning along its length, flames shooting out of the hold, and drums of burning fuel were rocketing up out of the opened hatch, tracing fiery arcs across the smoke and sky. But to Suzuki, all this was happening in silence—he had been deafened by the bombs.

In the distance, all in silence, he saw a ship under a banner of smoke and surrounded by columns of water from exploding bombs. As he watched, it began to sink. He thought it was either *Shin-ai Maru* or *Oigawa Maru*, but *Oigawa Maru* was known to be afloat as night fell. Suzuki turned and went to No. 1 hold and told a group of soldiers there to get overboard, the ship was finished. He went into the sea after them.

In the water, Suzuki found nearby Engineer 2nd Class Kato, who soon died from loss of blood; his leg had been severed. Engineer 1st Class Koba had died on the bridge, and none of the engine room crew are known to have survived. Also nearby was the Captain, Fumio Takiura, who had been wounded in the head while on the bridge; minutes later, he disappeared.

The first mad onslaught was over, and the attacking squadrons were re-forming on the way back to New Guinea, to refuel and re-arm, while from the higher-level B17s final counting went on. At 10.22, the 64th Squadron reported a damaged destroyer sinking, and at the same time, from their higher level, the 63rd Squadron counted eleven ships, two of them burning. Japanese radio monitors intercepted the 63rd Squadron message sent to Moresby at 10.25, reporting two ships burning at 148 degrees 30 minutes East, 7 degrees 15 minutes South. Already it was realised by the aircraft crews that significant damage had been done to the convoy, but in Rabaul and Lae the first reports of disaster were yet to arrive.

Lieutenant Jack Jones, of the 39th Squadron, was out of ammunition and had taken his P38 down to sea-level. On the way back to New Guinea, some 20 miles from Cape Ward Hunt, he watched Lieutenant Hoyt Eason's P38 land on the water and saw Eason emerge. As Larner's 90th Squadron was returning to New Guinea, four columns of smoke from the burning ships could be seen as much as 40 miles away. An unidentified aircraft was seen to crash into the sea only a mile or so from Cape Ward Hunt, and a man was seen swimming to shore. This may have been one of the other of the three missing P38 pilots—Faurot or Shifflet.

While these devastating attacks occurred the A20s of the RAAF 22 Squadron had been searching other parts of the area for a reported destroyer, but nothing was found. They prepared to join the next attack on the convoy.

John Smallwood, who had attacked in Ed Larner's leading flight of the 90th Squadron and been hit by anti-aircraft fire, brought damaged B25 #978 back to the 7-Mile Strip at Port Moresby, the only landing strip with a parallel emergency crash-strip for such situations. Bill Blewett, his Australian radio/gunner, recalled that the bomb doors could not be raised and the wheels could not be lowered; it was to be a belly landing; the radio was destroyed, so the base could not be informed.

When the emergency system for lowering the landing gear was tried, it was out of action. The nose wheel however, went down and possibly locked; the main gear remained up. The nose wheel could not be raised. Smallwood gave the crew a choice of parachuting or riding out the crash, and all chose to ride it out. Tests showed the B25 stalled at about 140 mph, much faster than the usual 110 mph. Smallwood and co-pilot Robert Lock-hart prepared to belly the B25 in with props feathered, and attempted to break off the nose wheel by side-slipping a little just before touchdown. The rest of the crew were to take up crash positions inside the fuselage, but unknown to Smallwood, Sergeant Martin decided to watch the landing from his top turret. Smallwood brought the airplane around onto finals and remembered nothing more until he woke up in a hospital bed 21 days later.

The approach was good but fast, he was told by witnesses, and the extra speed resulted in the B25 not touching down until reaching the second quarter of the pierced metal strip runway. Instead of collapsing, the firmly locked nose wheel held and bounced the airplane back into the air, sending it along the strip in a series of kangaroo-like hops. Even so, it was slowing, and if there had been more runway the crew would have walked away laughing. 'Unfortunately,' said Bill Smallwood, 'there was a fairly deep ditch at the end of the runway which changed the story into a tragedy.'

While still travelling, at 25 mph, the B25 arrived at the ditch, the extended nose wheel went into it and slammed the airplane to a sudden stop. Martin, in the top turret, was flung forward and his head crashed onto a gun-butt, killing him instantly. Sergeant Richard Martin was the only fatality suffered by the 3rd Attack Group on this mission. Smallwood was knocked out and came to 21 days later to see three figures come into focus at the end of his bed: Larner, McCoun, and Scott, the squadron adjutant. Three months later he was back flying with the renowned 'Pappy' Gunn. After 34 months in the SWPA, Smallwood and his Australian wife returned to the U.S.A. He later returned to Australia and now lives north of Sydney.

Bill Blewett woke up four days after the crash, in a U.S. hospital, bandaged from head to foot. He asked what had happened, and was told he had head injuries and had lacerations all over his body, arms and legs. He was also told he was the sole survivor of the crash. Over the objections of the U.S. doctor, he was transferred to an RAAF hospital, and three weeks later sent back to the 90th with a chit for '7 days light duty.' Ed Larner said there was no way Blewett would be fit to fly in seven days, and sent him on four weeks' leave. Blewett went to Townsville on the Lockheed courier. Next morning, he and another passenger were told they had been removed from the passenger list and they watched as two nurses climbed aboard the C47 going south. It crashed, killing all aboard. Blewett sent a telegram to his wife in Adelaide, telling her he was on his way. On arrival he found she had just given birth to their son. She had received a telegram saying he was 'missing, presumed dead.' Blewett never did get back to the 90th Squadron. He spent additional time in hospital recovering from his head injuries, and then finished the war on radar-equipped Liberators. He lives today in Adelaide, South Australia, having for over 40 years believed he was the only survivor of the crash.

Meanwhile, on the burning Japanese transports, it had become obvious that the vessels would never reach Lae, and orders to abandon ship were given.

Leaving *Teimei-Maru*, Sergeant Hosoda, from guncrew duty, clung to a log with nine other men—they would be like that for the next two days. Eiki Kiyo, an oiler, swam for the next five hours, before coming across a boat holding survivors of *Oigawa-Maru*. Sergeant Aoki, from the Shipping Engineer Medical unit, did not see any panic. The men were calm and the usable lifeboats were lowered. As on other ships, men clung to whatever floated.

Ropes were brought up on *Shin-ai-Maru* and thrown over the side; the ship was still burning. Private Akimoto, of 115 Regiment, surveyed the scene, and 'could not locate even one of our ships which was unscathed.' But things were not so well disciplined on *Shin-ai-Maru*. There were insufficient lifeboats, and Sergeant Ishihara of 50 AA Battalion saw most of them capsized in the rush. He and two others clung to the front half of an overturned rubber boat for the next day, before they managed to right it. Fourteen men, including Sergeant Major Endo, of 51 Engineers, got into a collapsible boat, and were for the moment relatively well off. Another member of the Engineers, Probationary Officer Seime Suzuki, was below decks, but on the order to abandon, he checked that all his men were safely off or accounted for, and then joined a boat with twenty men.

Colonel Endo and the Color Guard from 115 Regiment climbed into a ship's boat. There were 31 men in all, including the color guard, seven other men of 115 Regiment, eight from other units, and seven from the ship's crew. Colonel Endo was killed by strafing, though it is not clear when this happened. Captain Shiro Tsukahara, a Medical Officer in the Engineers, climbed into the rear half of a collapsible boat. The body of Colonel Endo was also placed in the boat.

Private Seiji Kojo, of the Debarkation unit, clung to a hatch plank, and looked around, unable to see a single undamaged ship. A Private in 115 Regiment, Takeki Horiguchi, on not finding a boat, climbed down from a rope ladder and swam to a nearby bamboo raft. On the deck of one of the sinking destroyers, a soldier of 115 Infantry Regiment looked around and later wrote in his diary, 'all the ships are burning.' He went into the sea with the others, and after two hours was picked up by another un-identified destroyer.

Another soldier on DD *Arashio* wrote that the ship had stopped after hits by the first attack, and that a transport ship had come alongside. Then the second wave attacked, one bomb exploded in the hull near the officers' quarters, then a second bomb hit, and the ship was finished; he went to a lifeboat. Later, Captain Matsumoto of *Nojima* swam to the boat. He also noted that DD *Tokitsukaze* had been hit four times by 10.15, and was abandoned 35 minutes later; the starboard boats could not be used. The crew was taken aboard *Yukikaze*. Also on *Arashio* was Chief Seaman Yasuo Yokoyama, a machinegunner with Sasebo Special Naval Landing Party (SNLP). After some time in the water, he was rescued by the DD *Asashio*.

The undamaged destroyers were busy rescuing survivors. DD *Asashio* came alongside *Arashio*, and took off some passengers, wounded, and confidential documents. The crew of the damaged destroyer were to remain and attempt to save the ship. Reiji Masuda looked at the faces of his friends and colleagues aboard the undamaged ship as it drew away. They were calling out encouragement to those remaining. None survived the afternoon. *Uranami* lowered its boats and the Army craft, sending them to pick up swimmers and bring them aboard. Private Yokichi Kitamura, of the Shipping Engineers, made four trips, and estimated that 300 people had been brought back to the destroyer before he set out on his fifth sortie among the hundreds of soldiers and sailors in the water.

From *Oigawa-Maru*, civilian Hisao Nakazawa swam to a raft and climbed aboard. Private Takao Nagata climbed into a boat with twenty others. One additional person was pulled in from the water. Nagata had only been inducted into the Army on 22 December 1942, and had had only nine weeks military service, some of it en route to Rabaul. Private Yamada (the man who had wished that his officer stop talking while the enemy planes were approaching) survived the three hits amidships, climbed onto a raft, and then swam to a small boat where he met others from his unit, 115 Regiment. The unconscious Sergeant Kojima, of 50 AA Battalion, with leg and head wounds, was carried from the ship and put into a lifeboat, which shows there could have been no panic in that group, at least. A carpenter with 115 Regiment, Sergeant Torao Abe, found himself on a raft with three other men, and they began four days of drifting. A Private in the Debarkation unit, Setaro Nagatomo, saw a B17 hit his ship with two bombs before he went over the side.

Sergeant Sasayama, who survived after seven of his section had been killed manning the aft anti-aircraft guns, got into a collapsible boat. *Oigawa-Maru* was still afloat, but drifting away, and he watched her throughout the afternoon. Tsukasa Koizumi, from 1 Machinegun Company, 69 Battalion, 115 Regiment, survived, but all his platoon, including the commander, Noguchi, drowned. Later, he would find that only 33 of 108 men would survive, none of them officers. A good infantry soldier, Private Kanami Mayeda of 88 Independent Infantry Battalion, tied his rifle to a board and dropped it over the side, intending to locate it when he was in the water. He never saw it again. The steam pipes were ruptured, and the boats could not be lowered, so he jumped in after his rifle, and swam to a small raft, where he sat alone, looking around at the sinking ships.

A soldier of 50 AA Battalion thought that *Oigawa-Maru* was the last to be hit, and that was only a minute and a half after the attack began. Within ten minutes the flames were pouring out, and within 30 minutes of the onset of the attack he was told to abandon ship. He thought that three MLCs and about twenty collapsible boats were launched. He was not a good sailor and became seasick.

Artilleryman Seiichi Hagihara climbed into a collapsible boat with 18 other men. He saw one of the remaining MLCs reserved for some high-ranking officers and the standard-bearer of 115 Infantry Regiment. (The account of the saving of the colors has the men in a ship's boat.) The man who thought he was last to leave the ship was Corporal Rihei Koido, Headquarters 3 Battalion, 14 Field Artillery Regiment. During the attacks, and in the next few hours and days, he saw men of low and high rank 'suffer bravely and die.' He found a raft, and with a couple of others, hauled himself onto it; it was small and they lay on it up to their waists in water.

Below decks, Private Saburo Shiraishi, of a truck unit, knew the *Teiyo Maru* had been hit. When the order came to abandon, he went up on deck. There were no usable boats, only rafts, and he went straight over the side into the water and became one of 12 men on a raft. Ryuji Sakieda, a Probationary Officer in 51 Division Signals, also counted two direct hits, and when the order to abandon was given, he made sure the soldiers were safely over the side on the rope ladders. He was then was among the officers who followed. With his lifebelt, he clung with 17 others to the sides of a raft among the wreckage.

In a collapsible boat with 13 others was Yoshio Watanabe, from a Sea Duties unit. They had left the ship on orders and launched the boat with little difficulty. *Teiyo-Maru* had six Dai-hatsu MLCs on board, but none was usable, though the small boats and rafts and a smaller motorised landing craft were put over the side successfully. An experienced soldier aboard *Teiyo Maru*, Warrant Officer Shichi-Hei Matsushima of 115 Regiment, climbed into a ship's boat with about a dozen others; they found themselves in the middle of a large cluster of other boats and rafts. Mikiwo Omiya, of 51 Division Signals, swam to a raft. He and some other men then lashed floating bamboo to it, to increase buoyancy. Another member of 50 AA Battalion, Yoshio Aoki, was ill with malaria and wished to die quietly on board. His commanding officer pulled him on deck and made him abandon ship, and Aoki obediently climbed into one of the small boats.

Discipline held, and Sergeant Chikui of 115 Regiment related how, after the order came, the unit began leaving in good order, with 1 Platoon leading. 'After leaving the ship,' he said, 'we drifted on the sea, hanging onto a box of hard biscuits. We started singing military songs.'

Survivors and crew on *Aiyo-Maru* found themselves victims of earlier generosity—many of the ship's boats had been given to *Oigawa-Maru*. Only a few remained, and only six collapsible boats were assembled and launched. Private Juichi Okamoto, of a truck unit, thought that none of the Daihatsu MLCs or the ship's motor boat had been launched, because there was no steam pressure for the winches. On deck were large numbers of bamboo poles and 6-foot by 1-foot planks; these were thrown over by the troops and used when they were in the water. Akio Fujiwara, 8 Shipping Engineers, was one of those who jumped into the sea. He knew that the transports had been annihilated, but thought the destroyers were not badly damaged and hoped they would return to rescue them.

At 10.30, *Nojima* sank. DD *Arashio* was still afloat, and at about this time *Tokitsukaze* began to sink. The order to abandon her was given at 10.50, but it was not possible to lower the small boats and MLCs. The 28 wounded from her crew were rescued by *Yukikaze*, and others went to different ships. At 11.30, Rear Admiral Kimura and the other survivors from *Shirayuki* left the sinking destroyer and transferred to *Shikinami*. The other destroyers, with survivors from all the sunk and sinking ships, were told to leave with the personnel they had collected. *Asashio* remained to pick up more, especially the naval crews. They were to go to the east of Long Island and meet ships coming from Rabaul or Kavieng, tranship the survivors, and return to the battle area. DD *Arashio* had been a focal point for some of the floating men. It has been battered by the strafers, with the Captain killed, bridge destroyed, and steering useless. At about noon, five men from *Taimei Maru* found each other among the crowded survivors on deck: Radio operator Suzuki, Helmsman Fujihira, Stoker Setouchi, Cook Aibara, and a Quartermaster also named Suzuki.

It was apparent to all that the Allied Air Forces would return to the scene of the disaster, and the weight of air power amply demonstrated in the morning's attacks would probably be applied to any ship in the area when the aircraft returned.

FOUR

COUP DE GRACE

3 MARCH 1943—AFTERNOON

To assist the strike force which would go out again to attack the ships, pressure had to be maintained on the Japanese airfields from which Zeros would fly cover over the battle area. At midday, the 8th Squadron, 49th Fighter Group, attacked Lae airfield. In a combat with Zeros, Lieutenants Harris, White and Blakely, and Captain Wright from Group headquarters, claimed four planes as destroyed and three as probables. A little later Lieutenant House of the 7th Squadron claimed two Zeros.

A Japanese report to 18th Army HQ stated that there was no damage to the airfield from P40 or P38, bombing and strafing, but made no mention of losses in air combat. Another message reported that five of the convoy ships were on fire, heading ashore to run aground, that *Shirayuki* had its magazine explode, Rear Admiral Kimura was wounded, and that *Yukikaze* and *Arashio* were damaged. The Japanese also intercepted messages from U.S. aircraft over the convoy, the first reporting that two ships were on fire, and another that four ships were on fire. (1)

At 14.10, from a 321st Squadron B24, four warships were sighted at 06.40 South, 148.05 East, course 300 degrees, speed 30 knots; that is, going north-west away from the battle area at high speed. 5th Air Force pondered this sighting of four warships 'apparently in good condition leaving the scene of battle with hundreds of thousands of enemy troops in life boats, on rafts, or in the water.' 5th Air Force came to part of the correct conclusion—that the destroyers had already picked up many survivors, but that they were taking them to Finschafen, which was incorrect. The four destroyers had left the area ahead of the imminent second AAF attack, and were going to meet two additional destroyers coming from Rabaul. They would transfer survivors to these two DDs, and take fuel from them, before the four DDs returned to the battle area.

Those who were picked up by the destroyers included some from *Teiyo Maru*, by DD *Uranami*; some from DD *Arashio*, picked up by DD *Asashio*; *Shin-Ai Maru* survivors of 2 Company 51 Engineers were saved by DDs *Asagumo* and *Uranami*; *Oigawa Maru* survivors were picked up by *Asagumo*, which had at one time 127 men rescued aboard. *Yukikaze* picked up others, including 18 men of 11 Company, 115 Regiment. The destroyers steamed north, where 1,400 survivors were loaded onto DDs *Hatsuyukaze* and *Urakaze*. Fuel was taken on by the original convoy escort before the two steamed back to Rabaul with survivors, and the others returned to the battle area. (2)

DD *Asashio* had remained in the battle area in order to honour a promise made by her captain, Commander Goro Yoshii, that she would continue rescuing personnel from *Nojima* and *Arashio*.

In the battle area by mid-afternoon, four or five transports, and DD *Arashio*, formed a ragged east-west line—all were burning to some extent. North of them, *Asashio* was busy collecting survivors, and to the west and drifting was another large destroyer with fuel oil from her burst hull forming a large slick on the northern side. *Shirayuki* had sunk, so this may have been the 1,700-ton *Tokitsukase*. Photographs of the ship show quadruple torpedo tubes, a design feature of *Tokitsukase*; the *Asashio* and

Kagero Class also had such mounts. *Fubuki* Class had three triple mounts. *Arashio* may still have been afloat at the western end of the line of burning ships.

After analysis of Allied and Japanese reports, the author believes the most probable locations of the destroyers in the convoy area at about 15.00 are in the diagram below:

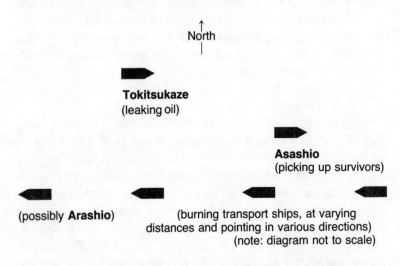

North

Tokitsukaze
(leaking oil)

Asashio
(picking up survivors)

(possibly **Arashio**)   (burning transport ships, at varying
distances and pointing in various directions)
(note: diagram not to scale)

Kembu Maru and *Nojima* had already sunk. Various survivors say that *Aiyo Maru* sank at around mid-day, but she may still have been afloat as the second wave of attacks developed.

Around the burning hulks and patches of wreckage were several thousand Japanese soldiers and sailors of all ranks (up to Colonel), who had just received a lesson in the use of air power. Only a year before it had been the Japanese air forces which had swept the seas, ruthlessly sinking and strafing the fleets of ships fleeing Malaya, Singapore, Java, Sumatra and the Phillipines. Those stories by survivors from the ships had been preceded by others of Japanese behavior in the war in Manchuria and China; tales of the Bataan Death March had leaked out; the Japanese had caused many civilian casualties in bombing raids on Darwin and Broome, in northern Australia.

At Broome, many Dutch women and children, evacuees from Java and Sumatra, were killed when the moored flying boats they were aboard were strafed. In the fighting across the Kokoda Trail, and at Milne Bay, Buna, Gona, Guadalcanal, and other places in the Solomons, the Allies had found evidence of what happened to prisoners taken by the Japanese. A diary captured on Guadalcanal describes experimental surgery [vivisection] carried out on two Americans, who had been shot in the feet to prevent their escape. In New Guinea, captured documents and prisoners described killings that took place on 13 August 1942 on the beach at Buna: European men, women and children, with a 16-year old girl left till last. The murderers in the Japanese Navy unit, Sasebo 5 Special Navy Landing Party, botched this beheading, and had to hold the wounded and frantic girl down on the sand, still screaming and crying out while they finished the job of cutting off her head. Earlier on this 3 March 1943, Moore's B17 crew had been murdered in full sight of the AAF aircrews attacking the convoy. Many who did not see the incident quickly learned of it on return to base at Port Moresby. (3)

Now the Japanese in the Bismarck Sea were to pay for all that.

The AAF strike squadrons were returning to finish the destruction of the convoy. Losses of one B17, three P38s and a B25 were minimal, and everyone was keen to get back out to the battle area. The implacable and impartial weather intervened to lessen the strength of the second blow, but a considerable force crossed the Owen Stanley mountains and approached the convoy area at 15.00 hours.

Allied Air Forces had planned another massive afternoon strike to really annihilate what remained of the convoy. Because of the duplicated sightings by aircrews, and the almost impossible task of quickly and precisely compiling an accurate report from the multiple claims from the morning mission, the convoy was still thought to be larger than it really was. But, as ever, the implacable New Guinea weather intervened. The daily buildup of dangerous flying conditions over the Owen Stanley Ranges had, by early afternoon, boiled up to the degree that some of the squadrons which had returned to Port Moresby could not get through. 30 Squadron RAAF, with the powerful Beaufighters, tried but could not make the passage. They took off at 14.00 hours from Ward's Strip, and returned after trying for an hour. Led by Tommy Lynch, the 39th Fighter Squadron, despite a difficult time getting across the island because of the buildup of clouds, did make it in their P38s.

Aircraft based north of the Owen Stanleys, on the Dobodura airfields, waited for the Port Moresby squadrons to join them, and then returned to the convoy. They left the rendezvous area in the following sequence: 65th Squadron B17s, 90th, 71st, and 405th Squadrons' B25s, 64th Squadron B17s, and 22 Squadron RAAF in A20 Bostons. With them were Lynch's ten P38s of the 39th Squadron.

DD *Asashio* was almost at a standstill picking up survivors, but *Uranami* had already departed at high speed when the first of the returning aircraft were sighted. Private Kitamura, on his fifth trip to pick up survivors in a small landing barge from the destroyer, watched in dismay as she sped away from him and the other boats. His dismay turned to contempt when he realised she would not return. He did not yet know of the approaching planes. (4)

Also dismayed was Sergeant Chikui. He and the others had been keeping up their morale by singing military songs. They saw a destroyer approach. 'Anxiously we waited for a rescue boat to come. At last we embarked on a boat. But upon hearing a second air raid warning, the destroyer hastily departed, leaving us behind.' Warrant Officer Matsushima, the 22-year veteran, was another disappointed survivor. They watched a destroyer picking up people all around them, until the decks were crammed with an estimated 500 men. It then departed as an air attack began. He was not sure if it escaped safely.

This ship was almost certainly DD *Asashio*, and those men not collected by it were fortunate. The decision by her Captain to remain in what had become a killing zone was commendable from the point of view of honour, but had little relevance in modern warfare. *Asashio* had just seen what concentrated air attack could accomplish. It would have been prudent to have left the area before the estimated turn-around time for the aircraft had elapsed, and so have lived to fight another day. In the Mediterranean, in April and May 1941, the British Royal Navy had continued to operate during the evacuation of Crete, under the determined and experienced Luftwaffe dive-bomber units. Including the Greek Navy, combined losses were four cruisers and 13 destroyers sunk, and another 25 battleships, aircraft carriers, cruisers and destroyers damaged. Thirty of these British and Greek ships had been sunk or damaged by Axis air power in May 1941 alone. The Royal Navy had continued to operate for several reasons, one of which was their heritage of support to the Army. Commander Yoshii should have been aware of what could happen if he remained in the battle area as the sole operable ship.

The RAAF A20s of 22 Squadron attacked at 15.03 hours, with five aircraft holding 250-pound semi-armorpiercing and 500-pound instantaneous-fuzed bombs. On finding a stationary destroyer (*Tokitsukaze*) in an oil slick, they circled it and broke off into individual dives of about 35 degrees, from 4,000 feet to 1,500 feet, attacking despite interception by the 25 or 30 Zekes (Oscars) now over the convoy. Direct hits were scored by Flying Officers Skinner and Hunt; all other bombs were near misses. Sergeant Grant was taking photos from the rear compartment of his A20 Boston, when the Oscars came on them so fast that he did not have time to grab his machinegun. Grant realised he had to point something at the Japanese, so he pointed the camera.

Single-engined Japanese fighters were often called 'Zeros' or 'Zekes' unless positively identified as a particular type. In the afternoon reports of 3 March, Allied crews spoke of both Zeros and Zekes. However, according to the convoy's fighter escort program, the afternoon duty was allocated to Army fighters, so in following passages they are named as Oscars.

The RAAF crews reported four merchant ships burning and two destroyers, all stationary. One large transport of 8,000-tons was seen to blow up. The destroyer they attacked was seen to be very low in the water, and the other was seen to blow up after hits from B25s or B17s. The fighters attacked, and were disagreeably surprised when Flying Officer H. Craig turned into them with his four nose .50s. Another Boston with an Oscar after it went under a formation of B17s whose gunners shot down the fighter. RAAF crews saw another Oscar hit the water, and B25s were seen strafing as the Bostons returned to land at Dobodura.

The other Japanese destroyers, busy transferring survivors and refuelling to the north, received a message from the *Asashio* saying she was under attack by some 30 aircraft. Then there was silence.

At 15.05 hours, the 63rd Squadron watchers from altitude of 8000 feet counted five burning ships and two destroyers, the warships steaming north. One destroyer was well to the north, apparently steaming away, and six B17s of the 64th Squadron were seen to go after it. Ten minutes later, the 65th Squadron reported that a transport had sunk. At almost the same time, another report confirmed that five burning ships were in sight. It was this continued duplication of such sightings that led to confusion over just how many ships were disabled, how many were sunk, and how many remained.

As she showed signs of activity and did not seem to be badly damaged, *Asashio* attracted her share of attention from the arriving force. Aircraft of all types went after it, bombing from mast height to 8,000 feet. Perhaps the experienced destroyer crew could have coped with one type of attack, but not so many, coming all at once and from different angles. The assembled men and ship's crew on her decks were about to suffer one of the worst horrors of modern warfare—the effect of bombs and machineguns on a human mass gathered into a small area.

Major Ed Scott, of the 63rd Squadron 43rd Bomb Group, who had hit *Kyokusei Maru* the day before, took off at 13.40 with Lieutenant Dieffenderfer, but Dieffenderfer had to turn back with engine trouble. Over Cape Ward Hunt, Scott met five other B17s (65th Squadron), and they flew to the convoy area. They sighted the ships at 15.05 hours as the strafers were beginning to attack. Two other B17s attached themselves to Scott, who was in #574 *Tuffy*. They selected targets and began bomb runs.

Below the B17s, twin-engined strafers dived for low-level attacks. When the B25s dropped out of the clouds, the remains of the convoy were straight ahead. They went into the attack at once. The 90th Squadron, with eleven aircraft, claimed four hits on a large destroyer and four on a smaller one, leaving them sinking. Two transports were hit again, and left sinking or with raging fires.

Scott led his formation of three north-east, past the burning ships and large oil slick with wreckage dotted across it, and made a run on a destroyer busy on the northern edge of the area of destruction. The destroyer was almost certainly *Asashio*. At 15.12, from 7,000 feet, Scott aimed two 1,000-pounders at *Asashio*. His 65th Squadron wingmen each dropped four bombs, enveloping the target in smoke and spray from hits or near misses. Scott believed he hit her on the stern. He watched her slew to port and come to a stop, leaking oil fuel.

The two 65th Squadron B17s thought *Asashio* had slowed and stopped as the eight 1000-pound bombs had exploded off the bows of the ship. This was probably the attack witnessed by several other squadrons. Both B17s went down to 200 feet and expended 2,000 rounds on strafing attacks. As they were leaving the area, the Oscars attacked. They broke away in pairs from a 15-plane formation and made passes from below, despite the low altitude of 200 feet. The combat lasted 25 minutes, and four enemy planes were claimed destroyed, with two as probables. The B17s landed at Moresby at 17.30 hours.

Even as the bombs from the B17s were on the way down, B25s were preparing to attack. Before the spray from the explosions cleared, Scott's crew saw one B25 skip-bomb the destroyer, immediately followed by others from the 90th and 405th Squadrons who bombed and strafed it.

1st Lieutenant Melville Fisher, in the 90th Squadron's #793, had Flight Sergeant J. Stephen RAAF as co-pilot and Staff Sergeant P. Malito as gunner. Fisher was flying Number 3 in a 3-ship V. When the convoy was sighted, there were four burning transports in an east-west line, and a cruiser and destroyer about four miles apart, thought to be steaming west at speed. The westernmost cruiser was *Tokitsukaze*, and the destroyer, *Asashio*, was to the east. The B25s flew along the northern side of the burning ships, then at 15.15 turned north onto the destroyer. The flight slid out into echelon right, and at 1,000 feet and two miles from *Asashio*, they began their runs.

The first two planes scored hits, and Fisher saw the ship was already enveloped in smoke and flames as he began his run-in, so came in from dead astern, jinking as much as possible, though he saw no AA. At 600 yards, now at 100 feet and 240 mph, he stopped jinking and opened fire. Smoke obscured his vision and the first two bombs overshot. He went on ahead, then turned and came in broadside, noticing flashes every six or seven seconds, and presumed these were from the destroyer's guns. He did not take evasive action, went on in and dropped two bombs which hit amidships. Fisher then strafed lifeboats and rafts, expending 1,000 rounds. They saw A20s strafing, and the water covered with debris and men. The destroyer he attacked was halted and burning when last seen.

1st Lieutenant James B. Criswell, 90th Squadron, was in the convoy area from 15.15 to 15.45, as Number 2 in a 2-ship formation approaching from the southwest. They flew over burning ships, wreckage and personnel in the water. On the eastern side of the target area they approached *Asashio*, then moving at about eight knots. When the B25s separated to attack, Criswell could see water churn from the destroyer's stern as the propellors increased rpm. Criswell swung out, then came in from the stern, mast height, at 220 mph. When the destroyer was hit by the leading B25, it swung to the left, presenting its side to Criswell, who was somewhat hidden by the smoke from the stack, and in any case saw no firing at himself. He strafed, then skipped a bomb into the side, passed over the ship and turned 90 degrees to port. Criswell considered the destroyer to be sinking, so went to the centre of the battle area and strafed.

These attacks took only about seven minutes to execute, from the time Scott's B17s went overhead, through the 90th Squadron attacks and Major Ralph Cheli's low-level runs with the 405th Squadron (described later). The ship was almost literally battered to pieces by a continuous stream of bombs. The effects of blast and concentrated machinegun fire on the crew and survivors crammed in the ship and on deck are beyond description. And yet, people survived. Chief Seaman Yasuo Yokoyama, a machinegunner with the Matsukawa Butai of the Sasebo SNLP, had survived not only the attacks on *Arashio*, been picked up by *Asashio*, then survived the maelstrom which engulfed that ship, but had somehow managed to get aboard a raft. (5)

Meanwhile, aircraft attacked other ships in the area as well as the barges and boats littering the surface of the sea. Still angry at what had been done to the parachuting crew of Moore's B17, Ed Scott took *Tuffy* down to low level and his gunners began firing at Japanese in the boats and wreckage below. He also dropped two 1,000-pounders on a transport, but missed. Twelve Oscars were in the area, but did not attack.

One of the ships strafed by a B17 was *Oigawa Maru*. Kojiro Narisawa, 33 Mountain Artillery Regiment, wrote that Sadao Arai went overboard with a steering oar when the B17 machinegunned them, adding: 'The Boeing is most fearful. We are repeating the failure of Guadalcanal. Very regrettable. All the transports are sunk. Our lives of tomorrow are uncertain.' (6)

It must have been frightening for a man on the deck of a burning ship, out of sight of land, confronted with other stricken naval and merchant vessels in all directions, with the surface of the sea littered with small boats, barges, wreckage and survivors, and columns of smoke drifting over the scene, to see the huge four-engined olive-drab bombers, engines roaring, machineguns hammering from nose, belly, sides and tail, relentlessly circling. Hurtling past at twice the speed of the B17s were the B25s, often preceded by the horrendous wall of water and debris flung up by fire from the eight massed .50-caliber machineguns in the nose. On damaged DD *Arashio*, the strafers inflicted more destruction, killing many more men on her decks. Her captain, Commander Hideo Kuboki, had been killed earlier, and in the afternoon attacks all the other combat officers died. Blood ran freely across the decks.

2nd Lieutenant Edward Solomon, in B25 #112946 of Ed Larner's 90th Squadron, had Sergeant Redus W. Harrell as gunner, and two RAAF men aboard—co-pilot Flight Sergeant J.H. McLellan and Sergeant A.L. McDonald as radio-gunner. When the B25s came in at 2,000 feet and split up to make attacks by elements on separate targets, Solomon attacked a blue-grey

3,000-ton 'cruiser' five miles from the convoy, which seemed to be in process of rescuing men from rafts and boats. From Solomon's written mission report, it seems he attacked *Asashio*, but the accompanying sketch indicated an attack on *Tokitsukaze*.

At 250 mph, Solomon continued to dive for the warship, diving and climbing until he reached minimum altitude, while giving it the most difficult full deflection shot for its guns. Forced to pull away because of B17s bombing, he circled and then went in again at the bows, firing his eight .50-calibers at 1,000 yards. He was again forced to break away because of level bombers. There were no near misses or hits, but some bombs exploded within 100 feet of the Japanese ship. This time, Solomon attacked from astern and wrecked the rear gun position, sending a large column of black smoke into the air. Light anti-aircraft fire ceased when Solomon opened the eight .50s on the decks.

Solomon strafed barges and rafts, then went in broadside to a transport ship to put a bomb in its side. The transport began burning furiously. He noted that the enemy were still wearing battle equipment. During this time, Oscars attacked twice, pressing in close, so Solomon made violent turns at low level, and avoided the fighter attacks. He saw six enemy aircraft—two attacking B17s, two attacking A20s, and two attacking him. Solomon was at an altitude of 50 feet or less during his time in the convoy area, and in all, expended 2,500 rounds of .50-caliber ammunition, and all his 500-pound bombs. In his report, he commented on the excellent co-ordination of the attack, but presumably this did not refer to the B17 attacks which broke off his own attack runs.

After leaving DD *Asashio*, Lieutenant Criswell began his runs at boats and wreckage clusters from 200 feet, continuing in the pass until water and debris thrown up by the massed fire of the .50-calibers made it necessary to pull up. He made four strafing runs, then turned onto a 5,000-ton transport, the easternmost in the line, and attacked personnel on the deck at mast height and at 220 mph. The gun on the ship's stern was not manned. When the eight nose guns of the B25 were fired, Criswell reported that 'a marked effect was noticed among the troops on deck'; his bombs overshot. He expended more ammunition on

A B25 crew of the 90th Attack Squadron. At rear left is Flight Sergeant Bob Guthrie, RAAF, co-pilot, and right is Lieutenant John E. Sbisa, pilot. Front left is Sergeant Allister L. McDonald, RAAF, radio operator, and right is Corporal Ashton E. Carter, gunner. (RAAF)

Flying Officer (1st Lt) Maurice Carse, RAAF, co-pilot, and Lieutenant Bob Chatt, pilot of B25 "Chatterbox" hit a destroyer in the attacks. (RAAF)

Lieutenant Edward T. Solomon, right, piloted a B25 of the 90th Attack Squadron on the afternoon mission on 3 March and hit a destroyer. At left are Sergeant Eugene P. McCarthy RAAF, radio/gunner, Staff Sergeant James M. Hume, turret gunner, and Flight Sergeant Ivan Wilkinson RAAF, co-pilot. (RAAF)

B25 crewmen of the 90th Attack Squadron. Left to right are, Staff Sergeant C. H. Maupin, gunner; Staff Sergeant Charles C. Thompson, radio/gunner; Flight Sergeant Noel Stibbard RAAF, co-pilot; and Lieutenant John B. Criswell, pilot. During the afternoon mission of 3 March, Criswell, Thompson and Maupin bombed a destroyer and a burning transport ship; Stibbard flew with another crew. (RAAF)

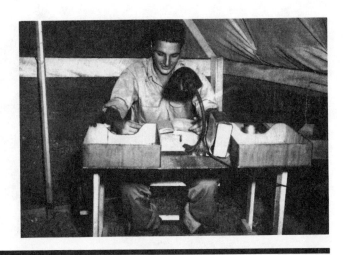

Major Ralph Cheli, CO 405 Bomb Squadron, 38th Bomb Group, led the squadron on low-level missions against the convoy. Later he won the Medal of Honor in an attack on the Japanese airfield at Dagua, was captured, and is believed to have been killed by the Japanese at Rabaul. (AWM)

B25 #971 "Dirty Dora" of the 405th Squadron, 38th Bomb Group, as the crew arrive for the mission. (RAAF)

Wing Commander Brian "Blackjack" Walker, commander 30 Squadron RAAF, who flew an unscheduled mission against the convoy rather than be left out of the action. (RAAF)

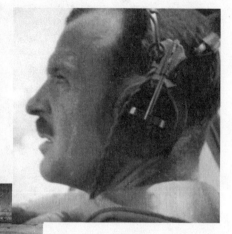

Loading belts of 20mm ammunition into the belly hatches of an RAAF Beaufighter. Two cannon are on either side of the center-line. (RAAF)

Flying Officer Fred Cassidy, navigator in 30 Squadron RAAF, flew the Bismarck Sea strike missions. (Cassidy)

Australian Bristol "Beaufighter" of 30 Squadron RAAF passing through the New Guinea mountains back to Port Moresby. The Beaufighter mounted four 20mm cannons in the nose which were devastating against the gun crews on the convoy. (RAAF)

Beaufort torpedo bombers of RAAF 100 Squadron flew through tropical storms on the night of 2 March 1943, to attack the Japanese convoy. (RAAF)

A20 "Bostons" of 22 Squadron RAAF. On the afternoon mission 3 March, they attacked a destroyer despite fighter interceptions, and scored two hits. (RAAF)

Below: The tail surfaces of B17 #41-24455 "Old Baldy," of the 63rd Squadron Bomb Group, after pilot James Dieffenderfer put it into a near-vertical dive on 2 March 1943 while under attack. He flew it back to Port Moresby, and the Boeing Company representative was amazed that the airplane stayed in the air. (RAAF)

Many attacking crews saw this spectacular explosion and smoke ring. Australian Dick Roe was strafing a transport loaded with gasoline and ammunition when the 20mm cannonfire from his Beaufighter detonated part of the deck cargo. (Alf Nelson)

Taimei Maru just after attack by the Beaufighters. Smoke is steaming from the bridge area where 20mm cannon shells exploded. The ship was changing watch and many casualties were suffered. (Fred Cassidy)

Lieutenant Gordon McCoun, 90 Attack Squadron, flew #433 "Mortimer" on the 3 March convoy attack mission. (RAAF)

Bombs bursting alongside 6,870-ton *Teiyo Maru* as the attack develops. (RAAF)

strafing until his flight leader called him back, and he gradually drew into formation on the flight to the New Guinea coast. During the attack, he and his crew saw B17s and other B25s strafing; the aircraft performed well, with no malfunctions of equipment.

Many Japanese realised that the only protection against the bullets was in the water. As the strafers approached, the men would jump off the rafts and out of the boats until the aircraft had passed, then try to climb back again. This was repeated many times and each time used valuable strength. Medical Captain Shiro Tsukahara, who was in the boat with the body of the commander of 115 Regiment, Colonel Endo, saw six people in the boat killed or wounded by strafing, and joined others in the water, holding on to the boat's sides. Men nearby in the sea were killed as the attacks continued. A boat that Masami Yamada climbed into with five others was strafed and sank. They relied on their lifebelts to stay afloat, but drifted apart. (7)

When 2nd Lieutenant Charles Howe, in B25 #980, returned to the scene, he counted seven ships, roughly in the same position as the morning attack. Six were stopped or moving very slowly, all but one were burning. One 5,000-tonner was firing, but only blindly through its own smoke. The northernmost ship, probably a cruiser, was damaged and moving slowly. From the sketch accompanying his mission report, it seems to have been the 1,700-ton *Tokitsukaze*. Flying north through the center of the line of burning ships, Howe attacked *Tokitsukaze*.

He passed over the ship from the stern, machineguns firing, and dropped two bombs, scoring a hit at the waterline that caused the already weakened superstructure to collapse. Then Howe turned to port and went for it broadside, dropping a bomb while in a dive. The bomb did not skip, but went into the water and exploded under the surface, about 20 feet from the hull. Howe then attacked a burning cargo ship, which was afire at the stern, scoring a direct hit with his fourth bomb and causing another explosion, presumed to be ammunition or a magazine.

Japanese fighters attacked in one formation of two, and one of three. Howe went down to water level. The fighter attacks were diving passes from rear, and his turret fired back. As the fighters passed, Howe tried to fire his eight .50s at them, but the

B25 was not manoeuvrable enough. The fighters pulled away, and Howe then began strafing the survivors and supplies which were 'strewn as far as the eye could see.' He flew out to the eastern edge of the chaos, turned back to port, and made a strafing run against the destroyer *Asashio*. After seven seconds of fire from the .50s, Howe released the trigger and witnessed lifeboats overturned and crowds of men 'definitely out of action.' During the mission, he attacked five separate ships, and expended 1,500 rounds of .50-caliber ammunition and four 500-pound bombs.

Captain John 'Jock' Henebry, 90th Squadron, came up from the southwest, made a strafing pass across the westernmost ship in the line, possibly *Arashio*, and continued north to attack another damaged destroyer, *Tokitsukaze*. Placing a 500-pound bomb into it, he swung back to port and attacked all but one of the burning vessels, starting a fire on the easternmost ship. Henebry made a total of about 15 strafing passes, including a final run on the drifting *Tokitsukaze*. He was attacked by six enemy fighters, and while Henebry kept the B25 flat out on the water, his gunner, Staff Sergeant William H. Epperson, shot one down, and the other five did not press their attacks. Henebry went on to become Group commander, and after the war achieved general rank.

The 90th Squadron had launched 11 aircraft, expended 24 500-pound bombs and 15,000 .50-caliber rounds, and claimed ten hits, eight of which were on the two warships north of the main group of burning ships. All crew members agreed that none of the ships would reach land. This type of attack was hazardous, and few men would survive a badly damaged aircraft hit flying at low-level going into the sea or jungles.

The following men of the 3rd Attack flew in the Bismarck Sea battle and later were lost on operations: Lieutenants Harry Hamilton and Raymond Tabb of the 13th Squadron; Captain Roger 'Dixie' Dunbar, Lieutenant Richard Ruby and Staff Sergeant Joseph Fox of the 89th; Lieutenants Walter Lee, Richard Lockhart, Roy Moore, Keith McKee, and Harlan Reid, Staff Sergeant Bennie Estep, and Sergeant Redus Harrell of the 90th.

Meanwhile, in the lifeboat, the color guard of 115 Infantry Regiment was repeatedly machinegunned, and according to one account it was here that Colonel Endo died of a head wound.

Seven other soldiers were also killed in the strafings. A few minutes later, another strafer wounded standard bearer Lieutenant Kondo. Kondo was hit in the leg, presumably by a .50-caliber bullet, and bled heavily. According to the same account, his last words were, 'The regimental flag!' (which was undamaged). Sergeant Namiki then assumed command of the flag party, and all the survivors were aware of their responsibility to save the colors, regardless of cost. Three rifles tied to the flag ensured that it would sink long before it could be captured. (8)

The 38th Group's 71st and 405th Squadrons began attacks at 15.17 hours, claiming three hits on each of the two destroyers. Crews counted eight burning ships. The attacks described here were going on more or less simultaneously, with aircraft crisscrossing the area, pilots talking to each other and sometimes arguing about who was going to attack which ship. On several occasions, aircraft had their attack runs interfered with, or endangered by, another keen strafer or bomber going for the same ship.

The 71st Squadron assembled at Cape Ward Hunt with more confidence than they had on the morning mission. The squadron approached the ships from the south, and after some initial confusion began a bombing run with five aircraft at 4,800 feet in a staggered line. They claimed three hits and six near misses on a stationary destroyer on the western edge of the group of ships. The post-mission sketch shows this ship probably was *Tokitsukaze*. Oscars attacked from above and one B25 was hit, but fire from the top turret guns drove them off.

As the 90th Squadron B25s and Scott's B17s bombed *Asashio*, Major Ralph Cheli approached with four B25s of the 405th Squadron 38th Bomb Group. It was 15.20. They saw the convoy from 6,000 feet, counted four burning ships, and saw *Asashio* in the distance. Cheli brought the small formation round in a counter-clockwise direction, going down to 500 feet. They watched the other attacks on the destroyer, saw the 90th strafers score one direct hit and a near miss, and bring the ship around to port, slowing to a halt, so he decided to attack it, and slid down to 200 feet.

He had a different crew in #903, with Captain G.B. Marzolf

as pilot. His wingman was 1st Lieutenant E.W. 'Ed' Atkins, in #899 *Filthy Lil*. As they were approaching at 500 feet, Atkins noticed the large quantities of wreckage and men bobbing on the surface of the water. Flying on Cheli's right, Atkins saw another strafer begin an attack on the destroyer, just as a bomb from higher altitude exploded amidships. Atkins watched muzzle flashes and tracer coming at his aircraft from *Asashio's* guns, but this fire stopped after the strafer whipped over its decks, and then came the explosion of the B25's bombs.

Crossing the destroyer, Cheli dropped five 500-pound bombs at its portside, and Atkins released one. Cheli scored two hits and three near misses amidships, and Atkins' bomb hit the bow. As Atkins passed over, his plane rocked from an explosion in the ship, possibly caused by a bomb from the preceding B25 strafers. As they left *Asashio*, and turned sharply to port, the 405th pilots and crews saw flames, explosions and smoke belching from the destroyer.

After bombing *Asashio*, both Ralph Cheli and Ed Atkins began attacking the Japanese in the water, and Atkins' gunner, Staff Sergeant J.R. Franklin, saw a lifeboat capsize as the Japanese jumped into the water. Cheli began a strafing run on a burning transport, but Atkins zipped in front of him, dropping two 500-pound bombs at an 8–9,000-ton ship. The bombs fell short and exploded as near misses. They flew back to New Guinea.

In the other 405th Squadron element, 1st Lieutenant W.D. Brandon was flying #905, with 2nd Lieutenant Bill Pittman on his wing in #908. As they approached, they could easily see the burning ships and a destroyer (*Arashio*). Brandon climbed to 3,500 feet for a bomb run, but while they were approaching, he saw bombs from a B17 formation (Scott's) explode around it, scoring one direct hit. Brandon then turned onto another destroyer, but this one was also attacked by B17s and B25s, both strafers and medium bombers—probably from the 90th and 71st Squadrons, who attacked a few minutes before the 405th. The *Asashio* was seen to explode, burn fiercely and then settle in the water.

Brandon turned to a third destroyer seen some fifteen miles

away, heading for Finschafen. This was probably *Tokitsukaze*, which other formations had reported as stationary. To Brandon, it seemed to be manoeuvring violently, dodging bombs from B17s, and also able to fire at Brandon's formation, as four anti-aircraft bursts appeared 1000 feet below him. Brandon went in on his bomb run at mast height, and released three 500-pounders as the destroyer headed towards him, firing another six shells at him. Bill Pittman, on Brandon's wing, released five bombs, and both aircraft machinegunned the destroyer on the way in.

Pittman passed over the bows, and his crew reported two near misses on the port bow, one hit amidships, one on the port side, and one miss. Pittman pulled up and turned left to witness the damage to the destroyer. Two hits, one amidships and one forward, were seen by Brandon's crew, so he turned left and made another run. Before they could bomb, another salvo from B17s fell on the ship, but missed. Brandon went over again, dropping two more bombs, which were near misses. After this attack, crewmen in both B25s saw the destroyer explode and begin to disintegrate. They also saw the destroyer attacked by Cheli and Atkins on fire, with flames shooting out of the hatches.

There was a large burning transport close by, with Japanese abandoning ship in boats and barges. Brandon went for them, firing his nose .50-calibers, while Pittman flew through the mass of burning ships, strafing boats and clusters of Japanese in the water. At least one transport was not on fire, but seemed to be abandoned, and Pittman described it as 'wrecked and battered.' They flew back to New Guinea, staying overnight at Dobodura.

The exhilaration among returning crews at Dobodura was as high as it had been on the morning mission. Everyone had stories of direct hits, near misses, burning ships, exploding destroyers, Japanese abandoning ships, strafing boats and ships' decks, falling Zeros, the amount of wreckage and anything else which had made a visual impact on them. There was no doubt that Allied air power had gained a victory.

Back in the convoy area, Sergeant Sasayama, 50 AA Battalion, survived the Beaufighter strafing and the bombs, and fought the fire on *Oigawa Maru* before finally abandoning ship. He climbed into a collapsible boat, and was strafed. Several men were killed, but when it was over, there were 14 still alive. Still drifting, they watched *Oigawa Maru* until nightfall. Shiro Sato was a man who could not really care about such things as machine-guns. He had become seasick in the small boat. When it was strafed he just lay in the bottom while the others leaped over the sides. He survived the attack. Private Ueno had seen *Oigawa Maru* hit by bombs after they had abandoned it, then saw men die what he called 'heroic deaths' in the strafing. Seven of the 12 aboard the collapsible boat launched by Private Takeo Yanagizawa, of 115 Regiment Signals were killed, and the five survivors drifted for days. Sergeant Abe, a carpenter with HQ 115 Regiment, had the other two with him on his raft killed. (9)

P38s had been tangling with the Japanese Army fighters, at a much lower level than the morning combats. Charlie King was aware of the amount of debris in the water, and later wrote:

Had our hands full with the Zekes we encountered. They were skillfully flown. Several of us had one isolated for a few minutes, and several got hits on him, but he did finally get away from us. My best shots were at a Zeke which was chasing a P38 while being closely followed by another P38.' Later, King found it was Tommy Lynch in the last P38, who 'complained later that he thought my bullets were coming as close to him as to the Zeke. It was quite a melee. We didn't do anywhere as well as we had in the morning as far as confirmed victories, but it is my impression we did what we were assigned. We provided the bombers and strafers with an environment in which they could survive. A far cry from what would have happened if we had only P40s and/or P39s. We did it with relatively small numbers, especially on the afternoon mission.

The skillful Japanese fighter may have been flown by Major Sawada, commander of the Army's 1st Fighter Sentai, who was airborne on the last mission of the day, and failed to return.

Between 15.20 and 15.30, aircraft from the 13th, 63rd, 64th, 65th and 321st Squadrons reported hits on destroyers, or seeing sinking destroyers, and that four, five or six transport ships were visible, on fire or stationary. Another eight B17s of the 64th and 403rd Squadrons, in two elements of three and one of two, began their attacks at 15.25. The pilots, some on their fourth combat mission in two days, were Major Ken McCullar, Captains Giddings and Nelson, Lieutenants McMullen, Schultz and Olsen, with Captain Smith and Lieutenant Gowdy of the 403rd. The bombers approached from the south-west, passing between a stationary destroyer, *Arashio*, on their left, and five burning transports on their right. The leading element of three came under fighter attack, but made a circle to port and passed over the destroyer, which showed no signs of life. They went on, still under fighter attack, to bomb one of the transports, and claimed a direct hit on a 6,000-tonner. They then circled back to starboard, shooting into the chaos, and flew away to the south.

The second element, of two, also passed over the lifeless destroyer near the burning ships, and turned starboard to attack the same ship bombed by the leading element. Over the burning ships, they came under fighter attack, which the Japanese continued intermittently as the B17s circled over the easternmost ship of the burning group. The B17s bombed and strafed, before passing through to the south and New Guinea.

The third element of three B17s flew on to the north, attacked *Asashio* just after an attack by B25s, and claimed a hit and two near misses. They swung back to the center of the convoy and also went down to strafe. Crews saw a transport sink at 15.12 and a destroyer sink at 15.18. Fighter attacks went in on the B17s, some persisting from the target area all the way back to Cape Ward Hunt.

Five aircraft of the 65th Squadron split into a three-plane element and a two-plane formation. The two-plane element had attacked with Major Ed Scott, 63rd Squadron. At 15.20, the element of three B17s, led by Captain Easter, was attacked by fighters as it approached the convoy at 6,000 feet. The Japanese made low frontal attacks in pairs, their gunnery was good, and hits were made on the leading aircraft, wounding several crew members in Easter's ship. The formation turned port, Easter salvoed his bombs, and as the turn continued towards New Guinea, he left and returned to Buna. The other two bombers flew northeast through the burning ships, and dropped eight 1,000-pounders on a 5,000-ton transport. All bombs fell on the starboard side, and there was an immediate explosion and large fire amidships. Two 65th Squadron aircraft were holed, and five crewmen injured. In total, the B17s claimed seven fighters destroyed and one probable.

From 5,500 feet, a five-plane B25 formation of 13th Squadron, 3rd Attack Group, attacked at 15.25, claiming two hits on a destroyer. From their height, the crews watched the other B25s strafing, and saw the B17s and B25s hit destroyers. The 13th's B25s, flown by Lieutenants Joseph R. McWhirt, Kenneth P. Christiansen, Thomas H. Cline, John S. Bromage and Ralph C. Payne, circled one destroyer already under attack by the 90th and 22nd Squadrons, then attacked the center one of the three warships below, *Arashio*. They dropped twenty-five 500-pound instantaneous-fuzed bombs, claiming four direct hits. Crews counted five unidentified ships burning, with smoke rising to 3,000 feet. They had seen a flight of B17s bomb a destroyer as B25s were attacking the same ship, and watched the bombs fall 50–100 yards short, but confirmed several hits by three other B17s on the easternmost destroyer. They also confirmed the hits on the bows of the westernmost destroyer by the 38th Group—Pittman—and hits by Larner's 90th Squadron and the RAAF A20s strafing. This report and identifications by the 13th Squadron, specifying which destroyer was attacked by which squadron, tend to confirm that Brandon and Pittman did bomb *Tokitsukaze*, the westernmost destroyer. Aboard *Arashio*, many men were killed and wounded in the attacks, but about 150 survived and began to make rafts. Some alcoholic drinks were brought out and shared around. The ship sank lower in the water.

Overhead, to the east, the 13th Squadron crews saw the P38s and Zeros or Oscars in combat, but did not report any fighters shot down. On return to base, pilots reported that the tactics used were successful, but there seemed to be too many Allied aircraft over the target at the same time. In the afternoon combats, Curran Jones of the 39th Fighter Squadron, claimed one destroyed Zero as his second victory of the day and the last in his total of five.

Ken Sparks, Ed Randall and Harris Denton made claim to having damaged one plane each. Japanese figures admit the loss of one on this mission, but the number of damaged planes was not included. The strafers and heavy bombers claimed a total of 7-2-0 Japanese fighters in the last combats of the day. Japanese documents admit the loss of twelve aircraft destroyed in the air on the 3rd of March; Allied fighter claims for the entire day, from Lae to the convoy area, were 26-4-4. The Japanese claims were for 20-6-1; six B25s, nine P38s, and three heavy bombers were included in the 'destroyed' claims. It seems the Japanese rotated three 'shifts' of fighters over the convoy, with about 12 to 15 aircraft in each. Jones may have shot down Sawada. On the final mission of the day Major Sawada, 1st Sentai, was listed as lost, last being seen on fire, and was believed to have 'fought to the end.' (10)

Gradually, the hunting aircraft turned away for New Guinea, and only single reconnaissance planes circled above the scene of burning ships and wreckage. The battle area was not far from shore, and Allied HQ realised that rescue of many Japanese soldiers and sailors was possible, or that they could find their own way to shore. The Japanese who reached shore, by whatever means, would be dangerous to future Allied operations. Orders were given to attack the boats and rafts and to destroy as much as possible of the force aboard the convoy ships. The aircrews received these orders with mixed feelings. Some were openly pleased at the prospect of continued destruction of the Japanese and saw it as an opportunity to repay some of what had been done by them to the Allies. Some accepted the orders as necessary but distasteful, and still others were sickened by it. All over the sea were clusters of boats, rafts, makeshift floats, and MLCs, plus hundreds of men clinging to planks, barrels, bamboos and whatever else floated. There are no accurate accounts of the numbers killed in the strafings, as so many Japanese died in the bombings and strafings in the next days before they reached shore. But the massed machineguns and cannon of the aircraft which criss-crossed the scene would certainly have inflicted heavy casualties.

Akio Fujiwara, from *Aiyo Maru*, was machinegunned four

times in the afternoon, and estimated that by nightfall there were 100 dead men around him. He knew of only three other survivors who were being kept afloat by life jackets. Three survivors from *Teiyo Maru*, clinging to the raft with Ryuji Sakieda, died of wounds from strafing, and Mikiwo Omiya saw seven men near him killed. Yoshio Aoki was also strafed, but still sick with malaria, knew little of it. A bomb landed in the middle of a fleet of rafts and boats, capsizing all except the one in which Sichichi-Hei Matsushima had watched the destroyer steam away with her decks full of men. He knew there were many killed by bombs and machineguns, but had no idea of the numbers. Sergeant Chikui also survived the attack, though his boat was holed by bullets. They had a motor attached, but no fuel, and so drifted helplessly. (11) Captain James DeWolfe, who had seen Woodrow Moore's B17 shot off his wing, and watched the men in parachutes machinegunned, was back over the convoy at 15.25, for a four-and-a-half hour sortie, strafing and counting the burning ships. His gunners fired 4,500 rounds of .50-caliber and 500 rounds of .30-caliber ammunition into the targets below them. He radioed that every cargo ship was burning, and the sea was covered with wreckage and debris.

The 115 Regiment color guard was strafed again late in the day, but no one was injured. The occupants of the boat had taken inventory of their food and water. For two dozen men, there was a small quantity of rice, dried fish, dry bread, wheat gluten, and about eight gallons of water. Sometime before noon, the boat picked up Lieutenant Haruo Kozaki, of the same academy class as Kondo. Kozaki had been wounded in the face while still aboard *Oigawa Maru*. He decided to assume command of the soldiers in the boat, and to assume responsibility for the regimental colors. (12)

On battered DD *Arashio*, radio operator Suzuki, who had survived the destruction of *Taimei Maru*, gathered with the survivors on the fantail of the ship. Still deafened, he was handed a note by an officer there, which told him the other man was also a mail steamer engineer, who had been called to the Service and sent to the destroyer; he was Reiji Masuda.

A B24 from the 321st Squadron of the 90th Bomb Group,

circling the scene, reported that at 15.19 there were four transports smoking and a destroyer stationary, but at 18.30 the B24 reported that there were three 4,000-tonners on fire, a large destroyer (*Tokitsukaze*), stationary in an oil slick, and another small destroyer riding very low in the water. The B24 went in to bomb the stationary destroyer in the oil slick, dropped six 500-pounders, and missed by 300 feet off the bows. The Japanese intercepted the messages from the afternoon attack and reconnaissance aircraft. They were well aware of what was reported to Port Moresby. The B24 bombing was the final Allied attack on the convoy that day. (13)

Back at Moresby, the high level of excitement continued. In the 90th Squadron camp, there was what Bob Guthrie recalled as 'a state of euphoria, as the whole convoy had been wiped out, and it was claimed 25,000 Japanese had been killed. Everybody was thrilled to the back teeth,' said Guthrie. Royce Johnco, who had flown in #487 with Bob Reed, paid a special tribute to the squadron's ground crew: 'We sustained quite a few bullet holes, and by next morning the ground crews had replated them, and had the ship serviceable and ready to go again. A mighty effort.'

The P38s of the 39th Fighter Squadron from the afternoon mission went as far as Dobodura and stopped there for the night. 'We were really worn out,' recalled Charlie King, 'and had to spend the night on borrowed cots.' Pressure on the Dobodura flightline was such that the fighters were able to be refuelled but not re-armed, so they did not fly the morning mission on 4 March.

While the Allied aircrews celebrated, the Japanese destroyers met east of Long Island, and began refuelling and transferring the packed Army survivors on their decks. Some 1,400 soldiers were put aboard the arriving ships and taken back to Rabaul. Well aware of the power of Allied strike aircraft, the original convoy escorts began to return to the battle area, knowing that they should not be caught there in daylight.

Slowly combing the area, the returning Japanese destroyers found 170 of the crew of *Arashio* in the water at 01.15. The stricken ship had begun to tilt to port at about midnight, though the survivors on it still hoped for rescue, and out of the night appeared *Yukikaze*. 45 minutes later, the rescue ships found the abandoned hulk of *Tokitsukaze*, still with two men aboard. At 02.30, the destroyers again turned away, heading for Kavieng with the survivors they had found by that time. Behind them was an area of sea some twenty miles across, dotted with men alone or in groups, on rafts, boats of various types, or clinging to planks, bamboo poles or floating boxes and drums. Dawn was not far away, and there would be no more large surface ships of the Imperial Japanese Navy entering the Vitiaz Strait to search for survivors.

Allied signals intercept stations had been trying to record the large number of Japanese messages sent as a result of the action. One deciphered message from DD *Yukikaze* reported that the commander of 51 Division had been rescued, with 1,000 other men, and would be delivered to Lae at 01.30 4 March (Tokyo time). The flood of traffic continued until 22.00 3 March, and then slackened. Unfortunately for MacArthur's Intelligence staffs, technical difficulties meant that only fragments of the messages could be read. (14)

4 March 1943 would see a bloody manhunt by the Allied Air Forces. The Japanese had shown little mercy during their advances and occupation of Asian and Pacific territories, and the repeated murders and massacres of military and civilians alike had reduced their image to that of a sub-human beast which had to be eliminated, whatever the circumstances.

FIVE

RETRIBUTION

That night at Port Moresby, the Allied staffs tried to make some sense of the many reports from the many squadrons, and despite repetition and duplication, it became obvious that the day was a victory for Allied air power in the SWPA.

It now remained to sink whatever was left, and to kill as many as possible of the Japanese still in the water or small boats. If reconnaissance found more ships still afloat, they would be attacked, but now there was the overall ground war to support along with missions against Japanese targets in New Guinea and the neighbouring areas. Ground crews worked long hours to prepare the aircraft for the next day's operations.

This was the opportunity for the PT boats to come out into the battle area, approach under cover of night and attack what remained of the convoy. It was thought that several ships were still afloat, and would make good targets. Ten PT boats, under Lieutenant Commander Barry K. Atkins, set out from the base near Tufi on the north coast of New Guinea, but two hit debris and had to return. The other eight scoured the seas. At 23.20,

PTs 143 and 150 came across *Oigawa Maru*. One torpedo from each finished the destruction of the last of the eight Lae Convoy transport ships. Only two destroyers were left in the battle area, and the PTs did not find them.

During the night, DDs *Uranami* and *Hatsuyuki* arrived at Rabaul, and the survivors they carried went ashore. Shoge Akimoto, 115 Regiment, who when abandoning *Shin-Ai Maru* had not been able to see 'one ship that was unscathed,' was rescued by DD *Asagumo*. He noted that he was back in his old barracks, but that the platoon was only at half strength. (1)

The Field Diary of 2 Company, 51 Engineers, recorded the abandon-ship order on *Shin-Ai Maru* at 10.20, the pick-up by DDs *Asagumo* and *Uranami*, and the transfer to *Hatsuyuki* before the return to Rabaul. The survivors began the move back to Kokopo, and by 18.00 on the 4th, they had assembled forty from *Shin-Ai Maru* and forty-five from *Teiyo Maru*. *Yukikaze* delivered the men picked up in the night. Only three of the 49-man crew of *Taimei Maru* were recorded at Rabaul as survivors. Two of the five who had made it to the deck on DD *Arashio* had been lost in the afternoon attacks, having jumped overboard as the strafers approached. Two more were taken prisoner, making a total of five survivors from the entire crew of the ship. (2)

On the slowly sinking DD *Arashio*, survivors saw a signalling light then a dark shape crept closer and voices called that it was *Yukikaze*. Men on *Arashio* called back and 176 navy and army survivors were transferred. Soon after, *Arashio* disappeared in the black waters.

General Kenney was about to go to Washington, departing at 06.00 on 4 March, and the success could not have come at a more opportune time. He rang General MacArthur and passed on the assessed Japanese losses: 6 destroyers or light cruisers sunk, 2 others damaged; 11 to 14 merchant ships sunk; 2 others sunk in Wide Bay and Lae harbor; air victories of 60-25-10; and estimated Japanese personnel losses, as high as 15,000 men. Allied losses amounted to 4 aircraft lost and 2 crash-landed, 13 men killed and 12 wounded.

MacArthur sent the following message of congratulation:

Please extend to all ranks my gratitude and felicitations on the magnificent victory which has been achieved. It cannot fail to go down in history as one of the most complete and annihilating combats of all time. My pride and satisfaction in you all is boundless.

General Kenney composed one of his own, with a reminder that it was the power of the air forces which had achieved a significant success:

Congratulations on that stupendous success. Air Power has written some important history in the past three days. Tell the whole gang that I am so proud of them I am about to blow a fuze.

In Washington, Kenney was to find that despite the Air Force achievements in general, and of his own in particular, U.S. Army and Navy representatives at the meetings were reluctant to accept the capabilities and flexibility of military airlift. Far from being granted an increase in aircraft allocation, he had to make a case to avert a reduction in numbers, much less replace the losses. Then, in Hap Arnold's office, a group of engineering experts told Kenney that the B25 could not fly effectively with eight .50-caliber machineguns in the nose. Kenney let them talk, then told them and Arnold that the Bismarck Sea victory was largely won by his modified B25s.

Eventually, after a talk with President Franklin D. Roosevelt, Kenney returned to the SWPA with promises of one more heavy bomb group, two or three medium groups, three fighter groups and a troop carrier group, totalling about 500 aircraft. The European theater and the Soviets were first on the list. This had been decided at the highest levels, among Roosevelt, British Prime Minister Winston Churchill, and the Combined Chiefs of Staff.

Meanwhile, from Port Moresby, on 4 March the 320th Squadron sent a B24 over Lae and along the south coast of New Britain on armed reconnaissance. It dropped one hundred twenty 20-pound frags onto the airfield at 06.55, but saw no results through the darkness. Anti-aircraft fire was heavy, intense, but inaccurate. Apart from four Zekes taking off from Gasmata, and others on the ground, there was no other sighting on the mission.

At 08.00 hours, a B24 of the 320th Squadron arrived in the convoy battle area for a four-hour patrol. Five landing barges were seen 20 miles east of Finschafen, and heading that way. A stationary burned-out destroyer was sighted at 07.40 South, 148.20 East. Some 20 minutes later, three B17s of the 63rd Squadron attacked six powered launches with machineguns, sinking one and causing an unknown number of casualties among the fifty Japanese aboard. In their three-hour sortie, crews saw the sea covered with lifeboats, wreckage, boxes, crates and other debris.

The three B17s were flown by Derr, Murphy and Dieffenderfer. The center position was flown by Dieffenderfer, with Murphy on the right wing and Derr on the left. Before taking off, the Operations officer had reminded the crews of the attacks on Moore's crew as they parachuted into the ocean, with all its perils. The Japanese pilots were regarded as cowards to have done such a thing, instead of continuing to attack other B17s in the combat. The crews were told they were to attack anything afloat.

One of the boats turned so tightly to avoid the B17 gunfire that it capsized, and no sign of life was seen around it afterwards. In one boat, clearly visible to Fred Blair in the nose of James Dieffenderfer's B17, an officer stood up and fired his pistol in a futile display of courage. The four-engined B17 with .50-calibers firing from nose, sides, belly and tail roared over and when it had passed the Japanese was gone.

Then Blair noticed a Japanese fighter coming in for a pass from the 1 o'clock position. Quickly he changed his target, and fired 50 or more rounds at the Oscar, but it came on in, guns flashing, and Blair heard a loud bang and a rushing noise. He looked down, and his firing hand was covered with many small holes. Blair turned to the navigator, Bill Grosenburg, and said, 'That Jap was a poor shot. He missed us by an inch!' The Japanese, one of six counted attacking, came right for the B17, seemingly intent on ramming, but at the last second Dieffenderfer dropped his left wing and the Oscar flicked by, missing them.

Fred Blair had reason to be thankful for his foresight. A few days before, he had helped to remove from a B24 a dead bombardier, who had been killed by a shrapnel hit in the temple. Blair took note, and at once went to supply and drew a steel helmet, which he wore on missions. This helmet took most of the blast and fragments of shrapnel and plexiglass from the hit on the nose. Grosenburg and Dieffenderfer were also slightly wounded by fragments and the tip of the bullet lodged in the left side of the pilot's cockpit. After several passes, the Oscars withdrew and the B17s continued their strafing mission, finally bombing land targets before returning to base.

A B17 from the 65th Squadron arrived at 09.10, and covered the area at heights of 100 feet to 6,000 feet, strafing lifeboats and making two hits on a destroyer. There was no other shipping in sight. The crew reported debris over a 20-mile area, and counted at least thirty rafts. Then, at 09.20, twenty Army Oscars arrived and a combat began at 100 to 200 feet over the area. Oscars (with a lightning-bolt painted along the fuselage), attacked in pairs from the sides or rear, and damaged the B17, putting one engine out of use. Four Oscars were claimed destroyed. According to the program of fighter escort, the morning of 4 March was the Japanese Army Air Force's turn to provide aircraft. The fuselage marking was one that had been used by the 11th Sentai, and this unit had arrived in the New Guinea area in December.

Watching this combat from the water was Sergeant Chikui and his boatload from 115 Regiment from *Teiyo Maru*. During the night they had been worried when a large silent black shape had closed on them, thinking it might be enemy, but it drifted past. It was probably one of the abandoned ships. As dawn broke, they saw a ship to the west, and raised the Japanese flag, but there was no reply. They then recognised her as a damaged destroyer. As they started rowing towards the destroyer, then the B17 headed towards them.

With vivid memories of the low-flying aircraft on the previous day, the boat load jumped into the sea. Then they saw fifteen Japanese fighters approach from the north, and attack the bomber. 'Machinegunned by our planes, they flew away,' wrote Chikui. They again began rowing to the destroyer, passing among all sorts of floating materials from the transports, but no food of any kind. (3) The regimental color party of 115 Regiment was also attacked, but no one was hurt and the flag remained untouched.

On the island of New Guinea, the airfields at Lae and Malahang had been attacked. The intention had been to catch the Japanese fighters refuelling after combat over the convoy area, and it was successful. At 12.05, eleven Beaufighters of RAAF 30 Squadron destroyed six Zekes and a petrol truck, reporting that all aircraft were camouflaged with palm fronds, and that one had an inline engine, with a yellow spinner, possibly a Messerschmitt 109. This was probably one of the first Kawasaki Ki-61 'Hien' or 'Tonys' to arrive in New Guinea. Airborne Zekes were seen, but did not engage. The sweep also covered the area off Finschafen and the Huon Gulf, but no ships were sighted. Japanese records confirm the destruction of six aircraft on the ground at Lae on 4 March. (4)

30 Squadron had two aircraft damaged. Flying Officer Dick Roe and Len Vial destroyed four fighters and the petrol truck, but Roe had engine damage, and Flight Lieutenant 'Torchy' Uren, who had taken cameraman Damien Parer on the convoy attack, sustained 12.7mm bullet hits in the fuselage that damaged the cannon and radio mountings. If Parer had been filming with Uren, he would have been killed. After leaving the Australian Department of Information, Parer was killed while filming with the U.S. Marines on Peleliu in September 1944.

George Drury and Dave Beasley, in A19-75, realised they had problems with the starboard engine when strafing Finschafen, possibly caused by hits from ground fire there or back at Lae. Drury turned back for Dobodura, escorted by Bob Brazenor. The

Beaufighter climbed to 7,000 feet before one of the engines sputtered and gave up. Drury tried to go on with one engine, but it also seemed to be giving less than full power and the aircraft gradually lost height. One mile from the end of the strip at Dobodura, Drury realised he was not going to make it and decided to go into a clearing, about 200 yards across, which was right under the airplane nose.

As he turned tightly over the kunai grass, the port wingtip touched the ground and spun the Beaufighter around. It lunged across twenty yards of grass into the trees, smashing its way along. The big plane's massive engines and wings mowed down the trees and tore a path into the jungle. 'The noise was incredible,' said Drury. When it halted, it was completely covered by the trees, but neither man was hurt. Silence. Drury and Beasley each yelled to the other, then Drury called, 'Out!' They rapidly climbed out and ran back along the swathe in the trees, in case it caught fire or exploded. When they were some distance away, they dived to the ground. But it was not 'ground.' 'It was swamp water,' said Drury, 'one foot of 10,000-year old swamp water. The stink, the stench, the insects!'

They waited for a while, but there was no explosion or fire. They peeked at the wreck, and saw smoke coming from the engines. More time passed, and they realised that the smoke was really only steam from the swamp water vaporising on the hot engines. They walked back and began removing personal kit and the valuable instruments from the cockpits, while Drury wondered what to do next. Then they heard an American voice calling out, 'You there, Aussies?'

A U.S. Sergeant in charge of a native roadmaking group had seen the Beaufighter slip below the trees and had forced his way through the jungle. It was so dense, and the kunai grass so high, that they had to shout back and forth to guide the sergeant to them. He led Drury back through the jungle to his unit, where the Major was sitting on a stool outside a tent, chewing tobacco. Drury was impressed by this officer's spitting accuracy, and watched him hit several of the small lizards nearby.

Drury was welcomed with hospitality and the generous loan of a jeep. Eventually, he and Beasley returned to 30 Squadron, but found that all the little luxuries they had collected, such as a pressure lantern, had quickly been taken by the other members of the squadron. Brazenor had seen the crash, but no sign of life, and they had been reported as 'missing, believed killed.' The two survivors then had to go round the tents repossessing all their belongings and ignoring the wartime jokes: 'Why did you have to come back? We wanted that lantern!' In addition, their next-of-kin had been informed they were missing, but were puzzled when the boys' letters continued to arrive as if nothing had happened.

In addition to the RAAF Beaufighters, the 89th Squadron, 3rd Attack Group, sent twelve A20s to attack Lae and Finschafen. They arrived at 12.20, fifteen minutes after the Beaufighters. The A20s strafed the airfield at Lae, flying through all types of AA coming from multiple positions. The A20 flyers noted a 'considerable number' of aircraft on the field.

Escorting the Beaufighters and A20s were P38s. Twelve Lightnings of the 39th Squadron fought a dozen or so Zekes, Lieutenant Ken Sparks claimed two—his eighth and ninth—Lieutenant Benjamin Widman claimed another, and 2nd Lieutenant John 'Shady' Lane claimed a probable. Sparks claimed two more victories to the end of July, returned to the U.S. and was killed test-flying a P38. As the Beaufighters swept the Huon Gulf, the P38s claimed again. Major George Prentice damaged one on his last flight before returning to Australia to command an operational training unit. Lieutenant Paul Stanch destroyed one, and Charles Sullivan and Ralph Bills claimed a probable each. John Dunbar damaged two and James Walters another. Prentice later commanded the 475th Fighter Group when it was raised in Australia. He returned to the U.S. but was killed in a crash.

Eight P38s of the 9th Squadron engaged ten to fifteen Zekes at 8,000 feet, and Lieutenant Harry Brown claimed one plane destroyed and another as a probable. 2nd Lieutenant John O'Neill claimed one destroyed, the first of his eight victories. Total claims for the day were 6-4-4. Japanese records, almost always incomplete, record the loss of a single plane in aerial combat, at Surumi. (5)

Meanwhile, out to sea in a debris-covered area near the convoy, Takeki Horiguchi of 115 Regiment, from *Shin-Ai Maru*, was without oars for the boat he and three others had climbed into. He was lucky enough to find one floating past and so he and the others paddled over to an abandoned destroyer. The stern was low in the water, and they climbed aboard in hopes of finding food and water. There were no sailors on her, only about a dozen soldiers from another transport. They found some bad water and tinned meat. Shortly thereafter, Allied aircraft were spotted. Horiguchi decided to leave what was an obvious target.

As they paddled away, they watched the aircraft score a direct hit. Later, Horiguchi saw what he firmly believed to be Japanese aircraft attacking and hitting her with bombs. Later in the day they picked up Akio Fujiwara 8 Shipping Engineers from *Aiyo Maru*, who told them that he had also been on the destroyer. (6)

Fujiwara and some other men had been kept afloat throughout the night by their life-jackets, but at dawn they had seen the destroyer and assumed she was rescuing survivors. They swam hard towards her, afraid she would steam away, but as they came closer they realised she was abandoned. There was a gaping hole in the starboard side between the second and third torpedo tube mountings, and she was listing to starboard, very deep in the water. At about 11.00 hours, they climbed aboard.

After capture, Fujiwara identifed the ship from photographs as *Fubuki* Class, with three triple mountings of torpedo tubes. *Tokitsukaze* had two mountings of four. Scattered about the deck were many water-soaked uniforms, all marked 'Toki.' By a process of elimination, it seems that the drifting ship was *Asashio*. She had been severely battered the previous afternoon and it was unlikely that *Arashio*, hit badly in the initial attacks, had been able to pick up survivors from *Tokitsukaze*. It was more likely that these men had been rescued during *Asashio's* work at the scene prior to the afternoon attacks. That the ship was well down by the stern and hit amidships on the starboard side tends to confirm the reports that were made about *Asashio* on the previous afternoon.

Exhausted by their adventures, the four soldiers lay on the

deck and went to sleep. Suddenly, about an hour later, five Allied fighters attacked, strafing the decks, killing two and wounding a third. Fujiwara was unhurt. He and the wounded man immediately went back over the side into the water. B25s began to attack, dropping about ten bombs, scoring two direct hits. The destroyer began to burn and ammunition exploded throughout the afternoon until the ship finally sank at about dusk.

These were probably the twelve P40s of 7th Squadron 49th Fighter Group which provided escort over Cape Ward Hunt for ten of Ed Larner's 90th Squadron B25 strafers. The B25s did claim two hits from six 500-pounders dropped and expended 18,000 rounds of .50-caliber machinegun fire in attacks on boats and rafts in the target area. The P40 pilots watched as the B25s attacked, confirmed them making two hits, and saw the B25s strafing an estimated 600 Japanese in a nine-square-mile area, on rafts, and in landing barges and lifeboats.

Fujiwara and the other man clung to a floating spar, and because of the fire and explosions, could not reboard the ship. At dusk, the other man died. Soon after, the boat with Horiguchi came by and picked up Fujiwara. (7) Another boat carried Sergeant Chikui and his men, rowing towards the destroyer with all their might:

> As we approached, saw a crowd of our men drifting. One Boeing plane came towards us. All at once we jumped into the sea. Another plane was approaching us. We jumped into the sea again. We were strafed twice. A formation of about 100 bombers and fighters (sic) attacked the disabled destroyer. We were attacked twice before but did not have any casualties. In this attack, most of our comrades were killed.

Sharks were seen near some Japanese clinging to wreckage. Pilots had often noted the large sharks in the sea below, and now they obviously had been attracted by the blood and activity. There are no survivors' accounts of shark attacks, but the chances are slim that anyone in the water would survive the shark feeding frenzy after the sharks became excited by blood from wounds. Only those in proper boats would have been safe.

An unknown diarist had noted 3 March in one word—'disaster'—and on the 4th recorded that he was with 11 other men and Lieutenant Fukuda, drifting. Seiji Kojo, of the Debarkation unit, was in a collapsible boat with 21 other men. Two were killed by strafing, but the boat did not sink as the bullets struck the top of the sides and not the bottom. Without oars, they picked up floating bamboo and used that with their belts as rowlocks. There was little drinking water. (8)

Private Takao Nakata, who had only just been inducted on 22 December and was in the battalion of 35-year olds, had his boat strafed. Five were killed and one was wounded. The boat overturned, and after the attack only the leaking rear half of it could be used. Then the wounded man died. (9)

Those with operable barges had been able to cover more distance, some making it to the Tami Islands. Three B25s of the 90th, led by Captain Launder, with 'Seabiscuit' Sbisa and Australian co-pilot Bob Guthrie in one of the strafers, crossed the Owen Stanleys and searched the area between Lae and Finschafen. They saw nothing on the open sea, and no Japanese fighters, but came on some barges in the mangroves on the island coast. Launder went in first, machinegunning, followed by the other aircraft, then Sbisa. As they passed, what Bob Guthrie described as 'a nice big fire started. A great big cloud of black smoke we could see for some time after.'

On 4 March Sergeant Masao Kojima recovered consciousness after being wounded in the legs and head during the attacks on *Oigawa Maru*. Others had taken him aboard a boat when they abandoned the ship. There were 12 men with him until strafing attacks killed two. The others were able to make a sail, and steer away from the danger zone and toward the direction of the islands they knew were close by. The commander of 12 Company, 115 Regiment, Captain Takahashi, was in a boat with 12 other men, including Warrant Officer Matsushima. They had only one oar, and despite trying hard to get to friendly territory to the east, found the current taking them southeast. Aircraft attacked, killing men in the water, but no one in the boat was harmed. From boxes of biscuits floating nearby, they had their first food since the sinking. (10)

Yasuhira Yamazaki, 2 MG Company, 115 Regiment, from *Oigawa Maru*, was one of those who kept a diary, and for this day he noted: 'We continued to drift. Friendly planes appeared on several occasions. We were strafed a number of times. Starting tonight, we intend to steer our course to the north. Sighted a vessel which appeared to be a destroyer. She was bombed by enemy planes.' (11)

A member of 8 Shipping Engineers from *Taimei Maru*, Ushiro Watanabe, wrote:

> The sea was very calm. Checked provisions carried by each man. Found that we had four canteens filled with water, six pieces of compressed food, eight canned goods, nine bars of sweet paste, four bags of confectionery, four bags of dry bread and one bag of oranges. to avoid the danger of exposing ourselves to enemy aircraft, we tried to get out of the tidal current, using a shovel as an improvised oar. (12)

In Rabaul, 18th Army Operations Section issued Order 11, stating that all eight transports, including a sea truck, were sunk. Three destroyers had been sunk, and one was drifting east of Lae. (13)

The drifting destroyer (*Asashio*) apparently survived the air attacks, and was finally sunk by Japanese aircraft, as stated by Takeki Horiguchi. Independently, Sergeant Chikui wrote in his diary: 'In the evening, eight of our ship-borne attack planes came. Three of our attack planes sank our destroyer. We headed towards the north-west and rowed all night.'

At the end of the day, at Rabaul one of the battalions of 115 Regiment could account for 245 men, but knew nothing of the whereabouts of Colonel Endo. A diarist who returned to Rabaul noted that his battalion was at only one-quarter strength, but did not identify the unit. He noted that 'one-half' of 3 AA were killed. (14)

Meanwhile, out on the open sea, hundreds of men were wondering what would happen. The relentless sun and sea would give no mercy, and it seemed the Allied aircraft were determined to hunt down every last one of them. Just as the rigid discipline of the Japanese armed forces made them a formidable enemy in battle, so it provided the base for order and survival in the lifeboats, barges and on rafts.

Having assumed responsibility for the colors of 115 Regiment, Lieutenant Kozaki issued orders in the lifeboat. He was a member of a shipping engineer unit, and had been in command of the unloading unit on *Oigawa Maru*. As no rescue ships had been sighted, Kozaki decided to sail to New Britain. He had noticed that the current was taking them northeast anyway. But as the boat was damaged and difficult to control, rowing was the only way to make progress. According to his account, still aboard were the bodies of Colonel Endo and the other dead soldiers. (15)

On New Guinea itself, the Japanese Army had supplies for six days normal rations or ten days emergency, and 90 rounds per artillery piece, 1,100 rounds for each 13mm machinegun, and 1,300 rounds for each 25mm cannon. (16)

In other sorties that day, Allied aircraft flew the following missions: three B17s of the 63rd Squadron on armed reconnaissance along the north and south coast of New Britain from 12.15 strafed six power launches, sank one before attack by four fighters, resulting in two B17s damaged; a single B24 from the 320th followed five hours later, bombing the airfield at Finschafen and strafing men and lifeboats in the battle area; three Hudsons from 2 Squadron RAAF attacked Saumlaki, igniting a large fire at an oil tank; another B24 of the 320th photographed Finschafen and Kavieng, despite attack by two Zekes off Finschafen, and sighted six barges heading to that port.

5 MARCH

It was obvious that the convoy was destroyed, and attention could now be turned to other matters. Nevertheless, it was still necessary to attack the Japanese in the boats, barges and on rafts and makeshift floats. Buna-Gona and Guadalcanal were very fresh in the minds of combatants and staff, and the Australian and U.S. units which had fought in those battles were not anywhere near ready for more operations. Once ashore, the Japanese soldier from the convoy could be relied on to fight at Wau, Salamaua and Lae as toughly as had his predecessors. It would be much easier to destroy the Japanese forces with air power while they were exposed at sea, rather than attack them in their formidable defensive positions on land, or withstand their attacks on Allied positions.

Japanese records state that at 06.25 on 5 March, two A20s attacked Lae airfield, setting one aircraft on fire, followed at 08.15 by a B17 which did no damage, and at 09.10 by ten P40s and twelve P38s who attacked and destroyed one Japanese plane. (17)

Four A20 Bostons of RAAF 22 Squadron trailed four 500-pound and six 250-pound bombs along the sides of the runway, starting two fires. One fire was obviously the aircraft referred to by the Japanese. Pilots also saw a large number of unidentified aircraft on the ground as they flashed by in the dawn light. The AA opened fire when the bombers were still two miles away, and despite flying through intense accurate fire from several positions, only one plane was hit and the pilot slightly wounded. The 7th Squadron 49th Fighter Group had sixteen P40s over Lae at 08.30, and they engaged Oscars at 8,000 feet, claiming three destroyed, by Captain Ray Melikian and Lieutenants Donald Lee and David Baker. The Japanese were camouflaged a tan color on top, with silver bellies. Lightnings confirmed the destruction of three Japanese by the P40s.

Only an hour later, P38s of the 9th and 39th Squadrons engaged in another combat, with Captain Robert Vaught of the 9th claiming two Zekes destroyed and Charles King of the 39th an Oscar damaged. The P38s had failed to meet the strafers they were to escort, and so continued on to Lae on their own initiative. Vaught saw two enemy planes just off the ground, dived and came in behind them, shooting both down, but anti-aircraft fire hit one engine. He decided to land at Wau, but power applied to the one engine he had operating during landing rolled the P38 onto its back. It crashed, and put Vaught in the hospital.

Vaught had an interesting flight out of Darwin the previous July, when he found a poisonous snake in the cockpit—after take-off. The snake bit him on the left leg, he grabbed it, identified it as poisonous, and threw it overboard, then began looking for a place to land and get medical attention. He put the P40 down at an abandoned farmhouse, increasingly worried about his swelling poisoned leg, almost got lost in a nearby swamp, and spent the night in the P40 cockpit, being bitten by hordes of mosquitoes. Next morning, deciding no one was coming to help, despite being found by squadron mates the afternoon before, he took off and returned to the squadron base, crash-landed, and was rushed to the hospital.

The Allied victory total claimed for 5 March was 5-0-1. Incomplete Japanese records refer to the loss of two aircraft in the air over Lae on this day. (18)

Five Beaufighters of 30 Squadron, led by Flying Officer Brazenor, attacked the Malahang strip, and were able to confirm the destruction of six Zekes from the attack the day before, but saw no other Japanese aircraft on this strike. While the P40s were engaged, both sides of the strip and buildings at the north end were strafed. All the Beaufighters returned safely to Ward's Strip at Port Moresby by 09.52. The squadron prepared for an afternoon sortie over the area of the convoy battle.

The 89th Squadron also attacked the airfield at Lae, making six passes from north to south across the strip, attacking AA and machinegun positions. Pilots noticed many unserviceable aircraft around the field. They also saw the Japanese fighters with P40s after them over Malahang.

A B25 of the 405th Squadron, 38th Bomb Group searched the convoy battle area from 08.00 to 12.00 hours, without contact by Japanese fighters. The crew believed that the missing U.S. pilot in the area had been picked up by Japanese boats. Floating below them were log rafts. These had presented a bit of a puzzle when they were first seen in photographs of the ship's cargo. Now there were many in the sea. Thirty lifeboats were sighted 30 miles northeast of Cape Ward Hunt, as well as an estimated 100 Japanese on fifteen rafts south of the battle area. The B25 fired over 1,200 rounds at the men and boats before returning.

On boats and rafts, the survivors hoped for rescue. They tried to sail or paddle to land, and wondered if the Allied aircraft would return. Yasuhira Yamazaki noted that his boat rescued Cadet Takashima of No.5 Company, bringing the total in the boat to nine: one from Regimental headquarters, six from the Signals unit, one from 5 Company and himself from 2 MG Company. At times they were attacked by planes, but no one was hurt. (19)

The boat carrying Naval Captain Matsumoto, captain of *Nojima*, was found by submarine RO-101, and the survivors were taken to Rabaul. Rear Admiral Kimura and staff were also rescued by submarine. (20)

Sergeant Chikui and his boatload looked around in the dawn light. He wrote: 'no islands are in sight. Heard gunfire. It seems enemy PT boats are machinegunning our drifting comrades. Only two or three boats are to be seen. I wonder where are the rest of them.' PTs 143 and 150 were searching for the U.S. pilot reported in the area.

A stoker from *Taimei Maru*, Nobukatsu Ishida, had been hanging on to a floating log since the ship received four hits and began to sink. On this day he drifted to a small MLC, was able to start the engine and cruised around picking up other swimmers—28 in all—until the fuel was exhausted. They then found a drum of gasoline floating past and restarted the engine, untroubled by aircraft. (21)

Another man in a boat with gasoline for the engine was Sergeant Aoki, 8 Shipping Engineers Medical unit. He had been in the water since the explosion on *Taimei Maru* but at midday was picked up and joined the other thirty men aboard the boat. Then the gasoline ran out. Also picked out of the water was Sergeant Hosoda, who had been on guncrew duty when aircraft attacked, and since abandoning *Taimei Maru* had been holding on to a log along with nine other men. An MLC came by and collected them, making sixteen in all. (22)

A single P38 in the area from 11.00 to 12.00 was looking for P38 pilots who had been shot down on the 3rd. Coming across fifteen rafts and boats with about 100 Japanese in or on them, he strafed them. The concentrated effect of the 20mm cannon and .50-caliber machineguns in the nose of a P38 was horrifying on such a target.

U.S. PT boats were searching for the pilots in the Tufi area, and found three boatloads of Japanese, and then a Japanese submarine. Before they could attack, the submarine dived. The PTs could not use depthcharges without endangering each other, and so turned back to the Japanese in the boats. The PTs sped past them, machineguns firing, and passed as close as possible, dropping depthcharges by the boats. The explosions from underwater swamped and overturned the boats, and an estimated thirty Japanese were killed.

At 13.50, five Beaufighters, led by Squadron Leader Ross Little, took off from Ward's Strip with a mission to attack the ten to fifteen barges reported at 08.05 South, 149.20 East. The barges were full of troops or cargo. Barges were found, under attack by a Lockheed Hudson, and within sight of the Trobriand Islands. The plane was A16-200, flown by Pilot Officer Carlin of RAAF 6 Squadron, from Turnbull Field at Milne Bay. The Beaufighters went in and attacked with cannon and machinegun fire. The Japanese were seen to be wearing green uniforms and military equipment, and some had life-jackets on. At first, the soldiers did not attempt to jump overboard during strafing runs, and the full force of the 20mm cannon and .303 machineguns struck home. The water around the sinking barges was seen to be red with blood, a sickening sight to some of the Beaufighter crews.

Alf Nelson, looking down from the rear of Len Vial's Beaufighter, described it as 'a "very bloody show." The water in the bottom of the barges was red with blood. You could see the sea was stained all around.'

Adding to the horror, sharks were seen nearby. But there was little compassion for the Japanese, after the long list of atrocities committed by them since the beginning of military operations against China, and since Pearl Harbor. A U.S. 63rd Squadron diary was blunt: 'What we didn't get the sharks got. Every man in the squadron would have given two months pay to be in on the straffing (sic). One gunner expended 1,100 rounds of ammunition and burned out two guns.'

After the attacks, the Beaufighter crews estimated that there were few survivors, and the barges were left sinking. Two others were attacked and left sinking near Cape Ward Hunt. It was thought that there were about 30 Japanese in each barge, and four were destroyed during the mission. One Beaufighter was hit in the wing by a bullet. It was thought, momentarily, that the Japanese were firing back, though the hit could have been a ricochet.

Another mission was flown later in the afternoon, to attack boats thirty miles off Cape Ward Hunt. Five Beaufighters, led by Flight Lieutenant Uren, took off at 15.00 hours. They located four separate groups of boats and barges.

The first was a cluster of five barges, four filled with 25 Japanese each, and a small boat carrying supplies. The attack destroyed all the barges and the boat. Most of the Japanese jumped into the water before the boats were destroyed, so there was no repetition of the bloody spectacle from the previous mission. The Japanese returned small arms fire but no aircraft was hit.

North of this group was an empty barge which had been strafed already, and paddling towards it was a man in a yellow life raft. The Beaufighter observer who saw him tried to tell the pilot, but the inter-comm was out, and by the time he realised this and went up to the cockpit, the aircraft had left the location. It was believed that this was the pilot of a P38 who had been shot down on 3 March, either Faurot or Shifflet. The nearest Japanese was a mile away at the time of the sighting. This was the last recorded sighting of any of the U.S. airmen. The Japanese nearby would not have been inclined to take prisoners.

The second group was a cluster of fourteen rafts, each with twelve men, and four lifeboats, each with six men aboard. Two of the boats had sails rigged and were moving towards shore. Only one aircraft attacked these, inflicting heavy casualties, until his ammunition ran out. The rest of the flight could not be contacted, and so did not turn to attack this group. The lifeboats were half empty, though there were many men hanging on to the edges of the rafts. It was suggested that the men around the rafts were soldiers and those in the boats were officers. A third group of four small empty barges were not attacked, and a few miles south-east of these the fourth bunch of four empty barges were also not attacked. Possibly these barges were those of survivors who had been rescued already by the destroyers during the battle, or later by submarine.

Both missions combined, the Beaufighters attacked a total

of 24 barges, boats or rafts, claiming them all as sunk or sinking, and estimated that 350 Japanese were killed. The squadron report stated that although the necessity was understood, the two missions 'were most distasteful for the crews involved.'

The strafers attacked Sergeant Chikui, who already had survived so much:

> Three enemy planes strafed us. Again we jumped into the sea. Four remained in the boat; two of them were killed and two wounded. Our boat looks like a bee hive.' Then, 'the boat which is our life-line capsized. Our end is coming. At the time of attack, we were drying our clothes, therefore most of us are naked and in the water.

'Playing possum' was one tactic that the survivors used in hopes that the pilots would think them dead and not strafe. Takeki Horiguchi, who had climbed aboard the abandoned destroyer, and paddled away from it when the bombers returned, lay still with the others in the bottom of the boat during a burst of fire. The plane circled but there was no more shooting, and he thought the pilot believed them dead. Still hopeful that destroyers would come to rescue them, they drifted on, wherever the current took them. From *Oigawa Maru*, Tsunoichi Honda recorded that he could see other survivors here and there that aircraft had come and strafed. And also that '12 Japanese planes appeared.' (23)

During the day, DD *Shikiname* and three other ships delivered 128 survivors to Rabaul. Japanese 18th Army Operations Section reported that there were 1,000 men on rafts and boats near a drifting destroyer fifty miles southeast of Cape Cretin, and that two submarines had arrived in the area to rescue survivors, with two more due soon. However, the intention of sending more MLCs from Lae was abandoned due to the distance involved and the power of enemy air attacks. (24)

In Rabaul, the troop losses were becoming known in detail as survivors arrived and rosters were checked at the barracks and hospitals there. Headquarters 51 Division reported that the destroyers on 3 March and two sea trucks had returned a total of 1,502 men. The day before, 52 men of 115 Regiment had arrived in Lae, and DD *Urakaze* had collected 88. 11 Company could only report three men known to be killed, but 50 were missing. 9 Company had an almost exact reversal of these figures—three missing and 53 killed. These units had been on *Kyokusei Maru*, sunk on 2 March by the B17s. (25)

The Japanese 20 Division, waiting to be shipped to Madang or Wewak, received a report from Rabaul informing them that the entire convoy had been sunk on 3 March, but DDs *Shikinami* and *Yukikaze* had rescued 128 men. Some '2356 men took refuge north of Long Island'—a reference to those rescued and transferred to the destroyers from Rabaul. The report also stated that two Navy and 10 Army aircraft were lost. (26)

At day's end, Sergeant Chikui's diary described the situation:

> The sun is setting in the western horizon. It is very cold. We are just waiting for death to come. We tried hard to repair the boat and tried to sail north-west, perhaps to New Britain. At length a big island appeared in the west, like a huge cloud. It must be New Guinea or some island in Dampier Strait. Hanging on to the capsized boat, we struggled towards the island. We must reach there tonight or the enemy aircraft will find us.

5th Air Force continued to search the New Britain coast for additional ships and signs of activity, as well as to send aircraft to attack distant targets. A B17 of the 65th Squadron bombed two ships in Lae Harbor, but a damaged bombsight caused a total miss. The aircraft then went to New Britain, but saw no other shipping. Four hours later another B17 from the same squadron checked the north and south coasts of New Britain and the 319th Squadron sent six B24s from Fenton (near Darwin), to attack Ambon, but five returned with fuel system problems.

6 MARCH

It was obvious by this day that all that remained for the aircraft to find were small scattered groups or individuals dispersing over a wide area, and there was little point in tasking

Above: Shin-ai Maru photographed as "Torchy" Uren's Beaufighter passes alongside. (RAAF)

Right: Captain Bob Chatt flew B25 #088 "Chatter Box" on the 3 March attack. (Maurice Carse)

Below: B25 # 088 "Chatter Box," newly painted after eight .50-caliber machineguns installed. (Maurice Carse)

The Imperial Japanese Navy ship *Nojima*, photographed from a RAAF Beaufighter which had just strafed its decks; smoke clouds the forward gun position. (Alf Nelson)

B17 #574 "Tuffy" flew twice on 3 March: a morning mission flown by Lieutenant Kirby and the afternoon mission flown by Major Ed Scott. (Steve Birdsall)

Deck detail of destroyer *Uranami* as Captain Bill Beck makes his run. Beck's bombs did not release from his A20. (W. Garing)

A Beaufighter crossing the combat area. In the background, explosions mask a Japanese ship. (RAAF)

The 3,800-ton *Shin-ai Maru,* with flames belching aft of the funnel. The smoke pattern shows at least two fires blazing. (RAAF)

Barges on the deck of *Taimei Maru* as bombs from 89 Attack Squadron hit the hull. (W. Garing)

Taimei Maru, seconds before the bombs exploded. The A20s flew over so low and the explosions followed so quickly that some Japanese thought the airplanes had crashed into the ship. (W. Garing)

Damien Parer filmed this burning ship from the cockpit of "Torchy" Uren's Beaufighter. (RAAF)

Right: J. W. "Bill" Smallwood brought his B25 #970, damaged by Japanese anti-aircraft fire, back to Port Moresby with no hydraulics, flaps, or radio. The plane crashed on landing and was destroyed. (J. W. Smallwood)

Above: Pilot Officer Bill Blewett, radio/gunner in Bill Smallwood's B25 #970, looks at the wreck after release from the hospital a few days later. (W. Blewett)

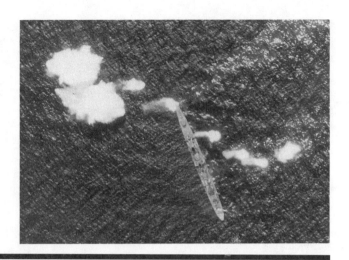

Above: **15.15 hours 3 March. Bombs from the 71st Squadron, 38th Bomb Group straddle a stationary destroyer already leaking fuel from bows and midships. (W. Garing)**

Right: **Three Japanese zeros destroyed during the strafing attack on Lae by Beaufighters of the 30th Squadron, 4 March 1943. (Fred Cassidy)**

On 4 March 1943, mopping-up begins. At 08.45 the 65th Squadron, 43rd Bomb Group attacked the abandoned DD *Tokitsukaze* from 6,000 feet, hitting its bridge. (W. Garing)

Two natives and Australian Warrent Officer Stanton on Kiriwina Island, with life-buoys from *Oigawa Maru* and *Shin-ai Maru* that drifted ashore and a samurai sword with which a Japanese tried to commit suicide. (Rev. Gordon Powell)

A Japanese life-boat towing half of a collapsible boat. Photographed by a RAAF PBY Catalina flown by Terry Duigan, who did not attack. This may be the boat in which the regimental colors of the Japanese 115 Infantry Regiment sailed to Gasmata, New Britain, in a month-long voyage. (Terry Duigan)

pilots and crews, using valuable aircraft to hunt for these people, when other targets of higher priority existed on land. Only one search of the area was made on 6 March, by four Bostons of RAAF 22 Squadron, who found only empty boats and rafts. However, the armed reconnaissance effort around New Britain continued. A B24 from the 321st Squadron checked the battle area, found no ships, then went on to Manus and bombed Lorengau; another B24 from the squadron flew along the west coast of New Britain, unsuccessfully bombing a small ship on a reef five miles east of Talasea, then making a low pass over three men seen signalling on the beach at Ea-ea. One was wearing a U.S. flight suit, and they were photographed; a third B24 from the 321st flew over known shipping lanes and sighted three submarines, which dived when the B24 attacked or approached. A fourth B24 from the squadron had an unsuccessful patrol along the south coast of New Britain.

Japanese submarines were busy rescuing survivors in the convoy battle area, and it is almost certain that the empty boats and rafts seen by Allied aircraft and PT boats had been abandoned by the Japanese after going aboard the submarines. On this day, I-17 delivered 156 men to Lae, and RO-101 took another 38 to Rabaul. During the next week, PT boats and RAAF Beaufort bombers searched the area, killed another 60 Japanese and captured 16. (27)

The survivors at sea were now coming closer to shore. Uchiro Watanabe and the other seven who had got into a collapsible boat and survived strafing had been rowing in one-hour shifts for the last two days, trying to reach three islands they could see to the south.

> After hard pulling without rest or water since yesterday, we neared the island. By this time our mouths were so dry that spittle hardly formed. Then, as if by the grace of Heaven, a squall came. We filled up our four canteens with water. A smile was now seen on the face of each man. We gave thanks to God, and gained confidence that we might be able to land today. Afraid it might turn out to be hostile, or uninhabited, we decided to land at night. (28)

For others, the day brought a relative improvement in their situation. Medical 2nd Lieutenant Hajimo Nakajima, 21 Artillery Brigade, had been on an improvised raft since *Oigawa Maru* was abandoned, but now was able to get into a collapsible boat. Lieutenant Kozuki and the color guard of 115 Regiment had been rowing throughout the night and day, drinking most of the water. Realising there was no prospect of a rescue ship, he had ordered the burial at sea of Colonel Endo and the other men. A sail was rigged at last, and the available wind used to make progress to New Britain. At times, clouds on the horizon were mistaken for land, and each time the truth was realised, morale sagged further. (29)

7 MARCH

General MacArthur's Headquarters issued a communiqué stating that 12 transports, three cruisers and seven destroyers had been sunk, with a loss of 12,762 men. A total of 59 Japanese aircraft had been destroyed. Not everyone accepted these figures and later, when more careful checking could only identify a total of 12 ships lost—eight transports and four destroyers—MacArthur wanted action taken against those who queried his initial figures. Washington was disinclined to do so.

Allied signals intercept had recorded many Japanese messages, but on this occasion the organisation was unable to clarify the situation. Many parts of messages were not received or were garbled, and it was only over a period of time that the sinking of eight ships and four destroyers could be confirmed. At first, it was thought 14 ships had been sunk, then ten, but later traffic confirmed the survival of four of the eight destroyers, identified the four lost, and the merchant ships sunk. Naturally, the confusion and lack of definite information experienced by the Japanese would be reflected in the signals intercepted, but it was a considerable time before the signals intercept analysis staff could report what had happened to the Lae convoy, and then this report confirmed what was already known from captured documents and prisoner interrogations. (30)

Post-war revelations of the 'Ultra' intercepts have sometimes led to exaggerated accounts of the value of the information received, with the implication that Allied commanders and staffs really had an easy time. In some instances, such as this battle, the truth is that 'Ultra' was of little value before or during the action, and served mainly to confirm what was known from other sources. During the 5th Air Force raids on Rabaul in October–November 1943, 'Ultra' was of even less use to the Allied staffs, and did not reflect losses or reinforcements on the Japanese side (author, *Into the Dragon's Jaws*).

Military organisations all over the world operate in basically the same manner. Commanders like parades with perhaps a band and a little pomp and circumstance. On 7 March, 51 Engineer Regiment at Rabaul was inspected by the CO, Colonel Araki. (31)

Personnel losses in the Japanese units were so heavy that the depleted battalions of 115 Regiment amalgamated under-strength sub-units. Thus 2nd Lieutenant Miyashita's 11 Company and 2nd Lieutenant Yoda's 12 Company, with a total of 31 men, joined with 1st Lieutenant Ogawa's, to form a No. 9 Mixed Company. As more men came ashore on 25 March the company expanded to 107. (32)

By now, the Japanese were receiving more reports of the rescue operations and the numbers brought in. Submarines rescued six officers and 159 men from ten different units, plus crew from *Aiyo Maru*. The 18th Army reported on the 7th that the following had been found by submarines: 115 Infantry Regiment, 55 men; 51 Engineers, 20 men; 50 AA Battalion, 17 men; 8 Shipping Engineers, 17 men, including Lieutenant Katsuda and Lieutenant Shimizu; 21 Artillery Brigade, 11 men; 2 Shipping Engineers, 7; 1 and 2 Shipping Artillery, six men; *Aiyo Maru* crew, the captain and four men; and other units, 17 men. I-26 brought in 14 men. Ten days later, it could report that 3rd Battalion of 115 Regiment, now reorganised, had 496 men. On 18 March, 45 men from seven units arrived at Sulumi. Private Ueno, 51 Division, was one of a boatload of 18 men rescued this day by a submarine. (33)

A submarine also rescued Sergeant Chikui, who had survived bomb hits on *Teiyo Maru* and several strafings, whose group had been struggling towards a distant island, hanging on to the sides of their overturned boat, but without clothes. When day broke, they saw the island was still a long way off, so separated to avoid presenting a clustered target to strafers. Then they saw what seemed to be a boat or canoe near the island, and raised the Japanese flag. The boat came towards them, and there was dismay when it was recognised as a submarine.

'We expected the worst,' wrote Chikui. 'Four days exertion seemed to end in vain.' [The submarine closed on them, then submerged. 30 minutes later, it surfaced on the other side, closed and again submerged. Chikui was irritated by these goings-on.] 'If we are bothered with this, we will never reach the island. We decided to swim. This time it closed in on us from the side, as close as 150 meters. They must be planning to capture us. We will take the food first then overpower them, the crew can not be more than 20. Three enemies came out on the deck with ropes in their hands and called out in Japanese. We are saved. Three days later we reached Lae and were hospitalised.'

Chikui wrote the account of his experiences while in Lae, with 7 Company 115 Regiment. His diary was captured in the Salamaua area, probably after his death in action. One entry reinforces the impression of devotion to duty which comes through Chikui's account, and also illustrates the discipline and readiness to do as ordered, regardless of the situation, which was a great strength of the Japanese, but also one of their great weaknesses, in that initiative was almost non-existent. On 8 August, Chikui wrote, 'Platoon commander, why did you not come back? We have waited for eight days. We are waiting for you in the water, without taking off our equipment. We might die. This is fate.' (34)

It is hard to imagine any platoon of Australian or American soldiers waiting for a Lieutenant, standing for eight days in the water without removing their equipment, or a sergeant who waited with them, without trying to find out what was going on.

Some survivors were coming ashore, and while there were no Allied troops actually waiting on the beaches, they were not far away. One Australian unit which suddenly found itself in a combat role was the RAAF 305 Radar Station, on Kiriwina. Being totally involved with radar work, they knew nothing of the air-sea battle. They had long expected a Japanese attack, and when a native runner arrived at 16.00 on 7 March, with the news that several boatloads of Japanese had arrived on the beach about two miles away, it was thought the enemy had come to destroy the radars.

At once, headquarters at Vivigani were alerted, and the defence procedures set up. The radars were prepared for destruction, but the operators kept working. RAAF men Ray Burton and Noel Lynam 'felt they were on a hot seat operating the radar in these circumstances,' said the unit history. Unit documents and codes were prepared for destruction also, but nothing was destroyed and the station continued to function. Milne Bay was also informed, and the RAAF men settled down for a long wait in the darkness, expecting a Japanese assault. An Australian Army unit arrived after a fourteen-mile march at night to get to their assistance, and this reassured the RAAF, who were not trained as jungle combatants. There was a minor alarm when some documents being destroyed by fire somehow had stray rounds of ammunition mixed in with them, and the explosions startled a few tired minds!

8 MARCH AND BEYOND

The Lae convoy had ended in disaster, but the other Japanese units coming from the north had arrived safely in New Guinea. The Advanced Headquarters of 20 Division, with some units, were delivered to Hansa, and the first and second echelons of 41 Division disembarked at Wewak, while the third echelon was at Palau. Allied air power could not reach that far north from its bases around Port Moresby and Dobodura. (35)

But at 09.00 that morning, 8 March, the Japanese on the beach at Kiriwina were attacked by Australian Army soldiers, who killed thirty-four, and captured three. Eight others managed to escape. This was reported to Milne Bay, and began a stream of similar events as survivors were killed or captured on the islands, along the New Guinea coast, and off shore. The three Japanese captured near the RAAF radar station were blindfolded and taken back to the camp area. One could speak English, and continually pointed to himself, asking the guards to hurry, 'All Japanese soldiers want to die!'

Elsewhere on 8 March, fourteen other Japanese were attacked on the coast near Tufi, eight were killed and six captured; twenty-five were seen on a raft near Goodenough Island; seven more were killed on Kiriwina; a PT boat engaged a boatload near Wanigela, killing forty-three and capturing eight. (36)

The RAAF radar men buried the dead Japanese with what military courtesies could be arranged at the time, as the bodies were placed in a common grave. It was only on 9 March that Flying Officer Bernard Katz, the RAAF commander, was told of the convoy action, and where the Japanese were coming from. More survivors came ashore in later days, but the first scare was over, and they were not regarded as a real threat to the radar station. Army and RAAF patrols were busy trying to capture the Japanese, who often would not surrender, and had to be killed, or taken by force. Eventually, some eighty-five were killed and twenty-five captured. The beaches became littered with barges, rafts, boats and various items which floated ashore. Attractive items such as swords, pistols, binoculars and so on were souvenired, and other material handed in.

The constant patrol contacts and knowledge that 'fanatical' Japanese were roaming the island did not make life at the radar station more pleasant, and night-time noises took on a menacing meaning to those forced to be moving about in the darkness, particularly to and from the radar equipment. As days went by, rafts were seen drifting past, with dead, emaciated, sunburnt and dehydrated Japanese aboard. Those who came ashore were helped and passed into the prisoner of war system, while the dead were buried. The Kiriwina natives had no love for the Japanese, and held a celebration, re-enacting, in dance and song, the destruction of the Japanese groups. (37)

Sergeant Hosoda, who had been doing guncrew duty on *Taimei Maru* when it was sunk, floated clinging to a log for two days with nine other men, finally got into an MLC and arrived on Goodenough Island on 7 March. The local people gave them food and accommodation in huts, but two days later, 9 March, Allied troops arrived, opened fire, and 13 of the 16 Japanese were killed. Hosoda was taken prisoner. (38)

On 8 March, 51 Division reported that 82 men had been delivered by submarine RO-101. But many other Japanese in small boats were still drifting or rowing closer to shore. Yasuhiro Yamazaki of 2 MG Company 115 Regiment, who had survived the strafing and was heading south to what that group of survivors thought was New Britain (sic), suffered from thirst.

> Our throats were burning and sore and we learned the value of even half a bowl of water. It appeared we had come much closer to our island. By 10.00 this morning, 96 hours had elapsed since we began drifting. The nine of us are all healthy. The island was further away than we had anticipated and heavy squalls hindered our progress. We are hoping to land tonight. (39)

Sergeant Aoki, 8 Shipping Engineers Medical unit, came ashore on Goodenough Island after finding fuel in a floating drum for the engine of the MLC. Looking for water, they came across natives who gave it to them, and traded bananas for cigarettes and biscuits, but also told the Australian military of the Japanese. The next day, 8 March, the sleeping Japanese were awakened by the Australians. There was a fight and only three of the 30 Japanese survived to be taken prisoner. (40)

About mid-morning on 8 March, the color guard of 115 Regiment had come across a collapsible boat drifting along. In it were ten men and 2nd Lieutenant Masuoka of the Shipping Engineer unit. Lieutenant Kozaki decided to gather all the healthy men in the lifeboat and put all the sick and weak in the collapsible, which was then towed along by the lifeboat, heading north-north-west with the wind.

Allied air power had shifted its attention elsewhere. 89th Squadron sent six A20s to attack Japanese defence works at Guadasagal; three Hudsons of 2 Squadron RAAF went north from Darwin to attack Toeal; six B25s from the Dutch 18th Squadron attacked the same target area; and the 320th Squadron, 90th Bomb Group, had three B24s on armed reconnaissance in the Salamaua-Lae-Madang areas and New Britain, but no shipping was sighted. The men on the beach at Ea-ea the previous day had been recognised from the photos as survivors of a B26 from the 22nd Bomb Group. Other Allied air operations were a mission by four Beaufighters from 31 Squadron RAAF north from Darwin to the Timor-Tanimbar areas; the 319th from the Darwin area sent two B24s on longer ranging searches of the area; one B17 from the 65th Squadron searched the area around Goodenough Island, where they saw three Sally bombers in formation at 1000 feet possibly on the same type of mission, but the B17 fired 6450 rounds at the Japanese below in boats and clinging to floating boxes, estimating that none survived the machinegun fire.

The men recognised on the beach at Ea-Ea were rescued by an RAAF Catalina, A24-17, flown by Squadron Leader Reg Burrage, while nearby Japanese positions were bombed. They were three men from a B26 which had gone down on New Britain, Private Stokie of the Australian Army, who had been evading the Japanese since the fall of Rabaul in February 1942, and three local natives. Strangely, six of the Catalina crew received U.S. D.F.C.'s (Distinguished Flying Cross) for the mission—Burrage did not.

By 9 March, the drifting engineless boats and rafts began to come ashore, many on Goodenough Island. The local people were not particularly friendly, but were not aggressive, preferring to tell the Australian authorities of the new arrivals. Only on a few occasions did the local people actually attack the Japanese, though native troops took part in actions against them. The U.S. PT boats were active, intercepting several boats. On the 9th, a U.S. PT boat captured Mikiwo Omiya and his three companions on a raft, off the coast. They were too weak to resist. Omiya, from 51 Division Signals, had seen seven men near him killed by strafing after escaping from *Teiyo Maru*. (41)

Stoker Nobukatsu Ishida, from *Taimei Maru*, reached the Trobriands in a MLC with fuel found in floating drums. There were 28 in the craft, three with rifles. When Australian troops appeared, the three riflemen fired, but were killed, and at midday on 9 March, Ishida was a prisoner. Some 14 Japanese in a boat from *Teiyo Maru* landed near Tufi on New Guinea; eight were killed and the other six captured. (42)

A few made the entire journey ashore alone. Private Kanami Mayeda, who had tied his rifle to a plank before going overboard himself, was alone on a small raft throughout the following days. He had emptied his waterbottle on 5 March, and when picked up by Australians some days later he was 'not in full possession of his faculties,' and did not know what had happened to him. (43)

17 men from *Taimei Maru* and *Oigawa Maru* arrived at the Trobriands, and after being fed by the people, fell asleep. An Australian patrol took them all prisoner, including Eiki Kiyo, the Korean oiler and rebellious student who had worked for Nippon Yusen Kaisha Line. (44)

Private Masami Yamada, 8 Shipping Engineers, survivor of *Shin-Ai Maru*, was still floating alone in his life-jacket when found on the 7th by 20 men in a collapsible boat. He had nothing to eat since the sinking four days before. On the 9th, they reached Goodenough and were approached by three Australian soldiers. The Japanese asked for water, but among themselves discussed plans for attacking the Australians and taking their weapons. They tried, but in the fight eight Japanese were killed and the other 13 taken prisoner. Another group of Japanese who were attacked by Australians were the 17 with Medical Captain Tsukahara, Headquarters 51 Engineers. As soon as they landed, the attacks began, and he was not sure how many were killed before he was captured on 13 March. (45)

Another man who was taken prisoner was Sergeant Ishihara, 50 AA Battalion, who had drifted to a small island and found an empty MLC. He and the other two Japanese with him tried to start the motor but could not, so rigged a sail and went on, to Goodenough, where they were taken by Australians. (46)

Similar events took place at many locations on the off-shore islands and along the coast of New Guinea as the survivors were either captured or killed if they resisted. Saburo Shiraishi, who escaped from *Teiyo Maru*, had drifted for three days with 12 others on a raft, then found an empty ship's boat. This capsized as they tried to climb aboard, but they righted it and picked up more men, finally coming ashore on Goodenough on 11 March. When Australians moved to capture them, two Japanese tried to escape but were killed, the others captured.

Another man who arrived on Goodenough that day was Ryuji Sakieda, a Probationary officer in 51 Division Signals. After surviving the strafing of his raft, he and another man swam to a capsized boat on the 7th, righted it and baled it out, allowed three more men aboard but ignored the others and drifted to shore and capture. Sakieda believed that much unecessary exhaustion was due to the crowding around the available rafts and boats. (47)

Yet, out at sea, some Japanese were found and rescued by brave men who went out to look for them, despite the power of Allied aircraft. On the 10th, 2nd Lieutenant Sato and 155 men of 115 Regiment were rescued by ship *Yo No.15*, from Lae. Next day, submarine I-26 brought another 54 men into Lae. The report of the submarine's arrival and number of rescued men was one of the messages intercepted and successfully translated by the 'Ultra' organisation. (48)

2nd Lieutenant Hirai, of 102 Infantry Regiment, with ten men, was senior officer of another small group which drifted about in collapsible boats. They had survived the attacks on *Shin-ai Maru*, and on 5 March arrived at a river mouth. Going ashore, they found Japanese grave markers and other material which identified the place as the mouth of the Mambare. Discreetly getting back into their boats, they carefully made their way north along the coast, and on 21 March arrived at the Nassau Bay positions of 3 Battalion, 102 Regiment, safe back in Japanese territory. They were given food and treatment, and sent on farther to the rear. There was no reference to 102 Regiment units in the captured documents which detailed the convoy loading, so perhaps Hirai and his men were part of a group put aboard at the last minute, like those on *Kembu Maru*. (49)

Meanwhile, out at sea, the regimental color guard of 115 Regiment continued their journey. Lieutenant Kozaki became worried about damage to the flag, so secured it to the mast and covered it with a canvas. On 9 March, one man died of wounds from the strafing in the convoy area. On 10 and 11 of March, aircraft flew over without attacking, and the men pretended to be dead. Food ran out, and starvation left little strength for rowing. Six men were to die of starvation during the voyage. Rain showers provided drinking water, though the rain made the nights cold and the men suffered after the hot sunny days. Still they went on to the north-north-west.

Other groups which survived reflected the disciplinary standard of the Japanese armed forces. Sergeant Major Nozaki, 51 Division Engineers, and 20 other men arrived in Lae on 16 March, with one light machinegun and twelve rifles, which they carried through the attacks, sinkings, into the boats and to shore, ready for duty. Captain Akiba and 19 men of eight different units from *Oigawa Maru* arrived at Sulumi on 18 March. (50)

Some men survived when many or all around them died. These sole survivors clung to life in the middle of the empty sea, hoping for rescue, determined to wait despite everything which had happened and which might come. Shotaro Watanabe, 50 AA Battalion, joined three other men from *Oigawa Maru* on a raft, and they drifted for the next 12 days. The other three died; Watanabe drifted ashore and was taken prisoner. The man who thought he was last to leave *Oigawa Maru*, Corporal Rihei Koido, 14 Field Artillery Brigade, had drifted for 11 days on a raft, without food or water, up to his waist in the sea, hoping always for rescue by Japanese forces. Rescue never came, and when Koido drifted ashore and was captured, he was too weak to walk. (51)

The search by both sides went on, and the fortunes of war decided whether the Japanese or Allies found the drifting men. Some who encountered U.S. or Australian patrol boats were the 12 in a boat containing Yoshio Aoki, 50 AA Battalion, who arrived at an island and bought bananas with Japanese coins. They were shot at, and so launched their boat again and put to sea. A U.S. PT boat attacked, sank the boat and killed seven of the Japanese, then captured the five survivors. The PT boats also attacked the ship's boat carrying Warrant Officer Matsushima, killing seven of the men aboard. The other five jumped overboard and swam ashore on New Guinea, where they were made prisoner by local people who handed them to the Australians. Matsushima's 22 years service in the Japanese Army was over. (52)

Noburo Yamada, Signal Company HQ 115 Regiment, had escaped from *Oigawa Maru*, was first on a raft, then swam to a small boat where there were men he knew from his unit. They drifted close to New Guinea, and saw a fast patrol boat approaching, but did nothing as they thought it was Japanese. Too late, they tried to escape, but PT boat 114 opened fire, killing two men. Yamada and others tried escaping underwater, but were captured. (53)

Some managed to remain free for a time. Sergeant Kojima, the cook who had been carried unconscious to the ship's boat during the battle, sailed to an island where the natives gave them food, and nothing happened until 21 March, when Australians arrived in a patrol boat and captured the eleven survivors. (54)

Lieutenant Kozaki and Sergeant Namiki continued to lead the group with the 115 Regiment colors. Kozaki made fish hooks and the party survived on fish and rain water till the end of March. Then they saw land, an island, and reached it at about 14.00 on 2 April. They were about six miles west of Cape Merkus, on New Britain, and so weak they could hardly walk. Natives offered local food, and they rejoiced at a safe arrival a month after the disaster of the convoy attacks. The natives told them of a Japanese garrison, and with some assistance from the Navy unit there, the survivors arrived at Cape Merkus late at night on 4 April. Sergeant Namiki was the standard bearer, and the colors were ceremoniously stored in the office of the garrison commander, Ensign Sakaguchi, head of the Gasmata airfield defence unit.

The colors were returned to 115 Regiment at Rabaul, and presented to the new commander, Colonel Matsui. On 21 May, the colors went to New Guinea, to Lae by submarine. After the war, Lieutenant Kozaki and Sergeant Namiki said they did not really understand how they survived the ordeal and brought the colors safely to Japanese custody, crediting their success to the intervention of heaven and the warrior spirits of the regiment's dead. Their exploit was described in an August 1944 military magazine, and later for the post-war history of army operations in the Solomons theatre. Captured documents also described the journey for Allied Intelligence staffs. (55)

Takeo Yanagawiza, another from 115 Regiment Signals, arrived on Goodenough with four companions. Seven had been killed by strafing. Allied troops killed two of the five, two other died later of malaria. Yanagawiza lived quietly with a native woman and some children in a hut, until the other local people handed him over to the Australians on 20 July, over four months later. (56)

Sergeant Major Yoshio Endo, 51 Engineers, was with 13 others in a collapsible boat which came ashore on the coast near Tufi. The people here were unfriendly, and killed two of three Japanese who went looking for water. The others split up into pairs, and separated, but were hunted down, some being killed. Endo was captured by the local people and handed over to the Australians on 5 April. (57)

From the Allied side, the many continuing small actions against the parties of Japanese coming ashore were included in the Daily Operations Report:

11 March—six killed, eleven escaped; nine killed, thirteen captured; eighteen captured on Trobriands.
18 March—one killed, seventeen captured on Kiriwina.
21 March—twenty-two killed, one captured on Goodenough.
22 March—six killed, eighteen captured on Trobriands.
24 March—sixteen killed, two captured in last two days near the mouth of the Kumusi River.
29 March—enemy in a barge seen near Oro Bay.
10 April—ten captured on Goodenough.
13 April—thirteen killed on Goodenough.
15 April—two captured at Tufi.
19 April—three killed on Kwaiawata Island.

When these figures are added, at least 300 Japanese were killed close in-shore or after landing on islands or the New Guinea coast.

Similar events befell the other survivors of the many units in the Lae Convoy. Some made their way safely along the coast to Japanese territory, but they were relatively few, and after medical treatment, were sent into the battles in New Guinea. Those who had been taken back to Rabaul were also sent on to New Guinea. Very few survived the next two and a half years of campaigning in the jungles, along the coast and in the mountains of New Guinea.

On 31 March, 51 Division reported that of the 247 officers and 4,110 soldiers who had set out on the convoy, 90 officers and 1,670 men had been returned to Rabaul. 3 Battalion, 115 Regiment was reorganised under Major Nishikawa, with a Headquarters and Companies 8 through 11, totalling 486 men. Others were in New Guinea and straggling ashore, or along the coast of New Guinea. One boatload sailed 700 miles to Guadalcanal, and when they arrived there were killed by a U.S. patrol. (58)

The fast cheap victories of early 1942 had not required the Japanese pay much attention to logistics. Now, a year later, in the face of increasing Allied battlefield capability, Japanese commanders at all levels were beginning to realise that fighting spirit alone was not enough in modern warfare.

In addition to the loss of the Lae Convoy, four other freighters and a tanker were sunk in the first eight days of March by U.S. submarines. However, Imperial Headquarters issued a communiqué on 18 March, stating that Japanese forces sank six enemy submarines from 6 to 11 March, and lost two ships during that time. One wonders how this news was received in the Lae and Rabaul areas. (59)

The Japanese were forced to use submarines and smaller surface ships, as well as destroyers for fast runs, in order to reinforce and resupply their forces in New Guinea. In April, submarines delivered 184 men from 51 Division, MLCs brought 293 and five destroyer missions carried 333, 269, 533, 250 and 195 men. (60)

On land and in the air, the Japanese situation had changed dramatically. It was apparent to Japanese commanders that the Australian and U.S. forces were planning a strong counter-blow, and on 17 July, Lieutenant General Hidemitsu Nakano, commander of 51 Division, saw fit to make the following announcement to his soldiers:

> The whole fate of the Japanese Empire depends upon the decision of the struggle for Lae-Salamaua. These strongholds must be defended to death. We must crush the enemy both on land and in the air. Whatever plans to land troops he may attempt, we must destroy speedily and decisively at the water's edge. Every officer and man must develop his strength and resolution so that one man is equal to ten. (61)

Two months later, by mid-September, the Japanese forces there had been defeated, and the Allies were developing the Lae-Nadzab area into an important base.

In the Battle of the Bismarck Sea, Generals Kenney and Whitehead successfully demonstrated some of the principles of war: surprise, security, flexibility, mass, offensive action, administration, and effective use of basic intelligence.

In addition, the battle probably would not have been as successful if the following factors were not present:

- The crews were experienced and well-trained.
- They were self-confident and keen.
- The maximum striking power was applied in the minimum of time.
- The tactic of minimum-level bombing and strafing had been developed and was employed.
- Fighter escort tactics were good.
- The Japanese made the following mistakes: not bombing AAF bases; not providing adequate AA and fighter escort; concentrating AA on the higher B17s; and having the destroyers steam towards the attacking aircraft, so leaving the transport ships briefly unprotected.

Leaving aside the factor of weather, which could have covered the area until the convoy arrived at Lae, if any of the above

■ **169**

had not been present, the outcome of the battle could well have been in the Japanese favor. Their army units would have landed and gone on the offensive, Lae would have been further developed by the units on the ships, and the course of the New Guinea fighting would have been different.

The Japanese themselves had taught the Allies in Asia and the Pacific that shipping in range of land-based aircraft is at risk, but until August 1945 and the surrender of Japan, their naval and merchant ships of all types were to be under constant air attack, losing destroyers, cruisers, aircraft carriers and even the giant battleship *Musashi* to air power. There were other, larger battles between ships and aircraft in World War 2, but, Midway aside, none where so much destruction was achieved so speedily at so little cost—and at such a crucial point in a campaign.

The U.S. 5th Air Force had demonstrated its growing maturity, and vindicated General Billy Mitchell as no other U.S. air formation had up to that time. The 5th already had achieved a high standard in providing close air support, air resupply and troop airlift in support of the land battles in New Guinea, and was gaining air superiority. Unaided by either army or naval forces, it now had defeated a major enemy reinforcement operation at sea. The 5th Air Force could look forward to future exploits in the application of air power.

On 19 March 1942 the first fighter unit to arrive for defence of Port Moresby had flown in—75 Squadron RAAF—with its Kittyhawks. They had less than two weeks training in the P40s. They held the line of air defence for some six weeks before the first U.S. P39 squadrons were available. On 1 April, the first puny U.S. bombing mission in New Guinea was flown by five A24s of the 8th Squadron, 3rd Bomb Group. The U.S. Army Air Force needed a year before all the positive factors of high morale, experience, suitable aircraft and enough of them came together for the Allied Air Forces in March 1943, and from that time the writing was on the wall for the Japanese in New Guinea and the South West Pacific.

The U.S. Fifth Air Force wrote several notable chapters in the history of air power, begining with its support for the Australian Army fighting over the Kokoda Trail, and for the Allied forces in the Buna-Gona campaign. Perhaps that time can be seen as its apprenticeship. Then came the Battle of the Bismarck Sea, when the 5th demonstrated its ability to concentrate an appropriate force for a massive blow.

In August 1943 the 5th executed the attacks on Japanese air units concentrated on the Wewak airfields, which changed the balance of power in New Guinea. In March 1944 the 5th again destroyed the Japanese around the Wewak airfields and followed this with the almost complete destruction of the Japanese Air Force on the airfields at Hollandia in April 1944. Then came the invasion of the Philippines and the move to Okinawa. By the end of the war, 5th Air Force planes were flying regularly over Japan itself, and, fittingly, a 49th Fighter Group P38, flown by Colonel Clay Tice, was the first U.S. aircraft to land on Japan.

No other air force in 1939–45 planned and executed such a series of successful operations which proved the value of intelligently employed air power. No other air force covered such a large part of the earth's surface, nor moved its units through such inhospitable areas for such long distances.

The first days of March 1943 had seen the first great victory for the U.S. Army Air Force. That victory had been achieved by an air force poor in all types of aircraft and supplies, but rich in the priceless attributes of courage, audacity and initiative.

APPENDIX 1

AIRFIELDS AND ALLIED AIR FORCE UNITS IN BATTLE
(Other units such as P39s and C47s are not included as they did not take part.)

Field	Squadron	Group	Aircraft
Port Moresby			
Durand	90th	3rd Attack	B25C-1s
	71st	38th Bomb	B25s
	405th	38th Bomb	B25s
	7th	49th Fighter	P40s
Jackson's	63rd	43rd Bomb	B17s
	64th	43rd Bomb	B17s
	65th	43rd Bomb	B17s
	320th	90th Bomb	B24s (also Ward's)
	321st	90th Bomb	B24s (also Ward's)
Kila	8th	3rd Attack	A20s
	89th	3rd Attack	A20s
	8th	49th Fighter	P40s

Schwimmer	13th	3rd Attack	B25s
	9th	49th Fighter	P38s
	39th	35th Fighter	P38s
Ward's	22nd	9 Group RAAF	A20 Bostons
	30th	9 Group RAAF	Beaufighters

Milne Bay

Gurney	100th	9 Group RAAF	Beauforts

Australia

Mareeba	403rd	43rd Bomb	B17s

APPENDIX 2

ALLIED AIR FORCE UNIT COMMANDERS

35th Fighter Group	Colonel R.A. Legg
39th Fighter Squadron	Major George Prentice
40th Fighter Squadron	Captain M.A. Moore
49th Fighter Group	Lieutenant Colonel R.L. Morrissey
7th Fighter Squadron	Major W.P. Martin
8th Fighter Squadron	Major M.E. Sims
9th Fighter Squadron	Captain J.C. Peaslee
3rd Attack Group	Lieutenant Colonel R.F. Strickland
13th Attack Squadron	Major H.V. Maull
89th Attack Squadron	Major G.W. Clark
90th Attack Squadron	Major E.L. Larner
38th Bomb Group	Colonel J. O'Neill
71st Bomb Squadron	Major E.P. Mussett
405th Bomb Squadron	Lieutenant Colonel M. Lewis

43rd Bomb Group	Colonel R.M. Ramey
63rd Bomb Squadron	Major E.W. Scott
64th Bomb Squadron	Major K.D. McCullar
65th Bomb Squadron	Major H.J. Hawthorne
403rd Bomb Squadron	Major J.P. Reusek
90th Bomb Group	Colonel Ralph E. Koon
319th Bomb Squadron	Captain Charles E. Jones
320th Bomb Squadron	1st Lieutenant Roy L. Taylor
321st Bomb Squadron	Major Cecil L. Faulkner
400th Bomb Squadron	Major Harry J. Bullis
8th Photo Reconnaissance Squadron	1st Lieutenant F.S. Savage
9 Operational Group RAAF	Air Commodore J.E. Hewitt RAAF
75 Squadron	Squadron Leader W.S. Arthur RAAF
77 Squadron	Squadron Leader R. Cresswell RAAF
6 Squadron	Wing Commander A.A. Barlow RAAF
22 Squadron	Wing Commander K.M. Hampshire RAAF
30 Squadron	Wing Commander B.R. Walker RAAF
100 Squadron	Wing Commander J.R. Balmer RAAF (on leave)
	Squadron Leader J.A. Smilbert (temp)

APPENDIX 3

THE BISMARCK SEA CONVOY: SHIP DETAILS

Ships in the convoy ranged from over 8,000 tons to 950 tons, and were of varying ages. Information in this appendix was gathered from Lloyd's register, Japanese shipping companies, the Japanese Maritime Department, the U.S. Strategic Bombing Survey 'The Campaigns of the Pacific War,' and ATIS documents. The shipping companies themselves have little or no information, as so much destruction was suffered during the war, particularly in the B29 attacks. In some cases they know only that the company did own such a ship. Photographs of the ships before the battle are rare, and those seen in the book are the best that could be located in Japan, Australia, Canada, the U.S. and the U.K.

Aiyo Maru–2,746 tons. Built in January 1942 and owned by Toyo Kisen Kaisha. In 1964 became Showa line.

Kembu Maru–950 tons. Built in 1942 and was one of many similar sized ships owned by the Sanko Steamship Company Limited. Had 30 crewmen aboard including Captain Kenichi Mano.

Kyokusei Maru–5,493 tons. Built in 1920 by J. Coughlan and Sons, Vancouver, and owned by Asashi Shoji K.K. of Tokyo. The ship's radio sign was JDCM.

Oigawa Maru–6,494 tons. Owned by Shin Yei Steamship Company Limited.

Taimei Maru–2,883 tons. Built in 1936 by Mitsubishi at Yokohama, and owed by Nippon Yusen K.K. The ship's radio sign was JJBK. The Captain was Fumio Takiura.

Teiyo Maru–6,870 tons. Built in 1924 by Blohm and Voss in Hamburg. Formerly named the *Saarland*, before being bought by Teikoku Senpaku K.K., Tokyo, at the time of the Lae convoy. The ship's radio call was JQAO. The Captain was Takezo Ishizaka. Also included a crew of two radio-operators, 31 deckhands and 30 engine-room personnel. (1)

Shin-ai Maru–3,793 tons. Built in 1921 by Fujinagata in Osaka, and owned by Kishimoto Kishen K.K. of Osaka. The ship's radio call was JTGB.

Nojima–8,125 tons. This naval supply ship was built in 1919 by Mitsubishi at Kobe. Captain Matsumoto was in command.

Personnel and cargo were distributed among the ships as shown in the list below:

Ship	Personnel	Equipment on board	
Aiyo Maru (2,746 gross tons)	252	fuel in cubic metres	500
		provisions/property in cubic metres	500
		fuel drums	350
		ammunition in cubic metres	500
		MLC large	5

Kembu Maru (953 gross tons)	50	gasoline in cubic metres	500
Kyokusei Maru (5,493 gross tons)	1,203	AA gun	3
		150mm howitzer	2
		battalion gun	2
		mountain gun	2
		light mortar	4
		carts	26
		trucks	12
		MLC large	4
		collapsible boats	10
		rowing boats	8
		unsinkable drums	500
Oigawa Maru (6,493 gross tons)	1,324	AA guns	3
		150 mm howitzer	3
		battalion gun	1
		machinegun	7
		light mortar	1
		mountain gun	2
		motor car	2
		passenger vehicle	1
		trucks	5
		MLC large	8
		trailer	2
		unsinkable drums	300
Taimei Maru (2,883 gross tons)	200	MLC large	11
		unsinkable drums	200
Teiyo Maru (6,869 gross tons)	1,923	100mm cannon	2
		field gun	2
		rear car	1
		passenger vehicle	1
		trucks	5
		tractor	1
		carts	23

	MLC large	6
	collapsible boats	15
	rowing boats	6
	unsinkable drums	500
Shin-Ai Maru 1,052	100mm cannon	1
(3,793 gross tons)	AA gun	3
	battalion gun	2
	regimental gun	1
	other type gun	1
	light mortar	2
	machinegun	3
	trucks	1
	tractor	1
	carts	5
	aircraft materials in cubic metres	500
	drop-tanks	100
	collapsible boats	15
	rowing boats	6
Nojima (8,125 gross tons)	3rd Naval Air Defence Unit, Yokosuka Yokosuka 5 Special Naval Landing Party (SNLP) Maizuru 2 (SNLP)	

On the seven ships there were a total of 6,004 men destined for the Lae-Salamaua area. Many Japanese documents give the total as 5,954, and do not include any on *Kembu Maru*, but in fact 50 men from the 51 Division units as well as from 221 Airfield Battalion were aboard. *Nojima* was not mentioned in any of the captured documents referring to shipping manifests, but did carry naval landing units, of which 69 men were reported lost. In addition, the destroyers carried a known total of 958 men, making at least 6,912 personnel in the convoy, as listed in captured documents. (2)

After several months of analysis of Intelligence information, staff at Allied Land Force Headquarters arrived at the above total, and assessed that 3,566 survivors of the convoy were landed, with about 1,300 delivered by destroyer, barge and submarine to Lae and Finschafen, and about 1,680 members of 51 Division returned to Rabaul. Using the figures above, it was estimated that 3,346 were killed in the attacks on the ships, died later at sea, or were killed or captured on land. (3)

The Japanese 18th Army Medical Report for March 1943 stated that 6,828 personnel took part in the convoy, and 2,978 were missing in action, excluding ship and gun crews. That is, only Army personnel were counted; Navy losses from the destroyers and *Nojima* were not included. (4)

The destroyers represented several phases in the Japanese development of naval ships. Following are brief descriptions of the ships and their combat careers prior to the Lae convoy, but much more information can be found in books devoted to the subject of naval vessels and battles. Also in this list are the names of the destroyer captains at the time of the Bismarck Sea action.

FUBUKI *CLASS*

The design of the 1923 Program ships was superior to any others in the world at the time. Conceived to operate with the new cruisers to be built, the ships were of advanced design and heavy armament. Modifications and improvements to the ships made them still a useful vessel in the Pacific war's early years, with a crew of about 197, six 5-inch guns, nine torpedo tubes in triple mounts, and a top speed of about 38 knots. It is not clear if some of the main armament had begun to be replaced with more anti-aircraft guns, but those in this *Fubuki* Class in the Bismarck Sea were:

Shikinami, completed in December 1929 at Maizuru N.Y., and commanded by Lieutenant Commander Akifumi Kawahashi.

Shirayuki, completed in December 1928 at Yokohama, and commanded by Commander Rokuro Sugawara (or Sugahara).

Uranami, completed in June 1929 at Sasebo N.Y., and commanded by Lieutenant Commander Chikara Hagio.

At the beginning of operations against the U.S. and Britain, all three were in action off Malaya, Singapore, in the Java Sea, and *Shirayuki* had been with the force which attacked Ceylon (Sri Lanka). On 1 March 1942, shore guns had made a hit with a six-inch shell on the bridge of *Shirayuki,* while in the same action *Shikinami* had been damaged on her port side. *Uranami* had been credited with sinking two Dutch submarines, *O20* and *K XVII* on 20 and 24 December 1941. On 15 November 1942, *Shikinami* and *Uranami* were part of Destroyer Division 19 in the action off Guadalcanal, when three U.S. destroyers were sunk, and a Japanese battleship and destroyer were lost.

ASASHIO *CLASS*

Ten destroyers were ordered in the 1934 Reinforcement Programme, with various improvements over preceding ships, and with six 5-inch guns, eight torpedo tubes in two mounts and a speed of about 35 knots, with some 200 men in the crew at full strength, those of the *Asashio* class escorting the Lae convoy were:

Asashio, completed in August 1937 at Sasebo N.Y., and commanded by Commander Goro Yoshii.

Arashio, completed in December 1937 at Kawasaki, Kobe, and commanded by Commander Hideo Kuboki.

Asagumo, completed in March 1938 at Kawasaki, Kobe, and commanded by Commander Toru Iwahashi.

After service in the Philippine Islands assault force, in the Battle of the Java Sea, *Asagumo* had been hit by gunfire, reportedly from HMS *Electra*, having No. 1 boiler room and engine room flooded. After repairs, the ship had taken part in the night cruiser battle off Guadalcanal on 13 November 1942, when the U.S. Navy lost three cruisers and four destroyers, against a Japanese loss of a battleship and two destroyers. On 15 November, the ship was present in another action, when three U.S. destroyers were lost, as were one Japanese battleship and a destroyer. *Arashio* had taken part in the invasion of Amboina, and *Asashio* had been part of the Malaya assault force, on 19 February assisting in sinking the Dutch *Piet Hein*. Both ships had been damaged by U.S. divebombers at Midway, losing a total of 59 men killed. *Asashio* also had been damaged by air attack on a run to Gona, 6 December 1942.

KAGERO *CLASS*

More destroyers were ordered in the Third Reinforcement Program of 1937. These ships included design improvements to solve the shortcomings of the *Asashio* class, though the two classes were almost identical in appearance. The two ships of this class in the Bismarck Sea battle were:

Tokitsukaze, completed in December 1940 at Uraga, and commanded by Commander Masayoshi Motokura.

Yukikaze, completed in January 1940 at Sasebo N.Y., and commanded by Commander Ryokichi Sugama.

Both had seen action in the Battle of the Java Sea, with *Tokitsukaze* receiving one hit. As part of Destroyer Division 16, the ship had taken part in the night victory off Guadalcanal, when the U.S. Navy lost three cruisers and four destroyers on 13 November 1942. *Yukikaze* had sunk *USS Perch* on 3 March 1942, and also been credited with the destruction of the U.S. destroyers *Barton* and *Laffey* off Guadalcanal on 13 November 1942, but had been damaged in the action off Guadalcanal on 14 November 1942, when six Japanese transports and a cruiser were sunk and four more transports were beached, while three cruisers and another destroyer were damaged, for no U.S. Naval losses or damage to ships.

APPENDIX 4

JAPANESE ARMY COMMANDERS ON BOARD SHIP

Destroyers

Arashio	Lieutenant Shimizu
Asagumo	Sergeant Takahashi
Asashio	Sergeant Matsubara
Shikinami	2nd Lieutenant Nagano
Shirayuki	Sergeant Nakao
Tokitsukaze	Lieutenant Matsui
Uranami	Sergeant Yasuda

Transports

Aiyo Maru	Lieutenant Shimizu [sic] 8 Shipping Engineer Regiment
Kembu Maru	2nd Lieutenant Hasebe 221 Airfield Battalion
Kyokusei Maru	Major Nishikawa 115 Infantry Regiment
Oigawa Maru	Colonel Endo 115 Infantry Regiment
Shin-Ai Maru	Lieutenant Colonel Hondo 51 Engineer Regt
Taimei Maru	Lieutenant Tsuchiya 8 Shipping Engineer Regt
Taiyo Maru	Lieutenant Colonel Watanabe 14 Artillery Bde

UNITS ABOARD SHIP

Destroyers

Asagumo	51 Engr Regt	6
	8 Ship Engr Regt	23
Arashio	51 Div HQ	40
	51 Div Sigs	19
	51 Engr Regt	6
	115 Inf Regt	63
	8 Ship Engr Regt	22
Asashio	51 Div HQ	21
	51 Div Sigs	18
	51 Engr Regt	6
	115 Inf Regt	63
	14 Arty Bde	20
	8 Ship Engr Regt	22
Shikiname	51 Div HQ	18
	51 Div Sigs	9
	51 Engr Regt	9
	115 Inf Regt	82
	14 Arty Bde	8
	8 Ship Engr Regt	24
Shirayuki	51 Engr Regt	6
	8 Ship Engr Regt	23
Tokitsukaze	18 Army HQ	44
	51 Div Sigs	9
	51 Engr Regt	6
	115 Inf Regt	46
	14 Arty Bde	22
	8 Ship Engr Regt	23
Uranami	51 Div HQ	24
	51 Div Sigs	9

	51 Engr Regt	9
	115 Inf Regt	84
	8 Ship Engr Regt	24
Yukikaze	18 Army HQ	50
	51 Div Sigs	9
	51 Engr Regt	6
	115 Inf Regt	62
	8 Ship Engr Regt	23

MEN AND EQUIPMENT ABOARD TRANSPORTS

18 Army Headquarters
51 Division Headquarters
51 Division Signals
51 Engineer Regiment
14 Artillery Regiment
115 Infantry Regiment
3 Field Hospital

Attached units:

21 Artillery Brigade
50 Anti-aircraft Battalion
18 Army command post
15 Independent Engineer Regiment troops
Army Signals troops
22 Airfield Battalion
209 Airfield Battalion
5 Air signals Regiment

Unloading force:

8 Shipping Engineer Regiment
3 Company, 5 Shipping Engineer Regiment
3 Debarkation Unit

APPENDIX 5

SIGHTING REPORTS FROM AIRCRAFT DURING BATTLE

There has been argument about the number of ships in the convoy and those claimed sunk almost from the time the strike forces returned. Below are the sightings and their time quoted in the Advanced Echelon 5th Air Force report of 6 April 1943, to give the reader some understanding of the problems faced by Intelligence and Operations staffs during operations such as the Battle of the Bismarck Sea. The reporting squadron is represented as, for example, 321st Squadron 90th Bomb Group = (321/90).

1 MARCH

16.00   14 ships–six naval, eight merchant (321/90)
20.30   received anti-aircraft fire; no sighting
21.30   nil sighted

2 MARCH

07.30   nil sighted
08.25   14 ships, including seven destroyers (320/90)
09.55   two hits on 9,000-tonner (63/43)
10.00   large ship seen burning (65/43)

10.05	two large, four or five smaller destroyers, and two large and four to six other transports (63/43)
10.15	one hit on a 6,000-tonner (65/43)
10.20	14 ships seen–five naval, nine merchant; one seen on fire, one listing and sinking (321/90)
10.29	ship exploded and turned over
10.30	14 ships; one hit on bow of 6,000-tonner (64/43)
10.32	5,000-tonner burning for'ard, 8,000-tonner listing badly, with fo'castle under water (64/43)
10.35	8,000-tonner burning and exploding, 5,000-tonner burning forward hold (65/43)
10.40	6,000-tonner exploded violently (64/43)
11.00	500–800-tonner on fire
11.10	two burning ships being left by convoy (63/43)
11.15	one hit on 6,000-tonner, burst into flames, rolled over and sank in two minutes; 5,000-tonner ditto (63 and 65/43)
11.30	two or three possible hits on 5,000-tonner
11.45	one hit on 9,000-tonner
	no aircraft present for some hours; comment in the report that as the listing ship was not reported again, it was presumed sunk
14.05	four transports and four destroyers sighted; this number was believed to show that three ships of the original 14 had been sunk
16.00	15 ships sighted; believed four or five joined as convoy circled at 05.00South-147.20East; six navy nine merchant (63/43)
17.45	16 ships sighted, including ten merchantmen, of which two were on fire (403/43)
18.20	two hits on 6,000-tonner, definitely sinking; near misses on two others (403/43)
18.30	15 ships sighted; 6,000-tonner assumed sunk; at 0505South-147.30East were seven destroyers and six merchantmen, and two cruisers further south (65/43)
	end of day resume: believed three ships sunk, two burned out, several others damaged

3 MARCH

08.30   convoy located, sixteen ships counted and accepted as accurate figure of number present when attacks began

10.00   90th Squadron: 15 hits on three destroyers and seven transports, with two sunk, one blew up and others all burning;

89th Squadron: 12 hits on seven ships, one of which exploded;

38th Group: five hits on three ships

10.10   three hits on two 6,000-tonners, one burned and probably sank (64/43)

10.10   one hit on 5,000-tonner, started fire; two hits on 4,000-tonner, exploded and sank (65/43)

10.15   one probable hit on 7,000-tonner, smoking (13/3)

10.18   15 ships seen, of which five were burning, and report admits by now it was difficult to keep track of which ships were being hit and sunk

10.22   destroyer seen to sink (64/43)

10.25   11 ships seen, and two others burning (63/43)

12.20   five ships burning, four others in area (63/43)

14.10   four warships seen, course north, 06.40S-148.05N

15.05   five burning ships, and two destroyers (63/43)

15.12   one transport sank (65/43) report noted that with this sinking, results so far were eight ships definitely sunk, one probably sunk

15.15   five burning ships counted (63/43)

15.15   90th Squadron: nine hits on two destroyers and two transports

15.18   38th Group: six hits on two destroyers, eight burning ships counted

15.18   one destroyer sank (64/43)

15.19   four transports, one destroyer, all smoking (321/90)

15.20   two hits on destroyer, exploded; one hit on destroyer, exploded; four burning ships and two disabled destroyers seen in area (65/43)

15.25   two hits on 5,000-tonner (64/43)

15.25	five transports and one destroyer burning, one destroyer stationary (63/43)
15.25	four hits on large destroyer (13/3)
15.36	explosions on 6,000-tonner (64/43)
15.45	one transport sank
17.20	three burning transports, one large stationary destroyer seen
17.57	undamaged destroyer at 07.11S-158.03E
18.30	three burning ships sighted
19.30	one transport and one destroyer only seen afloat

4 MARCH

Many reports of barges and boats in battle area, the only ship sighted was a stationary destroyer which was attacked three times.

There were other sighting reports from distant reconnaissance flights, before and early in the action, and 5th Air Force staff believed that some of these other ships joined the original convoy late on 2 March. A total of 14 transports and seven destroyers were believed to have been sunk, though captured documents, prisoners and photographers only referred to or depicted the 'original' eight ships.

APPENDIX 6

STATISTICS: SORTIES AND ORDNANCE EXPENDED

Total bomber sorties: 193

Total fighter sorties: 117

Aircraft	Destroyed	Badly Damaged	Lightly Damaged
B17	1	4	15
B25	1	—	3
A20	—	—	2
Beaufighter	1	—	2
P38	3	—	5
Total	6	4	27

Claims for enemy aircraft destroyed were:

Fighter claims   27-12-9
Bomber claims   32-12-0
Ammunition expended: 20mm, .50- and .30-caliber:
233,847 rounds

Bombs expended:
   253   1,000-pounders; 19 hits, 42 near misses
   261   500-pounders; 59 hits, 39 near misses

However, 48 of the 500-pound hits were by 137 bombs dropped in mast-height attacks. Only 11 hits were claimed for 124 500-pounders dropped from 4–8,000 feet.

SOURCES

The Battle of the Bismarck Sea was such a resounding success that reports were called for from many higher headquarters, and a variety of people at a distance from the action seized the opportunity to be associated with success, so created their own versions of reports on the action. All used the same basic information, as becomes apparent when these reports were read together. Those consulted for this book were:

'Report on Battle of the Bismarck Sea'
  HQ Advanced Echelon 5th Air Force, dated 6 April 1943 and signed by Major General Ennis Whitehead.
  from Australian War Memorial AWM 54 643/6/6 ('Whitehead Report')

'Tactical Reports of Attacks on Bismarck Sea Convoy, March 2, 3, 4, 1943'
  V Bomber Command, Office of A-2 (undated)
  from MacArthur Archives, MacArthur Memorial, Norfolk, VA ('MacArthur Archives report'; an excellent after-action report which provided the skeleton for this book)

'Report on Destruction of the Lae Convoy March 1–12 by the Fifth US Army Air Force and the Ninth Operational Group RAAF'
Intelligence Division, South Pacific Force, U.S. Pacific Fleet from AWM 54 Microfilm 754 Can 33

Allied Translator and Interpreter Section (ATIS) reports, including Interrogation Spot Reports and Interrogation Reports, Bulletins, Current Translations, from the Australian War Memorial (AWM), in the AWM 55 collection.

The many quotations from Japanese diaries and reports came from ATIS material in the AWM 55 collection.

Allied Air Force Operations Reports from AWM.
Allied Air Force Intelligence Summaries (Intsum) from AWM.
Allied Air Force Intelligence Situation Reports (Sitrep) from AWM.
The 'Ultra' signals intercept material came from Military Division, WW2, U.S. Archives in Washington, the SRH series of reports.

The saga of Lieutenant Kozuki and the color party of 115 Infantry Regiments was included in ATIS reports, in the Japanese history of the events, and in 'Southern Cross,' an account of his time in the theatre by Kane Yoshiwara. The detail of Colonel Endo leaving the ship with the colors came from 'South Pacific Army Operations, Vol. 3,' via the Japanese Military Studies History Division.

The transfer of the flag from the sinking destroyer leader is from AWM 54 423/11/199, Index B51, and U.S. Archives Military Division (WW2) SRH 287.

Sergeant Chikui's diary is from ATIS Bulletin 420.

The detail of the abandonment of the transport ships and destroyers is in ATIS PW Interrogation reports: 53, 57, 59, 60, 65, 66,

68, 74, 77, 79, 84, 90, 94, 99, 102, 107, 108, 115, 116, 117, 118, 120, 122, 130, 132, 138, 139, 169 and Bulletins 408 p.9, 425 p.15, 447 p.17, 461 p.3, 1463.

Where a Japanese officer, soldier or civilian was first mentioned, and annotation made identifying the source document, it is to be understood that later mentions and quotes are from that initial source. Footnotes are the banc of the modern writer of non-fiction, and this step is taken to reduce the number necessary.

Similarly, quotes from Allied flightcrews or other personnel are from letters or audio cassettes sent to the author, or from interviews.

Private records made available included:
Personal flying log-books of veterans of the action.
Personal photo-albums.

Other reports came to hand during research, but it was quickly obvious that they were using the three main reports above. One translation of a Japanese history written post-war showed that they also used official U.S. reports and histories, such as Craven and Cate; their own material had been destroyed during the war, or on 15 August 1945, when Japan surrendered unconditionally to the Allies.

Information on the Japanese merchant ships came from the shipping companies which owned them, Lloyd's of London Register, captured documents in the ATIS series, Australian War Memorial AWM 55 collection, and the History of the Japanese Mail Steamers.

Acknowledgment is due those many people who assisted with my requests for research material, or who put up with my questions and requests for the loan of personal records:

| Ian Affleck | Australian War Memorial (AWM) |
| Patricia Balfe | WAAAF: ACH Townsville |

Dave Beasley	RAAF; 30 Squadron
Bill Beck	USAAC; 89 Sqn 3rd Attack Group (89/3rd)
Fred Blair	USAAC; 63 Sqn 43 Bomb Group (63/43rd)
Jack Bleakley	Australian Army; 'Ultra' operator
W.C. Blewett	RAAF; 90/3rd
Edward J. Boone, Jr.	MacArthur Memorial, Virginia
Joyce Bradley	AWM curator
Arthur Brasnett	RAAF; 100 Squadron
John Brogan	USAAC; 8 Service Gp
Lorna E. Brown	SSHSA, University of Maryland
Fred Cassidy	RAAF; 30 Squadron
Glen W. Clark	USAAC; 89/3rd
George Drury	RAAF; 30 Squadron
Terry Duigan	RAAF; 11 Squadron
Charles Endersby	RAAF; 13/3rd
Bill Ewing	RAAF; 100 Squadron
A. N. Furler	RAAF; 100 Squadron
Bill Garing	RAAF; 5th AF HQ
Kevin Ginnane	photographer
Robert Guthrie	RAAF; 90/3rd
Doris Heath	Japanese linguist
Larry Hickey	publisher IR&P, Colorado, USA
Ron James	RAAF; 13/3rd
Royce Johnco	RAAF; 90/3rd
Charles King	USAAC; 39 Fighter Squadron
Richard Launder	USAAC; 90/3rd
Eugene McCarthy	RAAF; 90/3rd
Sir Neville McNamara	RAAF; 13/3rd
Bill Martin	USAAC; 321/90
Bill Moran	USAAC; 320/90 photographer/gunner
Alf Nelson	RAAF; 30 Squadron
Martin Radnik	USAAC; 8/3
George Robertson	RAAF; 30 Sqn

Henry Sakaida	U.S. air historian and author
Bill Smallwood	USAAC; 90/3
Cy Stafford	USAAC; 482 Service Sqn
Jim Staley	USAAC; 63/43 Bomb Group
Len Stibbard	Noel Stibbard family
Sam Tagaya	Japanese aviation historian
Jack Taylor	USAAC; 89/3
John E. Taylor	U.S. Archives
David Vincent	Australian air historian and author
Dick Vodra	USAAC; 8/49th
Brian Walker	RAAF; CO 30 Squadron

A special thanks is due to the staff of the following organisations, unsung and often unknown to the researchers, but whose prompt service makes it a pleasure to deal with them:

Research Centre, Australian War Memorial for their many, many sorties into the stacks to bring out to me the numerous files and volumes of reports for this book and other projects;

MacArthur Memorial archival staff, for their fast and efficient service, which has delivered into my hands material requested, and done so within a calendar month—a personal thank you;

WW2 Division, U.S. Archives, Washington, D.C., for the prompt service during my visit. It was a pleasure to meet and talk to John E. (Jack) Taylor, who is so knowledgeable and helpful in his field.

A special thanks to Philip Wigley, RAF fighter pilot, not involved in the Pacific campaigns, but who freely gave of his time and energy in England, trying to locate good photos of the Japanese ships from many different sources across the UK. Also, Larry Hickey kindly made available translations of Japanese accounts of the battle, particularly the destroyer histories.

FOOTNOTES

Note: ATIS = Allied Translator and Interpreter Section
AWM = Australian War Memorial
CICSPF = Combined Intelligence Center, South Pacific
Force; collection AWM 58
ATIS collection at AWM = AWM 55, and a full
reference would be: AWM 55 ATIS Bulletin 500.
Below it will be given as: ATIS Bltn 500.
Other ATIS abbreviations are: Current Translation = CT
Enemy Publication = EP
The WW2 printed records collection is AWM 54, and
the numbers which follow in the lists below indicate
the file number within that collection, for example,
AWM 54 423/11/200.

Quotations accorded individual Allied pilots in the text are from written reports or from interviews and tapes or letters to the author. Because of the large number of such references, these personal accounts, comments and remarks have not been included in the footnotes.

ONE: THE GLADIATORS

1. Australian Archives A708 9/1/1297
2. AWM 54 423/11/199 Pt 6 Index T12
3. AWM 66 18/2/1
4. tape, RH Guthrie–author Nov 88
5. R.H. Guthrie Nov 88
6. U.S. Archives Military Division SRH 144 Pt 2 p.445
7. AWM 55 ATIS EP 123 (AWM 55 deleted hereafter)
8. U.S. Archives Military Division SRH 144 p.482
9. AWM 69 File 76
10. ATIS Interrogation (Intg) 77
11. ATIS Intg 74
12. ATIS Intg 103; 129
13. ATIS Intg 59
14. ATIS Intg 78
15. ATIS Intg 65; 53
16. ATIS Intg 79
17. ATIS Intg 68
18. ATIS Intg 60
19. ATIS Bltn 495

TWO: FIRST CLASH

1. ATIS Bltn 419 p.10
2. ATIS EP 123
3. ATIS Bltn 358 p.5
4. ATIS CT 87 p.25c
5. ATIS Bltn 307 p.15
6. from Fred Blair
7. ATIS Intg 141, 130; Bltn 206 p.7
8. ATIS Intg Spot 12, 14; Bull 420 p.6
9. ATIS Intg 130, 115
10. ATIS Bltn 428 p.15
11. ATIS Intg 74, 77
12. ATIS Bltn 307 pp.15–16
13. ATIS CT 87 p.26c
14. CICSPF #1155

THREE: ONSLAUGHT

1. AWM 64 100 Sqn ORB
2. AWM 54 423/4/154
3. interview with author, 11 Jan 89
4. AWM 54 423/4/154

5. MacArthur Archives; copy of 'Tactical Study of Attack on Lae Convoy'
6. AWM 54 Microfilm 754
7. 'Tactical Study' ibid.
8. via International Research & Publishing, Boulder, Colo
9. 'Great East Asia War Summary' GHQ Tokyo 14 Apr 50
10. ATIS Bltn 461 p.31
11. ATIS Intg 74, 77, 108
12. ATIS Intg 59
13. ATIS Intg 66
14. ATIS Intg 117
15. ATIS Intg 88, 104
16. U.S. Archives, SRH 826
17. RAAF Historical Section records
18. RAAF Historical Section records
19. RH Guthrie, Nov 88
20. History of the Japanese Mail Steamers, via Japan Dept. of Defense Historical Studies Division
21. ATIS Intg 118, 128, 165, Bltn 414
22. ATIS Bltn 417 p.17
23. ATIS Intg 90, 120, 132, 139
24. History of the Japanese Mail Steamers
25. ATIS Intg 158
26. ATIS Intg 103, 119, 129
27. ATIS Intg 53
28. ATIS Intg 57
29. ATIS Bltn 420 p.6—and all other Chikui references
30. South Pacific Army Operations Vol. 3, pp.62–65
31. IR&P, Boulder, Colo

FOUR: COUP DE GRACE

1. ATIS EP 123; CICSPF #1155
2. RAAF Historical Office
3. ATIS Research Report (RR) 72 p.23, CT 6 pp.23–24, 43 BG reports
4. ATIS Intg 60
5. ATIS Intg 116
6. ATIS Bltn 186 p.3
7. ATIS Bltn 428 p.15, Intg 94
8. South Pacific Army Operations Vol. 3, pp.62–65
9. ATIS Bltn 453 p.22, Intg 109, 117, 138, 143
10. ATIS EP 123 p.36, Whitehead report 6 Apr 43; South Pacific Army Ops ibid.
11. ATIS Intg 77; ATIS Bltn 420 p.6, Intg 53, 57, 65, 115
12. ATIS Bltn 740, EP 123

13. CICSPF #1155
14. U.S. Archives SRH 287

FIVE: RETRIBUTION

1. ATIS Bltn 428 p.15
2. ATIS Bltn 414
3. ATIS Bltn 420 p.6
4. ATIS Bltn 528 p.4
5. ATIS Bltn 815 p.8
6. ATIS Intg 75
7. ATIS Intg 77
8. ATIS Bltn 199 p.7, Intg 79
9. ATIS Intg 88
10. ATIS Intg 104, 53
11. ATIS EP 123
12. ATIS EP 123
13. ATIS EP 123
14. ATIS Bltn 461 p.3, 1463
15. South Pacific Army Ops Vol. 3
16. U.S. Archives SRH 287 p.73
17. ATIS EP 123 p.44
18. ATIS EP 123 p.47
19. ATIS EP 123
20. ATIS Bltn 447 p.17
21. ATIS Intg 132
22. ATIS Intg 139, 90
23. ATIS Intg 75, Bltn 202 p.4
24. ATIS EP 123 p.44
25. ATIS Bltn 290 p.2, 326 p.4
26. ATIS EP 145 p.22
27. ATIS EP 123 p.44
28. ATIS EP 123 p.62
29. ATIS Intg 91
30. U.S. Archives SRH 144 Pt 2 pp.567–596
31. ATIS Bltn 414
32. ATIS CT 87 p.26c
33. ATIS Bltn 453 p.8, p.22, EP 123
34. ATIS Bltn 420 p.7
35. ATIS Bltn 297 p.6
36. AWM 54 423/12/5 Pt 2
37. History of 305 Radar RAAF, courtesy of RAAF Special Projects Office
38. ATIS Intg 90
39. ATIS EP 123

40. ATIS Intg 139
41. ATIS Intg 65
42. ATIS Intg 132, Spot Intg 13
43. ATIS Intg 145
44. ATIS Intg 68
45. ATIS Intg 165, 94
46. ATIS Intg 118
47. ATIS Intg 107, 115
48. ATIS Bltn 421 p.9, CT 87 p.41c, U.S. Archives SRH 287
49. ATIS EP 115, p.53, EP 145 p.72a
50. ATIS EP 123 pp.78, 82
51. ATIS Intg 149, 141
52. ATIS Intg 57, Spot Intg 12
53. ATIS Intg 102
54. ATIS Intg 104
55. ATIS Bltn 318, 342 p.1
56. ATIS Bltn 143
57. ATIS Bltn 128
58. ATIS EP 123 p.78
59. CICSPF #1154
60. ATIS Bltn 452 p.6
61. AWM 54 589/7/14

APPENDIX 3

1. ATIS Bltn 173, 175
2. ATIS EP 81, 123
3. AWM 54 589/7/14
4. ATIS Bltn 839

GLOSSARY

AA	Anti Aircraft
AAF	Allied Air Forces
A20	Douglas Aircraft Company twin-engined attack bomber with 2-man or 3-man crew
B17	Boeing Aircraft Company four-engined heavy bomber, crew of 10 men
B24	Consolidated Aircraft Corporation four-engined heavy bomber, crew up to 10 men
B25	North American Aviation twin-engined bomber, in the South Pacific modified to carry eight heavy machineguns in the nose for use in attack missions at minimum altitude
Beaufighter	Bristol Aeroplane Company twin-engined attack fighter, 2-man crew, built in UK and Australia; heavily armed for ground attack

with four 20mm cannon and six .303-inch
machineguns

Beaufort   Bristol-designed twin-engined bomber and
                 torpedo bomber built in Australia, 4-man crew

Buna   location on north coast of New Guinea; point of
                 Japanese invasion, July 1942; scene of heavy
                 fighting December 1942–January 1943 before
                 Japanese destroyed by Australian and U.S.
                 forces

DD   destroyer

.50-caliber half-inch caliber machinegun, standard weapon
                 fitted to U.S. bombers and fighters

Guadalcanal island in the Solomons group, where U.S. forces
                 first landed against the Japanese in August
                 1942; battles continued to February 1943;
                 severe defeat for Japan

Hap or Hamp clipped-wing version of the Mitsubishi Zero or
                 Zeke single-engined fighter (see below)

Kittyhawk   RAF/RAAF name for the Curtiss P40 single-
                 engined fighter

Kokoda   Australian government station and commercial
                 plantation area in mid–New Guinea, the focal
                 point of Australian-Japanese military
                 operations July–November 1942, the first land
                 defeat inflicted on the Japanese; campaign
                 known as the Kokoda Trail campaign after the
                 trail Kokoda–Port Moresby, on the south
                 coast

Lae   town and administrative center on northern coast
                 of New Guinea, occupied by the Japanese in
                 March 1942 and used as a base by them, with
                 two airfields

mast-height bombing	a technique in which the attacking airplane approached the ship at minimum altitude, avoiding AA fire, and dropped bombs into the hull of the ship at 'mast height,' then pulled up to avoid collision
Milne Bay	Harbor and airfields on the eastern end of New Guinea; scene of defensive battle by Australian units which defeated a Japanese invasion in August 1942, first such defeat to the Japanese
MLC	Motorized Landing Craft
Observer	RAAF flight crew member qualified as a navigator, radio-operator, gunner and photographer
Oscar	Nakajima Ki43 'Hayabusa' [Peregrine Falcon] single-engined fighter, code-named Oscar by Allied forces; light, agile, armed only with two machineguns
PBY	Consolidated Aircraft Corporation twin-engined amphibian patrol and anti-submarine aircraft
P38	Lockheed Aircraft Corporation single-seat twin-engined fighter
P39	Bell Aircraft Corporation single-engined fighter
P40	Curtiss single-engined fighter
RAAF	Royal Australian Air Force
RAAF ranks	Enlisted ranks much the same as U.S., but officer rank equivalents are: Pilot Officer—2nd Lieutenant Flying Officer—1st Lieutenant Flight Lieutenant—Captain Squadron Leader—Major

Wing Commander—Lieutenant Colonel
Group Captain—Colonel
(general ranks omitted)

skip bomb the technique of skipping the bomb across the surface of the sea into the hull of a ship, in the way a stone may be skipped across a pond or creek

Solomons island group in the southwest Pacific where the U.S. forces went on the offensive in August 1942 and defeated the Japanese in a year-long series of battles and invasions

strafer nickname for the heavily-armed B25s with eight .50-caliber machineguns in the nose, used for minimum altitude attacks

SWPA South West Pacific Area; the theater commanded by General Douglas MacArthur, included Australia, New Guinea, Indonesia, the Philippines and South China Sea; bordered to the east and north by U.S. Navy commands, North, Central and South Pacific Areas

Tainan Kokkutai Japanese Naval air unit equipped with Mitsubishi Zero fighters, in early–mid 1942 based at Lae, New Guinea, and included many proficient pilots and leading aces

USAAC U.S. Army Air Corps

USAAF U.S. Army Air Force

Wau mining town in the New Guinea mountains, scene of Australian defensive battles against advancing Japanese; Australians almost entirely reinforced and supplied by U.S. and RAAF airplanes

Zeke   Allied nickname for the Mitsubishi single-
                engined A6M 'Zero' fighter

Zero   Mitsubishi A6M single-engined fighter, a very
                agile carrier-borne airplane armed with two
                (later four) 20mm cannon and two 7.7mm
                machineguns, able to out-manoeuvre every
                Allied fighter, reigned supreme until Allied
                pilots learned to exploit the good points of
                their airplanes and the weak ones of the Zero

BIBLIOGRAPHY

Alcorn, John S. *The Jolly Rogers*. Temple City, California: Historical Aviation Album, 1981.

Altitude Minimum; 89th BS. Sydney: Angus & Robertson, 1945.

Arbon, J. and Christensen, Chris. *The Bismarck Sea Ran Red*. Marceline, Missouri: Walsworth Press, 1979.

Arnold, Elliott and Hough, Donald. *Big Distance*. New York: Duell, Sloan & Pearce, 1945.

Birdsall, Steve. *Flying Buccaneers*. New York: Doubleday, 1977.

Bong, Carl and O'Connor, Mike. *Ace of Aces*. Mesa, Arizona: Champlin Museum Press, 1985.

Crawford, William. *Gore and Glory*. Philadelphia: David McKay Co., 1944.

Gillison, Douglas. *Royal Australian Air Force 1939–1942*. Canberra, Australia: Australian War Memorial, 1962.

Graham, Burton. *None Shall Survive*. Sydney, Australia: F. H. Johnston, 1943.

Headhunters, The. 80 FS Association, (undated).

Hess, William N. *Pacific Sweep*. New York: Doubleday & Co., Inc., 1974.

Kenney, George C. *Dick Bong*. New York: Duell, Sloan & Pearce, 1960.

Kenney, George C. *General Kenney Reports*. New York: Duell, Sloan & Pearce, 1949.

Legg, Frank. *The Eyes of Damien Parer*. Adelaide: Rigby, 1961.

Long, Gavin. *The Six Years War*. Canberra, Australia: Australian War Memorial, 1973.

Lord, Andrew M. *Tales of the Jolly Rogers*. Auburn, California: Auburn Letter House, 1985.

McDowell, Ernest R. *B25 Mitchell in Action*. Warren, Michigan: Squadron/Signal, 1978.

McDowell, Ernest R. *49th Fighter Group*. Carrollton, Texas: Squadron/Signal, 1989.

Morrison, Samuel Eliot. *Breaking the Bismarck's Barrier*. Boston: Little, Brown & Co., 1950.

Nohara, Shigeru. *A6M Zero in Action*. Warren, Michigan: Squadron/Signal, 1983.

Olynyk, Frank J. *USAAF Credits (Pacific Theater)*. Aurora, Ohio: 1985.

Parnell, Neville. *Whispering Death*. Sydney, Australia: Reed Books, 1980.

Photo History of the 9th Fighter Squadron. Sydney, Australia: Angus & Robertson, 1944.

Reaper's Harvest, 3rd BG, The. Sydney: Halstead Press, 1945.

Rust, Kenn C. *Fifth Air Force Story*. Temple City, California: Historical Aviation Album Publication, 1973.

Sands, John. *The Jolly Rogers: 90th Bomb Group*. Sydney, Australia: 1944.

Scutts, Jerry. *B25 Mitchell at War*. London: Ian Allen Ltd, 1983.

Stafford, Gene B. *Aces of the Southwest Pacific*. Warren, Michigan: Squadron/Signal, 1977.

Stafford, Gene B. *P38 Lightning in Action*. Warren, Michigan: Squadron/Signal, 1976.

Stanaway, John. *Cobra in the Clouds*. Temple City, California: Historical Aviation Album Publication, 1982.

Stanaway, John. *Peter Three Eight*. Missoula, Montana: Pictorial Histories Publishing Company, 1986.

United States Strategic Bombing Survey (Pacific). *The Campaigns of the Pacific War*. Washington, D.C.: U.S. Government, 1946.

Wandrey, Ralph H. *Fighter Pilot*. Mason City, Iowa: Stoyles Press, 1950.

Wilson, David. *Jackson's Few*. Australia: Chisolm, ACT, 1988.

Wilson, Stewart. *Beaufort, Beaufighter and Mosquito in Australian Service*. Canberra, Australia: Aerospace Publications, 1990.

Wilson, Stewart. *The Spitfire, Mustang and Kittyhawk in Australian Service*. Canberra, Australia: Aerospace Publications, 1988.

ABOUT THE AUTHOR

Lex McAulay retired from the Australian Army in 1982, where he was a Vietnamese linguist and Intelligence analyst. He is the author of nine books published in Australia, the United Kingdom, and the United States.

INDEX